FRIENDS IN HIGH PLACES

Friends in High Places

A Season in the Himalayas

PETER MAYNE

THE BODLEY HEAD
LONDON   SYDNEY
TORONTO

For Jagut and Mussoorie

© Peter Mayne 1975
ISBN 0 370 01389 1
Printed and bound in Great Britain for
The Bodley Head Ltd
9 Bow Street, London, WC2E 7AL
by William Clowes & Sons Ltd, Beccles
Set in 10pt Linotype Plantin
First published 1975

CONTENTS

Illustrations

PART ONE

1

Something suddenly happens. The road surmounts a spur that comes in from the east and without warning the little wooded foothills world, that till now closed us in completely, splits wide open. The valley lies spread-eagled at our feet with the Himalayas climbing to the skies for backcloth. Immense and marvellous country! Richer, more beautiful even than I had dared remember it! And across the line of vision the River Jumna flows in swift and vigorous and young from hills that rise up sharply to the east, where Jagut lives.*

This is what I had sat waiting for, all the slow winding drag here from the rail-head, puffing and panting along in a worn-out station-duty hack of a taxi. Unchanged!

I made the driver stop and I got out and I looked and I looked and even when I wasn't looking any more I still stood there on the broad balcony of land that overhangs the valley at this point, eyes sated and unfocused, senses groping backwards for the feel of life when India was my scene, or let me think so. India? So huge, so utterly uncaring whether I was 'in' or 'out'; it wasn't really India but a certain Hindu family that let me 'in'—to their small parts of it, I mean.

Back again!

It was Jagut that I wrote to in the first place, a tentative first letter after years of silence. I suppose I wondered if I'd still be welcome. He wrote back, 'Come, come, come! Come for as long as you want and can bear the solitude of my country home. My only concern is the remoteness and the quiet. But you say you'll be

---

* Jumna, Jagut. . . . The short first vowel in both is the same short vowel in Hindi but Jagut transliterates it 'Jagut' and so shall I.

9

busy with some writing, and this gives me the courage to hope you won't be too bored. When will you be coming? Give me plenty of notice: you know what posts are in my back-of-beyond. Have you written to the others? Mussoorie? Baiji & Co? Mussoorie's been in Kathmandu since their 1950 Revolution, you know. Baiji's left Delhi for good and gone home to Jodhpur. You knew that too?'

Yes, I knew that too. And reading Jagut's letter was like hearing his voice again.

'So come soon,' he finished up. 'We don't seem to be growing any younger. There's no welcome you could possibly outstay.' He added a postscript: 'You aren't considered "guest". You're family-member.'

'Family-member' still? It warmed the heart.

The driver had left the taxi too by now and was coming up be-side me. I guessed he meant to try a bit more of his slender store of English on me. I was right. He'd been at it intermittently all the way. He now said, 'The air is good.' It was, too. I replied in English, to indulge him, 'Yes, the air is very good'—though I really wanted to indulge myself with whatever I could dredge up from the past of Hindi. He repeated my sentence, savouring it. 'Yes, the air is very good.'

It was certainly much cooler now we'd reached the hills. The night I'd had to spend in Delhi getting here—a small hotel, no air-conditioning—had seemed intolerably hot to me. The plains of India hold the heat of summer far into what is autumn in the west, and I'd evidently lost the habit of great heat, of dehydration, mosquitoes, ceiling-fans that churn the exhausted air. I had even written to ask if it would still be disagreeably hot by autumn up in Jagut's hills, and he had answered, 'Don't be a fuss-box! It won't be hot a bit!' And indeed here in the valley, though summer lingered, the air lay far more lightly on the skin. I might even need some covering at night.

By now the driver had prepared another speech in English. He smiled and pointed and then said, 'Jumna river.' And I said it too, feeling soft, 'Jumna river . . .'—the lovely Jumna river, away across the green and golden valley, too far to catch the sound of it as yet. How long was it since I last was here?

Too long. Though it was only the day before that I had seen the Jumna last, gazing out across it from the walls of the old red Moghul fort in Delhi. There it lay, aged beyond recognition in its short life-history from the Himalayas to the plains, a great flaccid old snake of a thing the colour of its own mud, flopped across a landscape bare as a stomach—a stomach, moreover, so vast and swollen that nothing less than the arc of the horizon could belt it in. Over this horizon, south from Delhi, the Jumna has its eternal rendezvous to keep, its confluence with Holy Mother Ganga. Once there it must abase itself before her and surrender all identity. Poor Jumna, to be destined to give up so soon.

But here the river was still vigorous and young, and in a little upsurge of emotion that I instantly regretted I heard my voice say sentimentally, 'I was here when I was young. . . .'

'. . . young?'—the driver's head spun round. Young himself, he stared into my face till I could see him wondering behind those eyes of his—how could this person ever have been young? So I felt older still and hard as stone and changed the key abruptly. Practicalities. Marvellous country this well might be, but in all the huge sub-Himalayan world set up before us, never a sign of man or even habitation. And the tea-shop I'd been told to go to? Where would that be, might I ask?

I asked the man, in English very cold and flat, 'And where's the tea-shop?' I'd gone right off him now.

He blanked his face and said nothing.

Didn't he know? Doubts filled my head. *He didn't know!* Jagut had written as if the whole world knew, and the taxi-man himself had claimed to know Lal Singh way back there at the rail-head. Or was it just a lie, to get himself a rich long-distance fare? We *had* to find the tea-shop!

'Tea-shop!' I told him loudly, angrily, and added for good measure, '*Lal Singh ka chai-khana!*'

His face went bright at once. '*Lal Singh ka chai-khana? Chai-khana*, you say, sahib?'

Obviously 'tea-shop' found no place in his vocabulary. 'Lal Singh. . . ?'—and he was off. Naturally he knew Lal Singh and his *chai-khana*, had he not said so at the station? Who didn't know Lal Singh? That's what his burst of Hindi meant. '*Aiyye, Sahib*,' he went on, 'be pleased to come.'

He was leading me to the edge of the natural balcony of land we stood on and at once a big tree came in view immediately below us where the road proved to have looped off right to zig-zag down and left again. The tree was near enough for me to recognise it as a *neem*, wide-spreading, leafy. A few shacks clustered round it. To right of it a small canal swings in from behind the rising ground still further to the right. The narrow metalled road accompanying it in parallel had caught my eye. Was that the way to Jagut's now? A new alignment? It would explain his letter telling me that he could 'motor right to the front door these days—not like the old days, is it?' A private metalled road? Two posts, a chain between them, closed the road to traffic just short of where it joined the highway and the canal slipped under it. But surely it must be miles short of Jagut's still, miles of private metalled road, then? A fortune! But of course! A government irrigation-project, canal and its attendant road: and they had granted Jagut right of way. Very handy.

Meanwhile, where was the tea-shop?

'And Lal Singh's *chai-khana*?'

'There, Sahib!'

He was pointing down at the shacks around the tree, and though I saw nothing remotely tea-shop-looking, I decided to believe him and said 'good' and meant it. I felt warmer towards the man again, quite warm, in fact. I think I even smiled at him, but can't remember that he smiled back. A nice young man, but timid.

I dipped into my pocket for Jagut's letter of instructions. It had awaited my arrival at Delhi airport two nights earlier—the last in the long ding-dong of letters back and forth, once I had started it all off, question and answer, catching up with time, all leading to this Himalayan valley and the Jumna and on up-river to the mountains. Indeed I'd been relieved to know from this last letter that he'd had my own last letter giving final times and dates—to know, that is, that he would be expecting me today. In country such as his, where cables come as letters and letters come cleft-stick, every sort of breakdown in communications must be amply allowed for—storms, snake-bite, human frailty. But Jagut was expecting me, and I was almost there already. A half-hour more, perhaps? Less, even, if the road up-river proved as good as its metalled surface looked from where we stood. 'Soon Saan,' he called his property. Strange name, but soft upon the ear. It means 'Solitude', so he had told me once. 'Not loneliness, you see, Peter. Solitude. I love it, and I'm never lonely here.' He had done a lot to the place over the years, as I knew from his letters. It might look very different. Would it *be* the same? And I . . . ? Was I still the person that I used to be? And Jagut . . . ?

'So you're nearly here,' I read again. 'And with day and date now firmly fixed and berth booked on the night-train Delhi–Dehra Dun, you should take the Chakrata bus from Dehra as far as the River Jumna. Three rupees per seat, approx. You'll find it waiting just outside the station, its departure geared to your arrival-time. I'd been hoping all along that I could send in for you—I told you that I've had a car on order eighteen months already (my dear old Buick met an honourable death that long ago). It hasn't come. I keep on sending them reminders. So it's the bus, I fear.'

But I hadn't taken the Chakrata bus at all. I was so dismayed by the tumbledown sight of it busily stuffing itself jam-pack with peasants and their bundles, its roof piled double-decker high with bundles too—so dismayed I was, that I promptly threw all question of economy to the winds and went a splash with this old taxi. Moreover I didn't care at all for Jagut's next bit: 'bikes' and 'baggage'.

'Get the bus to put you down at Lal Singh's tea-shop. I'll despatch one of my men on a bike as guide and escort. Ask for him. Hire a bike yourself and cycle here, with him to show the way. Just bring a tooth-brush. Leave the rest of your traps in the tea-shop. My *amla*-contractor will bring it in to us next day.'

Amla-contractor? What could *amla* be? Leave my baggage at a tea-shop? Never! Look at it! Gone the days when I travelled feather-light. And on top of that a bike possesses little charm for me. As it was, however, all problems had been magically resolved by the one simple expedient: my dear old taxi right to Jagut's own front door at a fraction of the cost I'd feared. Rupees forty-five— a gift!

The *neem*-tree proved to mark a staging-post for buses, and the tea-shop proved to be less tea-shop (as we picture it) than a hut with bench outside as lure for transit-passengers to sit on sipping tea. My guide-and-escort was sitting on it, waiting. A hill-Rajput from the look of him, a type I think I recognise. He got up as soon as he saw a European arriving (who else could it have been but me?) and I realise in retrospect that I noted how his eyes went sharp on seeing I had come by taxi, not by bus: and how he was scarcely through with his formal greetings (bows from the waist, palms joined together—*namaste, namaste*) when he was whispering something fishily furtive to my driver and my driver was nodding and turning back to me to make me understand that he could perfectly well get me to Jagut's without the escort's help—because of course the whole world knew where Jagut lived as well as it knew Lal Singh and his tea-shop. So after all no need of guide and escort. Then, to honour Jagut's guest, Lal Singh offered tea, so I can add for the record that his tea is nicely stewed to syrup with goat's-milk and sugar. All this took place under the sheltering *neem*, its lower branches sadly ravaged by wayfarers' snapping off its twigs for tooth-brushes; and this I can deduce because it always has been thus for the poor *neem* with its astringent saps. Its role in Indian life is 'tooth-brush'. 'O God of the Woods! I cut one of your small twigs to cleanse my teeth. Grant me, for this action, long life, strength, honours...' Honours? Honours and ... and something-something. 'Wit' comes into it. 'And power!' The Abbé Dubois quotes it. I had him in my book-bag and I'd look him up. Long life and all those other things—and *power!* A bit much to expect of the God of the Woods as reward for despoiling his noble *neem*.

Lal Singh unlocked the chain and let it fall to the road *clank-clank* for our taxi to pass over it. My guide and escort stood there bowing respectfully as we started off. That man, I was thinking, he's after something. He's stayed back for some girl. Well, why not?

The canal-department road is a very different affair from the jungle track my feet remembered still. Today the canal and roadway share a solid shelf cut into the hillsides and following their contours. The river, to begin with, is at least a half-mile distant across the valley, and perhaps some sixty feet below; but soon the valley starts to narrow and the river-bed is climbing, climbing, till some miles further on it is barely twenty feet below the road and drawing closer, its waters running swifter and more vigorous than ever (noisy, too), whereas the roadway rises at a gradient all along so smooth and gentle that the channel-waters slip back past it at no pace at all. And then, at a given moment I wasn't ready for, the road and channel round a rocky bluff and immediately beyond it curve off quickly riverwards. And there before me, not fifty yards ahead, I saw the familiar rough stone wall that demarcates Jagut's boundaries in the valley that the maps call Kata Pathar.

I stopped the taxi once again and I got out. And I looked and I looked. Mountains ring the skyline to all quarters but the west: they crowd so near that they mask the real Himalayan giants up on the borders of Tibet, not seventy miles away, and over in Nepal to the south-east. This background I was ready for: but Jagut's private foreground, the valley and the hills that rise north, south and east of it—I gazed about astonished. Now everything is richly, thickly, sumptuously green where once were stony outcrops, scrub, with here and there a group of stunted goat-molested trees. If I closed my eyes I still could see the spur high up ahead, the shape of it so clearly printed on my mind that I could draw it blindfold, the way it juts out from the hill-mass south of it as a man's shoulder juts out from the column of his neck. A naked shoulder, the house perched on the tip of it, and three giant mango-trees to serve as land-marks. From here the precipice beyond would be invisible. But the naked shoulder that I would have drawn is clothed today in greenery so extravagant that its shape is lost, and the little house is lost, and the huge landmark mangoes have been swallowed up in the general exuberance of vegetation that falls back from the shoulder in a variegated cloak of greens, smoothly, gently, down to the valley and the river, where the terraced paddyfields take over.

I climbed back in and hoped the driver wouldn't try to talk and wondered how the time was going. Rather than invite more talk by asking him, I squinted at his wrist-watch. Its big hand had slipped in up his sleeve so I couldn't see exactly; but even if I could have, how exactly could it tell the time, that watch of his? Its hour-hand suggested something nearer five than half-past four. Good enough. I'd be in time for tea.

A country-lane. A private country-lane.

The wheels of bullock-carts have rutted it so deeply that in the centre of it runs a wide green grassy ribbon leading upwards, thumping, bumping, up, up, up, through leafy tunnels bottle-green and luminous under the dark mango-trees, whole groves of mangoes. The lane is joined at intervals by tributary-tracks that come in from the hillsides on the right: all roads here evidently lead to Jagut's Rome. Then citruses; then a plantation feathery-yellow that I didn't know at all and would have to ask about, trees whose lacy foliage is dragged down to the earth under the weight of golden plum-size fruit. Then jack-fruit. Papaya. Persimmon—wasn't that persimmon? Custard-apples, guavas. Such prodigality, such abundance on every side, and none of it foreseen—all the way up, thumping, bumping, a mile, two miles.... I gazed about astonished.

At the top of this long wooded climb a gate stood open, a marble slab inset in one of the two gate-posts. The inscription is in the Nagari Hindi script (that I can't read, but I knew what it must be

15

before the driver had spelt it out for me): 'Soon Saan'; then 'JAGUT' (his given name); then the appellations he was born with.

To the left of the gate the ground slips down to woods and orchards and on the right there is at first just space enough for a line of cottages. But twenty, thirty yards ahead the 'shoulder' proper has been reached and the ground has flattened out. There always were a few small buildings here, but never, as today, this little village street with its one-room general store and a terrace obviously used as a tea-shop and a booth with a cross-legged tailor. Not many cars would come up here, and such as did could certainly be heard chug-chugging nearer from miles distant, and a car is an event, so people would of course be out and waiting for it, drawn by the noise of its approach in the high silence of these hills. They were out just now and leaning down and forward as we trundled by (even the tailor was on his feet by then), peering in under the roof of the taxi to see what could be inside. And I was staring out, at them, at everything in sight, looking for things I knew or thought that I remembered—where was the dispensary, for instance? Was that it, near the gates? It looked all closed. Don't say he'd closed it down! He couldn't have. It was part of Soon Saan life, intended for his own people primarily but serving all sorts of others who trudged in from the mountains too. They seemed to like it better than such government facilities as existed in those far-off days. I had enjoyed the sessions with the tubs of aspirin and epsom-salts, the disinfectants, balms and salves, the adhesive-plaster, the electric-shock machine, hand-operated. I had at least one convulsive faith-cure to my credit with that good little machine. I'd have liked to try my hand with the hypodermic, too— the *sui*, the needle—but Jagut never let me. He would normally reserve the *sui* for stubborn or undiagnosed cases, a *sui*-ful of distilled water, a form of magic not to be too lightly resorted to, and much more powerful than electric-shocks. Magic of all sorts is perfectly respected here. Practised too, naturally. White *and* black.

A sweet-sour smell. Cattle. Cattle-pens and sheds and a two-storey barrack of a place behind a long stone wall, the wall (alas) uncomfortably high for little cows to look out over. They were clearly trying to, to watch our rattling arrival. 'Cross-bred Jerseys, now'—so Jagut wrote to tell me. I could see their dark, wet, sponge-cake muzzles diagonally up-ended to let one eye peep over. Big trees cast heavy dappled shade on them, on us, on everything.

16

Some fifty yards or so inside the gates the level ground has fanned out wider still. Geese crossed our path, honking, unhurried, scarcely even bothering to turn to look. Not so the ducks, who were away into the safety of the woods below in a wild diminuendo of quackings. Two-wheeled bullock-carts rested quietly under a central farmyard tree, each leaning on its single shaft. I saw that one was rubber-shod today. That must be restful for it, too. A farm cat stood aloof and waved its long slow tail, though not in greeting; and there in the background was something else to give the memory a jab: six pi-dogs in a group, 'oh yes, of course! My pariah-pack still guards us night and day. You'll see.' I saw. They stood there absolutely still, watching.

We had reached and crossed a little culvert. It straddles a narrow channel that I remembered for its cold clear mountain water and the unceasing noise it made—still makes. A rock stuck on a larger rock stands up beside it now (not there before, I'm sure). They have fixed a brazen Buddha's head on top of it. Before I realised it the first two giant mango-trees were already over my left shoulder, with the third and largest just ahead of where we were coming to a stop on a pavement of big water-smoothed cobbles. Under the mango's lowest branches I could make out an open airy terrace to the right—would that be the threshing-floor? To left of the huge mango, close under the protection of its great spreading arms, the little house stood waiting.

Now that I'd actually arrived at last and the taxi had drawn up under the mango-tree and I was getting out, and some of Jagut's men were converging on me across the cobbles and from the half-seen open area beyond the tree, I could take a conscious breath and slowly let it out again. Thankfulness? There had been moments like abysses when I'd wondered if it wasn't utter madness to come back on tracks untrodden for so long. I was sighing with relief, I think, as well as thankfulness, because against all likelihood the essence of this place flowed over me again unchanged, the suddenly-remembered feel of it, the sound of running water (the channel close behind me, the distant river raging softly far below us in the valley). Unchanged! The tumbling lavish greenery all around was just a gentle benefaction, changing nothing of the place's real metabolism. Or was there, possibly . . . was there, after all, some subtle difference? This green exuberance, could it be green invasion—was the vegetable kingdom swallowing up Soon

17

Saan and poor Jagut with it? Where was he? Had he alone not heard the taxi coming—had no one told him? Where was he hiding? Who ruled here now? But no time for such dotty speculations—I had my role to play. The bidden guest.

The nearest of the men had started gesturing their greetings as they came forward, five or six of them, and except for one I took to be a local hill-man, all Nepalese, all bowing over hands set palm to palm—less bows, perhaps, than little forward jerkings of the head, *namaste, namaste*—Mongol-eyes all closed to slits by grins of welcome. Two other men had reached us from beyond the mango. Rajputs, I thought: they were bowing from the waist as Rajputs tend to, dignified, unsmiling. I'd started on my own responses, too—*namaste, namaste*—to left, to right: but to be truthful I felt a little sheepish. Are my hands too square and solid for these graceful gesturings? I'd lost the habit of it, also.

They were gathered round the taxi by this time, young men or youngish, helping the driver to unload my stuff, and though I didn't know a single one of them, they were just as I'd remembered that they'd always been, faces, movements, manners—three kinds of each, if you counted local hill-men as well as Nepalese and Rajputs. Their clothes were now more western than they used to be. However one of the Rajputs, a tall man, thin, emotionless, more handsome than the rest, wore the traditional long white cotton shirt—*camiz*—outside the wide-cut pantaloons they call *paejama* (leg-clothes). (We took the word from them—pyjamas—along with the plaited-cotton draw-string that holds them up.)

These men could well be sons of those I used to know. The youngest of them could be even sons of sons. Apart from Jagut's cooks ('old ladies now and only two of them', he'd written) there were evidently but few survivors from the earlier household, for instance Bal Bahadur—'He's my major-domo now. Do you remember him?'—and did I? I thought I did, and wrote to say I did, assuming he'd have been the Nepalese so much more Mongoloid than most of them, and so much more than ever Jagut seemed, despite the Mongol-Rajput mixture in his blood. It was obvious, anyway, that Bal Bahadur couldn't be among the men who now surrounded me: there was no one old enough. And Jagut, where was he?

'Maharajkumar sahib . . . ?' I asked the man assuming charge of things (the tall thin Rajput) and he answered absently in Hindi, articulating clearly, in case I couldn't follow. 'Rana-sahib just coming now—in a minute coming.' He had already turned away to consider my baggage, the great bulging suitcase packed for heat of plains and cold of mountains, my bed-roll hired from Thos. Cook in Delhi for the train, typewriter, tape-recorder, book-bag, overnight bag, thermos-flasks—yes, two of them. A formidable clutter. A barely-teenage boy was struggling with the suitcase, and a child appeared from hiding behind his father's billowing *paejama*'d legs—certainly he must be the Rajput's son. I handed him the smallest bit of luggage I possessed, a little wide-mouthed thermos. Proud child, he took and cradled it with care—at least I hoped he would. And this reminded me that I must get them to refill with ice. Would there be any ice? I hadn't thought of that.

With everyone so busy and no one staring any more and Jagut still elsewhere—though where, I wondered?—I could look round a bit. Women had appeared meanwhile, discreetly in the background. That would be one of the two Brahmin women cooks ('old lady now') outside a fly-screened door at the far end of the house. Little children came sidling nearer, shy but determined. In due course I'd know them all apart. For the moment they were simply Soon-Saan prototypes, men, women, children, there must have been an assorted dozen of them, and all to the expected scale. Whereas the house, the trees, the gardens, everything had grown much bigger, and so aggressively alive. Mostly we remember things too big—or is that only true of childhood memories, of the days when everything was far too big in relation to the child?

Ahh-h . . . ! The pariah-pack had turned up now. It must have made a fairly wide detour to stage its entrance face to face with me, all six of them in their various standard pi-dog shapes and sizes, one of them (the only male) much bigger than the bitches, though callow-looking. They had stopped well short of sniffing-distance. Their noses twitched, however. They bristled with uncertainties. I might well have known their great-great-great-great-grandparents, but they could hardly be expected to guess at this, or think more warmly of me because of it. Never mind. It was their duty to mistrust all strangers so they were busy with mistrust of me. For my part I would ignore them, for days if need be, as if I were a sort of god, or else a cat, in my moods benign or otherwise. Aloof, anyhow. It would be for them to make the first propitiatory advances, fawning. I would let that happen, and then see how I felt.

I had become keenly awake in the last few seconds of several knee-high creatures directly behind me breathing through their mouths. Human breath, not dog's. And turning round I found three little Nepalese girls, sisters surely, their clothes and hair and faces, noses too, all caked with mud-pie mud. For a second they boldly stood their ground, eyes wide, mouths agape, and then took flight like starlings, the smallest almost airborne, her two sisters having grabbed her wrists so that she flew out behind them, more bumpy kite than starling; over the culvert they flew, and away beyond the water-channel and the second-biggest mango-tree and out of sight. And I saw now that the water-channel bifurcates beyond the Buddha-rock. Its main stream passes down into the woods, doubtless to fill the irrigation-ditches, turn by turn. But its right-hand streamlet, just this side of the mango, narrows to become a waterfall, doll-size, to feed the topmost of two descending rock-pools I hadn't really taken in till now. These pools were never here before—but with the perennial never-failing water-channel here to keep them filled and fresh, why not lily-pools? And gold-fish too, no doubt, why not? And a causeway of old mill-stones you could walk across dry-shod. Water-lily buds stuck up on long thin necks, presumably waiting for the dusk and opening-time. A small bronze temple has been set in the middle of the upper pool. It is in the pagoda-style the Nepalese invented and stands on an island rock not more than two feet wide. A temple bell hangs in the air above it, from a tree, though out of reach for ringing. A weaver-bird's nest hangs up there as well, long as a loofah. Very nice. But head-in-air I'd just caught sight of something far from very nice. A snake. It was coiled around a branch high in a tree beyond the lower pool, too distant to represent immediate threat to me, but to me all snakes are threatful. I estimated this one must uncoil to five-foot plus, but very thin. Was there not something called a whip-snake? This was striped in disagreeable greens and yellows, everything about it disagreeable, even the fact of its absolute immobility. What was it looking at? Had no one noticed it but me? Should I say something? Its tree was very near the lady I took for cook outside her fly-screened kitchen. Was it watching her? She was most certainly watching me. Perhaps I'd say nothing about that snake, in case it were construed as cowardice. How long had it been there? How long had I been *here*? And where could Jagut be? Why didn't he appear? I had so carefully rehearsed all this, prepared myself, had been ready for it when the taxi stopped—but the timing had misfired. In fact I hadn't been here any time at all, because on turning to the house again I saw that they were still busy sharing out my baggage between them. Was I to have the same old room?

I was getting very nervous.

The house, now I came to examine it more closely . . . the house was . . . yes, basically, of course, it was just as I had pictured it and wanted it to be still—rough, rustic, the stone parts slapped with plaster, the wood parts all home-made. Had there always been two outside wooden stairways to link the ground with upper-floor verandah? There must have been: the one outside the room I was thinking of as mine, the other one whose steps came down and forward beside the biggest mango, to within a yard of where I stood there waiting on the cobbles. Of course I knew that Jagut had added to the house (long ago, possibly, though I had learnt of it only from a recent letter), but I didn't quite see where it had been done, nor how. The place seemed larger, yes. Wider, anyway. Yet it had no added-onto look. I'd say that it had simply put on weight, like someone spreading into middle-age. Organic growth. And being here again, such fancies seemed not fanciful at all. This was no longer 'outside world': this was a deep and private 'inner world' and I was well aware that gods and demons haunt its hills and valleys. Nature enjoys unnatural powers here. What easier than for her to lend some to the little house, enough to grow itself new rooms? Nature? 'O God of the Woods . . . !' But who would he be, locally? Who was it that they used to talk about in whispers? Mahasu the Horrible? No good calling on him, anyway. But whoever it may have been that made the rules for here it was way back in pre-history, and the rules are not at all the same as those that outside people live by. This is the country of the Hindu epics, the five Pandava brothers came this way during their twelve-year sojourn 'in the forest'—it's all recorded in the *Mahabharata*. King Asoka came here too, but then he went everywhere and put up those pillars of his. He put one up on the banks of the Jumna not a linear mile from where I stood. He was a late-comer, however, second century B.C. I was for the moment the latest-comer, and in considering the house and the mango-tree again my head let in a madder fancy still: that it was not, after all, to the little house that those unnatural powers had been assigned but to the mango-tree beside it. Those huge encircling wooden arms, that forearm in particular, hooked into the upper-floor verandah, all predatory, not protective, bent on rape, possession—and slap across this sobering

21

thought, across the years, suddenly, a voice that reached me louder with each word it uttered: loud from within an upper-room; louder, from the verandah that the room gave onto; then from the topmost rung of the wooden stairway louder still, that voice, urgent, staccato, authentic, unchanged:

'Prepare to greet a dark old skeleton!'
—and down the stairs came Jagut, two steps at a time, dark glasses, shorts, shirt, jaunty Gurkha cap, long-leggèd, barefoot, down the stairway with a mid-flight change of rhythm where the wooden rungs end up in widening steps of brick—out onto the cobbles he came leaping, to land up straight in front of me:

'Peter!'
'Jagut!'

Face to face we stood there rigid, numb with the horror of complete non-recognition.

I must have dropped my eyes, because a second later they had riveted themselves on Jagut's copper toe-rings.

2

It was Jagut who broke the awful pin-drop silence—a single word
rapped out as sharp and peremptory as an exorcism: '*CHAI!*'

I raised my eyes again. What was he looking at so fixedly from
behind his dark-glasses? My baggage? Alas, so much of it. Was
that what he was thinking too? Poor Jagut who so loves his solitude. Did he think that I must plan to stay forever? Or was he
staring at my baggage so as not to stare at me?

'Rameshwar! Bring tea! Give that bag to Tuman! Sarwa! Hot
water! The sahib will want to wash his hands for tea.'

New names and faces—Jagut's not new, but. . . . Heavens, how
thin he'd got! But I must not stare, we must not stare, not yet.
There was no mistaking Jagut's voice, in any case, the urgent
grittiness it always had had. I'd cling to the remembered sound of
it. Why was that woman staring so, outside the fly-screened door?
Did she recognise me? She could not possibly! But she might
know who I must be. Could *she* be Saraswati—once young and
bold and beautiful, the one that Jagut used to call 'First Lady of
Soon Saan'? His letters had made no mention of her. Perhaps. . . .
But I wouldn't ask; I'd wait for him to speak of her. His voice cut
in on this; I didn't catch the words, only the English sound of
them. I turned to find him staring at my taxi.

'Did you say something, Jagut?'

'Well, yes. . . . You see we thought that you'd be riding in by
bike.'

What did he mean exactly? There was no need, nor even time,
to ask him. He had escaped into another string of orders.

'Shambhu! Take that suitcase from Deepak; he's much too
small for it. Fateh! You! The bed-roll. Nanu, that other bag!'

Deepak, ten years old, at most eleven, now got my mini tape-recorder. More new names and faces. The major-domo—his was a name I knew, Bal Bahadur—but he was missing. What would he look like now?

'Your child, Tuman,' Jagut was saying sharply to the tall thin Rajput. 'What's that he's got? A thermos-flask? He'll drop it sure as sure. Jagdish! Give it here to me!'

Jagdish, five or six-ish, did no such thing: he hid himself and prize behind his father's ballooning *paejama*. I said:

'That flask, Jagut. Could I perhaps have a refill of ice for it, please? Or have you got a refrigerator now, possibly? It's . . .'— and then I didn't tell him what was in it. I'd wait till I felt surer of myself. I hoped the stuff would keep meanwhile.

Jagut's mind was elsewhere anyway. He had swung about, one foot now on the bottom rung of the wooden stairway straight ahead. 'Come on, Peter. We're putting you in your old room, for auld lang syne. Though the new suite is really nicer. Come on up and choose for yourself.'

As he ran upstairs I called out after him. 'One second! I've got to pay the taxi off.' At the same time I was wondering if the new 'suite' also had the river view I longed for. I shouted up to ask him.

His head whipped out over the verandah railings up above. 'Taxi? Not an anna more than thirty-five rupees. That's the rate from Dehra.' His head whipped away, then reappeared. 'No. The new room only looks out over lily-pools. You like my lily-pools?'— and Jagut was invisible again.

Action! That was the stuff for blanketing our little 'situation' with. Clever Jagut. I'd follow blindly. Action! Movement! And how quick his movements were, too. Of course they always had been; and again (of course) 'always' was away behind us in the past, and now it was the present, with Jagut still as agile as a monkey. No. Not a monkey. What was he as agile as? What was it somebody had had to say about agility in writing of the family's illustrious ancestor, Jung Bahadur, the year he left Nepal to visit Queen Victoria in London? Jagut's disembodied voice had snapped this thread as well.

'Thirty-five chips and not an anna more, mind! You Whites, you've always spoilt the market for us.'

I could hear his laugh, and the past moved in a fraction closer.

I gave the taxi-man the forty-five I'd settled for (of course I had to) and a tip on top of it—and this not generosity, alas: more

24

from fear of its being whispered round about how mean I was. Not a soul at Soon Saan but would know five minutes later how much or little I had given. They would have asked: the driver would have told them, volunteering smugly '—and five rupees bakshish. . . .'

The corner of my eye took in the predatory mango alongside me as I climbed the stairway. Jugut's voice was muffled, calling, 'I'm in here. Second door along—past mine. Your old room. Remember?'

Yes, I remembered clearly: Jagut's room, a narrow passage just beyond it to the back verandah, then 'my' room. I went in.

It was dark inside, after the strong sunlight, and empty. No, not empty. An old woman was standing in the shadows, head bowed.

'Where are you, Jagut?'

'In your bathroom—checking. Half a mo'.'

'My' old room. Fly-screened doors and windows darken it agreeably, these and the overhang of the verandahs, front and back. Outside underneath the trees the evening air had seemed about as hot as noonday in the sun of summers we'd call hot in England. Inside here it was cool as well as dark. My eyes moved round the room, small, rough and cottagey: part masonry, part wood-partitioning. Not so small, after all, but seeming so because so filled with outsize furniture, the same familiar Anglo-Indian stuff. How comforting to see. 'My' room. Why think inverted-commas, though? It was mine again.

Would the shadowy old woman be looking after me? She was Nepalese and very tiny. She had come forward now and was rolling back the bedclothes, laterally, across the width of the bed, as they tend to on board ship. Jagut appeared through the side-door of what I knew to be my bathroom. 'Everything's all right, I think,' he said. 'Soap, lav-bumph—or there's a *lota*, if you like. Sarwa will be up with the hot water in a moment. And towels. Wouldn't you like to see the other bedroom? The new one? It's all ready for you, too—just in case.'

'No, thank you. This is the one for me.'

There is a big low window opening on the view across the back verandah, a door beside it. Jagut's hand was on the door-knob and in the half-light I could see that he was busy with a rapid bedroom-check. A moment later he was saying, 'I told them flowers, I'll tell them so again. And where's the fly-swat?' He turned to the old woman and asked her and her hands made fainting gestures that seemed to have no meaning.

'Where are the flies?' I asked.

'You never know, there might be some. That's Afim, by the bed. Look, she's wishing you, Peter.'

I 'wished' her back—'wishing' is Anglo-Indian for greeting someone. My hands went *namaste, namaste*. She had left her hands in the raised *namaste* position and now allowed her old fingers to interlock themselves, soft and quiet.

'Come on!' Jagut had opened the back-verandah door and was going out through it—but I lingered, looking round again, determined not to rush this moment.

'But Jagut,' I said, raising my voice, gaining time. 'Afim? Surely that means "opium", doesn't it? *Afim? Afyun?* Two syllables, or three?'

'Yes, opium, of course. Two syllables for her, though. The others call her that.'

'All these new names and faces.'

'I expect it is a bit bewildering at first. It might be easier if they had descriptive nicknames. She'd be Mrs Midget. Come along, there's something else to show you.'

Mrs Midget and I stood looking at each other, her blank unblinking eyes part-closed by the epicanthic fold—was she 'high' on her blessed poppy, possibly? She is very Mongol in looks, and very midgety, I'm bound to say. I hoped she didn't know what midget meant. I tried her out for English, slowly, loudly, clearly. 'Do you speak English?' She just stood there looking vague and Jagut's head came through the doorway:

'What's that? English? She doesn't understand a thing in any language, even in her own. She's the silliest woman alive. But that doesn't make her the less glorious. Reflected glory. She's my major-domo's sister. His *full*-sister.'

It was calming, somehow, this dialogue with no demands to make, me in the safe, familiar, darkened room, Jagut outside, the way he spoke, his command of highly idiosyncratic English, his voice so reassuringly his own—even if there were a note of mild impatience in it now:

'Get a move on, you old slow-coach. I've got to dash. But I want to show you something first. Your annexe.'

'Annexe?'

'Yes. Come and look.'

By the time I was out on the back verandah he was already through a doorway in the end-wall, left, but the view from the verandah stopped me in my tracks, just as it had the first time I had seen it—that staggering view, the green, the gold, the blue for sky, the mountains, valley, the river far below us, the distant roaring of its waters so much louder here behind the house than from the cobbles out in front. I think I said, 'Oh look!'—Full-grown trees and foliage now conceal how the ground drops vertically away behind the house. But Jagut was a fidget, I could see that much in the periphery of my vision. Perhaps he really had a busy evening ahead, whereas I'd thought that he was merely stepping up the pace deliberately, to bemuse us both with Action! Movement!, give us no time to think.

'Your view's not going to budge, I promise you,' he said. 'Come on in. Look! Your private annexe!' I went in too.

'I thought that you could sit and write in here,' he said. 'What do you write, though, Peter? You never used to write. Is it books?'

'Not many.'

'How do you like your new private annexe?'

'I like it very much indeed'—and indeed I did, too. My annexe. The full Victoriana salvaged from sold-up palaces, no doubt. The family had had their share of huge great palaces and jumbo furniture and embellishments to fill them with. There had been one such in the mountains not so far from here—Fairlawn Palace. It was outside a little township, Mussoorie, a nineteenth-century Anglo-Indian invention called a 'hill-station', where the Whites escaped the horrors of an Indian summer in the plains. Jagut's youngest brother—youngest full-brother—was named 'Mussoorie' after it.

But my annexe was far too small for anything but the smallest palace sofa, the smallest overstuffed armchairs, the reds, the oranges, the braid and bobbles, and everything *capitonné* as deep as belly-buttons. This I took rapid stock of, as of the window on the river-view that almost fills one wall. The photographs would all be 'family-members', mostly of a generation further back, silver frames, a sort of royal progress in fading sepia tones round three of the four walls. I'd be examining them later, I'd identify them all, with Jagut's help. Which would be 'father', for example? That one! It had to be. When first I'd known Mussoorie, the youngest brother, he was the spitting image of this resplendent figure.

As it happened I knew a great deal more about the family in

27

general terms than Jagut realised. They'd never seemed to speak of it themselves in those far-off days. The past was already long since buried for them, I expect, a past set in the Valley of Nepal, in Kathmandu that only the oldest of the children had ever even seen—that too as infants, before their father's exile. They weren't much interested, I imagine. But I was deeply interested, and had been reading it all up in London where the Political and Secret files on Nepal are preserved in the old India Office Library and Records. I would speak of it to Jagut later. He could hardly have had a chance to see the official papers, but their father must have spoken of Nepal to them as children, there would be family tradition to throw a different light on things. All this could wait, however. For the present I was following impatient Jagut through a door into my bathroom, fourth and final element in a little intercommunicating private suite.

The bathroom is partitioned off in wood and narrow as a passage, a real old-fashioned Anglo-Indian bath-house. The big zinc tub, an oval, sloping sides, enamelled green outside and white within. The slatted wooden footboard by it, the wash-stand, all exactly as it should be. But in place of the traditional square wooden commode with the bucket hidden underneath the lid—the 'thunderbox', traditionally so-called—I saw a pedestal of finest porcelain, of palace-size, with flowers festooning all about in blue and gold on white. Could this splendid object flush itself? No, of course it couldn't! Was I mad? Not flush in any sense of pulling plugs and running water. Two buckets stood nearby for sluicing everything away and away, down a long-drop, doubtless. There was a third bucket in the room as well, on the ground beside the wash-stand, steaming, carried up by Sarwa. I could see him through the door into my bedroom, waiting, towel across his arm.

'Good,' Jagut said. 'If there's anything you need, tell Sarwa. I'll leave you now. To freshen up. In fact I'm terribly behindhand with the evening—I must hop it quick.' He hopped it, calling to me as he went, 'Tea on the front verandah. I expect it's there already.'

There was room for Sarwa to come in now, and he did so, silently. I watched him, thinking. I like the dual elements in Jagut's world, the Rajput and the Nepalese; I like this moment's respite, washing hands for tea, the ceremonial presentation of a towel to dry them on. I've forgotten what it's like to be looked after—but I like it. I thanked the man, nodding, smiling, forgetting also that this must strike him as a silly thing to do. What could there be to smile about? He wasn't going to smile himself, he wasn't even looking at me. These little western tricks, the gracious smiles, the nervous smiles, the nods and becks—I must put them all aside, and quickly.

Out on the verandah I found tea ready waiting. Jagut was down below: I could hear his voice, so I crossed to the railings and looked over. Yes, there he stood, talking earnestly to a couple of peasants, an older man, and a younger who was probably a son. Jagut said something, the old man answered, Jagut clicked his tongue in sympathy, then broke in with some vehemence, even with passion—not a command, it seemed to me. It sounded like an exasperated plea. The old man's manner could perhaps be called deferential, but in no sense obsequious. There never had been any hint of *zemindar* in Jagut's character. *Zemindars* were the old-style Indian feudal landlords. Too often they were absentees, concerned only to milk their holdings to the last miserable drop. Cows like it better than do peasants. Their peasants were the sorriest of serfs, and cruelly down-trodden. But the *zemindars* of other times have had their claws filed to the quick since then. Jagut seems to have had no claws to file. He may have sensed that I was watching him from up above. He looked up.

'Ah! There you are. Pour yourself some tea and start without me. I'll be with you in two-two's.' And he was once again engrossed with the two peasants.

I sat down, busying my hands with tea-pot, tea-cup, sugar, I ate a home-made biscuit, I looked about.

The room beyond mine—the new room, I suppose—projects some eight feet further forward than my own, so that its side-wall and my front-wall between them form a convenient sitting-place, with two small divans set at right angles to each other to flank a corner table. The verandah has widened here, moreover, to accommodate the second outside stairway. Jagut was coming up it now, and saying, '—at last I can swallow down a cup of tea.' He sat down and poured it, but this done he was on his feet again and at the railings, firing down his orders in machine-gun rasps of sound, his head flick-flicking left–right–centre. In fact he seemed deliberately engrossed. 'Afternoon tea' was being made a succession of attention-catching interruptions that Jagut snatched at and I too was grateful for. He didn't sit again, but stood directing from above the course of life below us on the cobbles.

There is no doubt that 'tea-corner' provides him with an admirable vantage-point. It covers not only the cobbled area—which I already sense must serve as Soon Saan's 'apron-stage'—but enjoys views long and unobstructed across the lily-pools to where an ochre-coloured cottage stands beyond the lower of them and the woods begin. I watched the woman I'd identified as cook climb slowly, heavily, up its outside stairway. Left of the lily-pools the three great mangoes arch and frame the village view, some fifty yards or more away. And that was something very odd! One of the two lesser mango-giants had lost the whole of its once-towering top. Lopped right off! Flat stumps stick up at various levels above the lateral branches. A Buddha's head in brass crowns one of them, a sugar-loaf-shaped stone another. Strange, but satisfying to the eye. What I call 'lianas' (from my childhood Tarzan reading) loop and festoon like great green garlands between the various trees. What a marvellous place this is! And as the afternoon wore on the light flowed in obliquely, softly yellow, below the lowest branches of the highest trees, flooding the farmyard, the idle bullock-carts, men as they moved about on different errands, the pariah-pack laid out tranquil in the warm dry dust.

Jagut at the railings had half-turned towards me, at pains to excuse himself for being so inhospitably unable to give me his attention, '—and you arrived this minute only!' But saying this he abandoned all pretence, 'There'll be loads of opportunity for talk. We've all our time ahead of us and if I don't watch out— like an eagle!—everything goes wrong. Look! Peter! Did you see that?' And *flash!* he was gone from me, was away along the verandah, had reached the head of mango-stairway, was half-way down it, leaving me wondering what it was that should have startled me. I stopped being startled, poured myself more tea and ate another home-made biscuit.

It was at this point that a man appeared at the stairhead alongside me, a pleasant-looking man, mid-brown, unlike anyone at Soon Saan that I'd seen already. He made *namastes* and politely introduced himself. He was the government stockman, he said, name such-and-such, and could I tell him where the Rana sahib might be, please? So I said he'd just gone down, and introduced myself politely and directed a couple of seated *namastes* at him, thinking that a seated *namaste* ought to pass—with one's juniors at least, but uncertain if I should invite him to sit too. I didn't. He was explaining that at Rana sahib's request he had come this evening to perform artificial insemination on a young cross-bred Jersey cow at present in her season. His English was rather good, an educated man.

This stockman could examine me minutely (as Jagut couldn't yet) and examine me he did, though not rudely in the least. He had no preconceptions about what my looks should be, so my present-day appearance perplexed him not at all. He took it quite for granted that I should look like this and be the person that I'd said I was, and of an age to be his father. His next sentence did perplex me, though. He said:

'You see, sir, we thought that you'd be riding in by bike.'

And I had started to reply, 'Yes, of course, I do see, but...' —but couldn't bring myself to finish asking why on earth this business, bike or taxi, should have so fascinated everyone. And then I realised that he wasn't even listening. He was peering down over the railings and saying, 'Yes, there is Rana sahib—down.' And purely for a social fill-in I half-rose, leaned forward, peered down too, and there indeed was Jagut in vital conversation with yet another peasant, this one barefoot as himself. The stockman was preparing to take his leave of me but paused a moment longer, pointing to a hole in the roof-timbers, quite a large hole that seemed to lead over what was probably the ceiling of the room next door to mine.

'That is where the roof-snake lives, sir,' he told me.

'...roof-snake lives—?'

'Yes, sir; and out she comes from there, and down.'

He was pointing again, this time with a gesture that finished in a spiral movement round one of the vertical wooden supports of the stairway. 'She comes down like this—and she goes about her business. Then she returns. But she seldom lets herself be seen.'

'Once would be quite enough.' I made my voice as light as I could manage. 'Is she thin, by the way? Possibly striped green and yellow?'

'No, oh no, sir! She is fat and the colour of ripened wheat.'

Ripened wheat? I perfectly well know that this is the preferred skin-colour for a northern-Indian male, the preferred colour for a girl being a few tones fairer—say 'ripening-wheat'. I had never heard snake-colours so expressed, however. I asked the stockman a second question:

'If she *were* green and yellow—and *thin*.... If. Would she then be a whip-snake?'

He pondered on this for a moment, then said, 'I do not know whip-snake, sir.'

'Please tell me. Is she very long as well as fat?'

With the greatest satisfaction he assured me that she was enormous, adding, to explain things, 'And that, sir, is why the hole up there must be so big.' He was again preparing to go, but first said, 'I hope Your Honour will honour us by being present at the insemination, sir.'

'How kind.' I gave him a seated bow.

'We shall be hoping for a little cow-calf this time.'

He seemed to enjoy talking English, and I liked him for it; I hadn't liked the taxi-driver for it, but that was because he spoke it so badly and I wanted to try out Hindi. I could not presume to talk my rusty Hindi to this cultivated fellow.

'Yes, a cow-calf is what we desire. It is milk we want. This season so far only bull-calves and what is the good of that to a Hindu gentleman like Rana sahib? I myself am Muslim, and for Muslims beef is good. But for Hindu gentleman, oh no, that would never do, never. The very thought would make him vomit. He could never be party even to selling off a bull for slaughter; and these beautiful little Jersey cross-breds are too small, too small, for draught oxen.'

Thereupon he left me to my thoughts. My first thought was, who made that hole so big? My second, what on earth would I do if the enormous lady roof-snake were to make one of her rare appearances while I was sitting there alone in tea-corner?

I then emptied out my head and simply sat, but after a little allowed myself a few simple unexacting speculations, such as, what will there be for dinner? (for I had had no lunch); and another speculation: will the westering sun at any moment now slip down low enough to send its yellow-orange-reddened rays in underneath the roof of the verandah I am sitting on...? But who would that be passing down below—what was his name, I meant. The man with the child—crossing the water-channel now, over the culvert, tall and thin, the child round and plump. Yes, they were Tuman Singh and his little son Jagdish. I was quite pleased at remembering so freely. I tried out a string of names, at least I was about to when Jagut came up the mango-stairway and along the verandah towards me, looking pensive.

'That old peasant there—you saw?'

'Bare feet? I saw.'

Jagut took a gulp of cold tea. 'That poor old man. His buffalo is sick. Since yesterday. His buffalo is his life. We are not yet quite sure what is wrong with it.'

'Perhaps the government stockman could . . .'

'Heavens! Thank God you reminded me. The insemination ceremony. Yes, he told me that you'd graciously consented to be there as well. We must hurry, Peter—or there'll certainly be no time this evening to inspect the buffalo. Even as it is, I doubt if . . . Come! We mustn't keep the assembly waiting. "Punctuality is the politeness of kings"—Father often used to say that. Off we go. The stockman's quite a dab-hand at the job. He's promised to withhold the climax till we arrive—but we mustn't try him too far. There is such a thing as *jaculatio praecox*, so I'm told. On with your shoes!'

'I've got them on already.'

'So you have. This way.'

He led me along the verandah. Just by mango-stairway there is a railed-in corner with a bench and under the bench an assortment of old shoes. Jagut chose a pair. 'Immediately after the insemination—*if* time—I much want to inspect that poor buffalo. Then for the Grand Tour!'

He had pulled the first shoe on and now took up the second. I said, in some surprise, 'Don't you have to take off your toe-rings when you wear shoes, then?'

'Oh no.' He pulled on the second. 'With smart tight town-shoes, or dancing-pumps, of course. Not with these clod-hoppers. Now. You'll need this.' He reached for a couple of staffs that stood against the railings and gave me one of them, a nice, straight well-balanced five-foot staff, agreeable to handle. His own, I noticed, had quite a curve to it which I would not fancy for myself, but he liked it so, presumably. He had unhooked an odd old cap that must be American armed-forces disposals, creamily-khaki cloth with a peak like a beak.

'Down we go!'

And down we went, out onto the cobbles, Jagut first, over the culvert with me asking, 'Do you suffer from rheumatism, Jagut?'—because I was still rather struck by his toe-rings. But the geese and their sudden honking as they withdrew on our approach distracted his attention; then it was the ducks and chickens; then the pariah-pack. The latter all got up respectfully as we drew near, shaking their pelts free of dust. 'Kalé!' Jagut said severely to the

33

biggest of them, the callow dog with the starey coat. 'Kalé! Stop it!'

Kalé wasn't doing anything to warrant this that I could see, so I said, 'Stop what, Jagut?'

'Fancying birds. Kalé's a convicted bird-fancier. He knows what I meant—don't you, Kalé? See him now, guiltily cringing? He was fancying that fat Rhode Island Red—*shoo!*' said Jagut to the thoughtless fowl who had ventured dangerously close to Kalé, and the bird ran off to safer distances. 'When he's not fancying birds, he's fancying his sister—that bitch behind him. The pretty one.'

'Mushroom and ivory fur?'

'Yes. That's the one—a half-sister only, actually. She came of age for the first time recently. We locked her up. We decided she was too small for Kalé still.' Kalé had stopped his guilty cringing and was wagging his tail and fawning on Jagut now. Faithful to my decision I remained aloof. 'Come on,' Jagut said. 'And just look! The world and his wife—all come to the insemination ceremony!'

There ahead, their dark-brown hillman skins turned greenish-drab by the golden horizontal light that streamed in on them, was 'All Soon Saan', men and women, their children of the varying sizes to get mounted on a shoulder or a hip or just left free-ranging with White Sussex fowls and fat Rhode Island Reds. Jagut now clapped his odd old cap onto his head, right down to his eye-brows, and instantly looked both beaked and birdlike. And in the same instant I could see that he was far from being 'bird', not even partly; he was.... What was he, then? Part-creature, anyway, as well as man. What creature?

The insemination. It may prove fruitful in the fullness of its time and if so, that will be its justification. Judged as pure spectacle it was a sorry disappointment to us all, I fear. The stock-man, understudying the male lead, gave as spirited a performance as could be expected of a stand-in so lamentably no match for the real thing, but the little Jersey cross-bred cast as leading-lady—frankly she made no attempt at all to conceal her boredom. Yet this was scarcely the poor stockman's fault, so Jagut was quick to congratulate him:

'Well done, something-sahib!' he said in English, perhaps to please the man. 'And will you stay and eat and stop the night? Please tell my major-domo to have it all prepared for you. No? You really must get back? Some other visit, then. Thank you again. And offer up a prayer, please, for a little cow-calf this time, will you? Come on, Peter. To the Rice Bowl.'

As we left the gathering Jagut whispered to me, 'I said "To the Rice Bowl!" to put the stockman off the scent. Someone may have told him about that buffalo, and I don't want him, or *anyone*, to know we're going to take a peep. We've just got time, I think, and light enough. We'll have a secret peep, without the owner's knowing, above all he mustn't know—' And before I had a chance to ask why not, Jagut was off, out from the farmyard where the inseminating rites had just now been performed, through the gates, Jagut leading, me following, downhill through the orchards, bearing left up the first tributary-track and climbing till he slipped in through a sort of natural leafy archway and slowed down. He turned, finger to lips to caution me to silence. Now he was making signals for a crouching passage under the protection of a built-up bank between two groups of trees. He stopped. I stopped too.

'Shhh-h-h.... I'll just take the first peep. To see if the coast's clear. Keep your head down, Peter. Yes. Yes, it's all right. Nobody about. And there the poor creature is, too. Flat on the ground. No, no, not on its back! On its *side*. You can safely look now. Yes, that little stone cottage on the left is theirs—mine, really; they're my tenants. Now. What would you say about that buffalo?'

'It certainly does look very sick.'

'We'd better crouch again—in case the old man comes out. He must be home now. We came a long way round. On purpose. To give him time, and not run into him. But the buffalo—sick, you said? Just simply sick?'

'Perhaps it's very sick indeed. And its head flat to the ground, too.... Dogs, yes, of course. But things like cattle, horses, surely they don't lay their heads flat to the ground normally. Is it sleeping? Did you notice? Its eyes looked closed to me, though it's hard to be sure at this distance. Shall we look again? Perhaps if we could get a little closer....'

'No, no, no—there's nowhere closer where we wouldn't be seen *at once!*'

'Would it really matter if we were seen, though? I haven't understood why it's so secret.'

'*I must not be involved!* I must not even allow myself to appear too sympathetic.'

'Why not? And anyway you've shown you are, already. And

35

you *are* involved. I saw you with the owner—I saw from the verandah. You were full of sympathy.'

'You're muddling it all up. That was with *two* men, another matter altogether—a matter where overt sympathy was quite in order, the poor people. But in the affair of the buffalo, no.'

'I honestly don't see why you didn't get the government stockman to give the creature a looking-over.'

'You haven't understood at all. But then, how should you? The wretched creature isn't sick in any animal-husbandry sort of way—from what its owner says. And mark you, peasants know much more about certain things than we educated people do. That buffalo has been bewitched. Yesterday fat and healthy (so its owner claims) and look at it today! We'll take another peep, a quick one, before we go. There! See its ribs? So thin and wasted? It's wasting away in the space of twenty-four hours. That buffalo isn't going to greet another dawn. We'd better crouch again.'

'Poor animal. But Jagut...—do you really.... I mean, you *do* believe in witchcraft, do you?'

'Don't *you*?'

'Well yes, I suppose I do.... In an evil-eyeing sort of way.'

'Exactly! And everything else. Living in these parts you simply have to believe—a bit, anyhow. And what is more the buffalo's owner is in no doubt about who's done it.'

'You have a sorcerer, then?'

'No, no, no! Of course not! It's only what some people say. A woman. Not a man. And a resident "pros"....'

'Prostitute, you mean?'

'Of course. But she's not on my establishment, naturally. Free-lance. I don't believe she's doing very well. A good, hard-working woman, she's said to be. But the other lady I was speaking of—that's quite a different matter. Tough? She's tough. Did you notice the other cottage? Further to the right—on a terraced area with a wind-break of trees?'

'I think I did.'

'That's where she lives, the lady in question. She's my tenant too. At least her husbands are.'

'A polyandrous lady?'

'She's got a couple of brothers.'

'Like Queen Draupadi marrying the Pandava brothers in the *Mahabharata*?'

'Exactly. All five of them. You know that little temple upriver from us, a mile or so away? That's supposed to be connected with the Pandava brothers. Built on the foundations of an ancient temple —something of the sort. Tomorrow may be a good day for temple-visiting, à propos. I'm sorry to say I haven't been for some time— did we ever go together?'

'No. I wonder why not.'

'In fact the resident *jogi* may rather expect it of me. You needn't come unless you want to.'

'Not want to? Of course I want to!'

'Good. It's the first day of our Dussehra festival.'

'Heavens! I hadn't realised. The ten-day festival? What a moment to have picked for my arrival. At random, too. I hadn't troubled to check. I do hope it isn't terribly inconvenient.'

'Not in the least. Except that you must forgive us if the household service isn't up to scratch. I've had to give some of the staff leave-of-absence for it.'

'But please.... I don't need looking-after. I'm not used to it, either—since my Indian days. I'm so sorry.'

'It doesn't matter at all, except for your sake. Right. Tomorrow we'll make our little *acte de présence* at the temple together. This one is dedicated to the goddess Durga.'

'It might not be a bad thing if the poor buffalo's owner were to visit her as well. You know—magic, and all that.'

'That's for him to decide about. I'm taking no sides in this. I must keep out of it. Tomorrow may be too late, anyway. You do see, now, though, don't you, how imperative it is that I avoid getting involved in any way? In a case of theft, yes. Possibly. Though thefts are rare in these remote areas. But arbitrate in a bewitchment dispute—never? They've got the Panchayat—the village-council thing. But of course they get paid: whereas they wouldn't have to pay me if I should consent to arbitrate—which I most certainly shall not do. We'd better get on, Peter, or we'll never be home before dark. And as for that poor buffalo, everybody says that since no one in these parts has knowledge of *mantrams* to unbewitch it with, it must simply take its chance.'

'It does seem sad. I suppose the lady in question must know how to remove the magic—if she wants to? Supposing the complainants paid her to remove it, instead of the Panchayat to pass judgement?'

'My dear Peter, if she doesn't know how to bewitch things, how can you expect her to unbewitch them? And if she could, would you have her bewitching all and sundry and making us pay ransom money?'

'Oh, yes, of course. How silly of me.'

'Off with us, now! We'll have to keep our heads down till we reach the cover of the mango-grove. I don't want the lady to catch us snooping in her vicinity, either—not today, not with her handiwork still breathing. Incidentally, one of her husbands has just absconded in a fit of tantrums. That will not have put her in her sunniest mood. But he'll be back. Enough! To the Rice Bowl!'

Directly we reached the mango-grove and could straighten up once more Jagut put on speed and away we went, with him leading, me following. '... they're *langras*, these mangoes...' he called back to me, '... best in all northern India, second only to those wonderful Afonsos we used to get in Bombay, remember?' And I did indeed remember, but was far too much concerned with keeping up with him to embark on raised-voice conversation. We had come to Jagut's 'private lane' up from the valley, two men were coming down it—the two I'd seen with Jagut on the cobbles at the house, or so I thought. As we crossed the lane I asked him. He paused to look, then forged ahead of me again, down into the trees beyond, his comments reaching me in snatches as I hurried after him. 'Yes...—father and son: you guessed? They have a problem, too—mind out here, this ditch. Are you all right?—a problem... and they will not listen to me. Perhaps.... I was saying perhaps—I'll be able to... to persuade the second son; he's much less... stubborn, a stronger character at the same time too.... The third son is a leper, poor boy. Well, not exactly "boy" by now—who is? He must be thirty....'

'Is he their problem, then?' It was difficult to make him hear, whizzing along behind him on a narrow track. We'd reached an open field, on either side of us a high-growing crop of what I took for lentils. 'What was that?' he shouted, slackening his pace a bit. I repeated what I'd said and he replied, 'Yes, the leper son's their problem. I must at all costs have a word with the middle son. And soon.' The pace was easier now. Wrong shoes, short breath. I was glad of a let-up.

'Somehow I must prevent things coming to a head,' Jagut was saying, 'If poss. No time this evening, though. But there's not all that urgency, I think. Not like it is with the poor buffalo. Why didn't the owner tell me days ago? It can't have been sickening only since yesterday. Nobody's *mantrams* could take the flesh off that quick. Do you think you can manage this wall, Peter? We could go on further up and through a gate, but—yes, of course you can manage it! Have a shot. Look!' And there was Jagut up it, on it, jumping down the other side and laughing triumphantly. 'Come on!' And I was scrambling over it as best I might. 'That's the way,' he called back in encouragement, and off we went, a quickened pace again, with Jagut shouting to me, 'I shouldn't really call it the Grand Tour—it's only a sectional tour each evening.'

Soon we were passing the feathery-yellow plantation with the golden plum-sized fruit I had failed to identify on my arrival. 'Those? Why, they're *amla*,' Jagut said over his shoulder in answer to my question. 'A-M-L-A. Not sure of the botanical name, but the English used to call it "star-apple" when they were here. All the vitamins–plus. You shall try it for breakfast: we make a preserve of it. And a chutney.'

And he was off again, skimming ahead of me, bird-beak cap and shorts and shirt and long brown legs—leaping irrigation-ditches, slithering down banks, and when we finally got to what he'd called his Rice Bowl, the terraced paddy-fields descending to the river, he was running along the knife-edge ridges that divide the differing levels. 'Look! Not long now for the harvest!' And I must follow somehow, puffing and off-balance. How dare he be as lithe as a young man still! Once he stopped to let me catch him up; once he paused in flight, his eye caught by something that he wanted, a big smooth sugar-loaf of a stone. He bent down, eased it out of its niche, rolled it onto the track. 'Not the very best I've seen,' he said, appraising it. 'A very imperfect cone, but never mind. They know I like such stones.'

'I've seen one in a tree. By the house. Very nice.'

'You have? Yes, it is nice, isn't it? I keep on telling them, all and any of them, never come empty-handed home. Even if it is only a fairly well-shaped stone like this one, or an armful of kindling, or fodder for the cattle; the time is coming, I can see, when I'll have to cut down on my dairy. Three grass-cutters aren't enough and I can't afford to increase my pay-roll. Had you heard about the new land-ceilings—and the bogey of expropriation if we don't reduce our holdings to the maximum now set at forty acres?'

'But Jagut . . .'

'I'll tell you all about it later if you're interested. Now. This stone. Here. Right in the middle of the path. Let it be a test-case. How long will it take for someone to see it and bring it up to me? Oh yes, I like such stones. And my mushrooms, did you notice them?'

'Mushrooms?'

'Big stone mushrooms. In front of the house by the lily-pools. *Not noticed them?*'

'A Buddha's head—on a rock: and another high in a mango-tree. Yes, and that sugar-loaf in a tree too. Mushrooms? Not yet. I've only been here an hour or so, you know. Give me time.'

'I was forgetting. And you're tired out—from the journey. I saw as much at once.' He gave me a quick look and away again quick. 'Yes, it's the journey, of course,' he went on hurriedly. 'Perhaps I'll let you off the rest of the Grand Tour tonight, and we'll go straight back home. But I must just—on the way—I ought to look in on my pigs. To make sure everything's all right. I've given my pigman leave-of-absence for Dussehra. He's left his daughter in charge. I'd like to see . . .'

Off again behind his flying figure, over another wall—perhaps the same one in the other direction, higher up. We were climbing. Then bent double for some fifty yards, not for concealment this time but because of tunnelled undergrowth—'I'm taking you the shortest way'—really the bed of some small streamlet seasonally dry at present, rocks and a little standing water underfoot. Out into the dying sunshine once again—and Jagut had nipped in under a tree to emerge dragging a big dead branch behind him.

'There!' He laid it squarely across the path. 'That's today's Test Case No. 2.'

We overtook a group of peasants on their slow way homewards up the hill; they stopped, and now stood aside to let us by, making *namastes* at us. Jagut gestured back and said a word or two to them, then a firm word for me: 'It's not like in the British Army where I believe the senior officer present takes the salute—and I'm senior only in years, mark you: oh yes, I must be older than you but . . . never mind. It doesn't do to brood. *You* should also wish them. It's very improper not to.' So I wished them all belatedly and they had to do it all over again for me, while Jagut rattled off their names and all about them, about their wives, their children, virtues, vices. And off again—a whirlwind whistle-stop tour, my first evening, it was too soon, too quick, I could not take in any more. I want so much to play an interested part in Jagut's whirligig again, a part as intimate as my increasing foreignness allows: I shall do my utmost to remember everything, everyone, name, community, virtues, vices.

Another wall to scramble on to and jump off again—jumping for Jagut ('Nearly there now!'), slithering for me. I am astonished at the elasticity of all his movements, his sure-footedness. And very envious. What is he as agile as? He had leapt from that last wall to the apex of a boulder and landed up—yes, in retrospect, I almost think of it as landing up on all four sharp little conjoined hoofs. He's a mountain-goat—the part that isn't man! He's part ibex! That's what he is, though I think it may be a little early yet to announce it publicly.

We had entered a coppice.

'Here we are. My pigs. We can rest a moment, Peter. And you can get your breath.'

We stood beside the sties, gazing over a zareeba-hedging at a great fat sow and a boar rooting about in their open run, with a second boar alone in a corner. We scratched at the back of the nearest animal with our staffs. A young girl came up, Nepalese, very pretty in fact, and aged perhaps sixteen. A plump little black-eyed partridge-chick that almost anybody might be pleased with. She was unusually shy and nervous for a Nepalese girl. 'My pig-man's daughter,' Jagut said, and added something to her. She nodded and went behind the sties. In a moment she was back with a basketful of rotting guavas.

'See that mingy creature, that boar in the corner?' Jagut took a guava from the basket. 'He's the new one. Government pig-farms. He's a cross-bred Yorkshire. They gave him to me, a fortnight ago now, to improve our stock. He was so fit and strong when first he got here. Look at him today. Just like that poor buffalo, but a very different reason. I expect he's used to finer fare where he came from than he gets from us, but that's not the reason either.' He tossed a guava in his direction. 'See that?'

Before ever the mingy could get at the guava the sow was on him, biting at his groin, and the other, the bigger, coarser, bolder boar, had buffeted him aside and got the guava for himself.

'He doesn't get his feed—he never gets a square meal, with those other beasts around. But just wait. He'll settle in and grow fat and strong again soon enough: and then let enemies beware! Like Kalé, the biggest member of the pariah-pack, the Bird-Fancier

—you saw him just now. He was a sort of runt once, too, in spite of being so big. But poor Mingy.... Meanwhile the others hate him. Take that!' cried Jagut—and had thwacked the big bully-boar over the shoulder with his staff so that it squealed and fled and Jagut could then drop another guava nicely within Mingy's reach—but did he get it? Not Mingy! The sow was once again too quick for him and had gobbled it down first.

'Your father's gone?' he asked the girl. She was still too shy to do more than nod. 'He's such an excellent worker, this girl's father. He well deserves his Dussehra leave—three days of it, I gave him; and it looks as if the girl can carry on till he gets back. Incidentally, Peter: your guide-and-escort. I don't think I've seen him around since your arrival. Didn't he ...'

I broke in quickly—why should I think that I must cover up his tracks, though? 'You see he really couldn't do much escorting —no room for the bike in the taxi.'

'So-ho!' Jagut said a little ominously. 'Absent-without-leave is he? Dussehra starts tomorrow, does it? Strange coincidence. Very well, he's got till eight this evening to report for duty. He knows perfectly well how short-staffed we are and that with your arrival I may have need of him—my real receptionist's away. I couldn't refuse *him* leave: it's for his son's hair-cutting ceremony, but what with Dussehra hot on the ceremony's heels, and quite soon our Festival of Lights, Divali, he won't be back for ages. I don't begrudge it to him, except for your sake, Peter. He's the only one who's ever really come across the Whites or knows how to handle them—not that we're counting you as White, of course. You're just family-member. I've told them so. Perhaps that was a mistake on my part. I fear they may be rather taking advantage of it.'

' "Family-member" ...'

We had left the sties and were walking quietly up the wooded slopes. A glum young woman *namaste*'d us. 'Glum,' I commented, when she had passed by.

'You'd by glum too, if you were in her shoes. Oh, an unlucky house—I mean the house they're living in. Up near the goat-pens, on the hill behind the cow-sheds: you haven't seen it yet. Since they moved in, nothing but tragedy. I think I'll have to get them somewhere else to stay. A brother died of rabies—and only a week or two ago a sister of snake-bite. Mother, sick—but she's the least of it. Oh yes, an unlucky house all right.'

I murmured something sad as we continued up the slope in

Indian file and the shadows thickened round us—uncertain of each other still. The approach of darkness somehow helped.

'Home again,' said Jagut.

Oil-lamps had been distributed and lit and now stabbed points of brilliance in the windows and from 'tea-corner'. Others had been hooked along the two verandahs, up and down. There was the prickle of wood-smoke in the nostrils. Somewhere out of sight they must be heating up the water for our baths.

Jagut led the way back over the water-channel, on to the cobbles and towards a grouping of a dozen big stone 'mushrooms' of a size to sit on (how could my eye have missed them from 'tea-corner'?). Rameshwar in his houseman's jacket waited by them with two mugs of what I discovered to be *lassi*, a buttermilk-based drink much favoured in warm weather. Indians speaking English call such things a 'beverage'. We chose a mushroom each to sit on. Mine was up against a smooth stone column, very comfortable to lean against. We sipped our 'beverages'. Someone came and took off Jagut's shoes, then took both our staffs. I said with vague relief, 'I'd feared our staffs might be for vaulting with. And that I'd have to try.'

'Vaulting? Vaulting what?'

'I didn't really know. Streams, or little ditches. Boy-scouts do, don't they?'

'Come now! Our staffs are meant for warning snakes with. What do you think I was at, then, tapping at the grass and undergrowth?'

'Ohh—h—h. . . . Yes, I do see now.'

'You'd better tap-tap too, next time. You wouldn't want to trample them, would you?'

'Oh, no, I'd hate to trample them. . . . Incidentally. The snake that lives in the roof. The stockman told me it's enormous.'

'Nonsense. I doubt if it's above five foot in length.'

I have a horror of snakes, those holy beings, but I didn't say so and hoped it didn't show too much. Not every snake in India is holy, I believe, nor even venomous. But it would greatly surprise me if the holiest are not also the most venomous. The hooded cobra is the holiest of them all. In the great god Vishnu's rests between his various earthly avatars he sleeps at peace on a sea-borne bed of cobras. They canopy his head with opened hoods, and rather his than mine.

43

'Now for a nice hot tub,' said Jagut briskly, swigging down his *lassi*. 'It will do you the world of good'—and as we climbed the mango-stairway to our rooms I was considering another thing. It's to be the tub for me, yes: but it's not to be the tub for Jagut, unless I'm much mistaken. He'll be squatting on a footboard, water-buckets hot and cold and dipper handy, and he'll soap and he'll dip and he'll sluice—a good Hindu would never lie back soaking in his own disgusting soap-suds, never! Leave such filthy tricks to the Whites!

I am a White, though, I am a filthy White, and gladly I lolled lamp-lit in my tub of steaming water, and languidly I soaped and dipped and sluiced, and soaped and soaked, the dipper dipping. I lay my head back up against the sloping sides, a sponge to rest it on, muscles all relaxing, the water filling with my own familiar scum, but growing chilly.

'Sarwa!'

How pleasant to call for people and to know there's going to be a willing answer.

'*Ji*, sahib?' Unseen Sarwa's voice.

'*Aur garm pani hai?*'—any more hot water?—successfully enunciated sentence.

Oh, yes, there was plenty more hot water—and I became aware that he was speaking through the panels of my annexe door. It must be that the back-verandah stairs come up beyond it. He knocked. 'Please open, sahib'—which meant my standing up and stretching for the latch. But in any case I'd have had to get out of the tub, for him to pour the water in. Or risk a scalding. Sarwa edged in with two buckets, eyes discreetly, disapprovingly averted. Shocked. I snatched a towel.

'And Sarwa,' I said, making a grand, not a contrite, voice—though in India one should not allow oneself to be seen stark naked in the ordinary social way—'has Rana sahib a . . .'—what was the Hindi for refrigerator? *Baraf*-something, certainly—'*Baraf-ka?*—I started. Sarwa helped me out: '*Frij*, sahib? In dining-room.'

'Good. Take the little thermos—the little one. In the bedroom there. Empty the ice-water. Put the tin back inside. More ice. Then put in fridge, please.'

'Very good, sahib.'

So that was that. No, I wasn't going to produce the tin the first night. I'd wait a day or two.

When Sarwa left me I could hook up the modesty-towel and lower myself into a tub that once more steamed its welcome. Carefully.... *Hot! Ahhh–h–h...!* Did Jagut still keep whisky in the house?

Bathed, dressed, refreshed—a moment just to check that Sarwa had in fact borne off the little thermos (he evidently had: good boy)—I went out on the front verandah.

An oil-lamp with a deep dark shade cast a pool of yellow light on a tray of drinks. Whisky. Good. An Indian brand that I had sampled back in Delhi. 'Black Knight.' Not bad. Which would be Jagut's habitual seat? I didn't know. I sat beside the drinks tray and poured myself a *peg. Chota peg.* Joke-words, they sounded now. At the mango end of the verandah straight in front of me a man came out of Jagut's door—to check if I was there yet, or so I thought, because he glanced my way then went back in again. In a moment Jagut was coming out. He was in a shirt and *loongi*, bare feet, bare head too, and his hair in most peculiar disarray.

'That's right, Peter. A *chota peg.* Only an Indian brand, though; Scotch is prohibitively expensive, alas.'

'It's rather good. Shall I pour you one, since I'm nearest?'

'No thanks. I've got my own local tipple if I want anything. Excuse my get-up. It's my shampoo-hour.'

He sat down on the divan next to my bedroom door.

'Nirmal! Where's that boy got to?'

Along the verandah the man I'd seen just now came out of Jagut's room again, carrying something carefully. He was half-lit by a hanging-lamp then dark again, then lighter as he came forward into range of the lamp beside me. Lamps with such deep dark shades to douse them can't do much to pierce the shadows, but the yellow glow they do give, down and up, is filled with peace and safety. I must memorise this new man's name—Nirmal— together with its allotted face. Not easy: just a shadow face. He was making a little bow towards me, bending over the thing he carried, a saucer. He stationed himself at Jagut's elbow. *'Chalo!'* Jagut said to him. 'Go on, then!' And to me, 'It's mustard-oil we use. So good for the scalp. For the whole body, for that matter. It's Nirmal's evening on shampoo-fatigue.'

'You have one every evening?'

'Yes, of course. *Chalo*, Nirmal, *chal!* What are you waiting for? He seems to think it most indecorous of me to have it done right here in public. In vain I tell him you're not "public"—GO ON, NIRMAL!'—and this time Nirmal did go on, dipping his fingers in the oil, applying it with care, a little here, a little there. He put the saucer down, and then with fingers cupped and stiff he set about the agitation of poor Jagut's scalp as if he would detach it from the skull; it was quite obviously painful, the hardened-rubber flesh-pads of his fingers inexorably at work. And then, for variant, palms of hands performing the same function, fingers stretched immobilised, perhaps less painful. Jagut's agonised expression had relaxed a bit.

He motioned to the man to stop and in the lull said: 'Would you like a shampoo, too, Peter? You would?' He clapped his hands and called out. A head, two heads, appeared at the stairhead alongside me. I suppose their owners had been sitting half-way down. Were they 'in waiting' too this evening?

'You, Shambhu,' Jagut said to one of them. Yes, that was Shambhu: I recognised both name and face. He had helped with the baggage. 'Bring oil. Peter sahib wants a shampoo.'

Shambhu left, to reappear with an oil-saucer, and I surrendered my head to him. Now we were both silenced, though at one point Jagut in a vibro-voice did manage to announce unshakable belief in massage, as it might be in the efficacy of prayer. I'm sure that massage must be good, but it was another of those things I'd lost the habit of. Shampoo. We take our word from Hindi, and Hindi has it from the Sanscrit. The Hindi verb *champna* (in the infinitive) makes *champo* for imperative, meaning 'knead' or 'press'. Shampooing, *champi*, is a commonplace of Indian life, a commonplace of mine in India once. It would hardly be possible to write of the intimate daily life of Indians without reference to this fatigue-relieving, calming, soporific ritual that can last for hours and hours —the scalp, the neck, the arms, the legs, the body. Ours didn't last so long, nor drop below the neck. Rameshwar's head appeared at the stairhead to announce that supper was ready to be served.

'Be very careful not to sit in draughts and catch a head-cold,' Jagut warned me. 'All those open pores.'

'We Whites catch cold through wet feet, not our heads.'

'Nevertheless we'll wrap you up in something.'

They wrapped my head up in a towel.

'I'm accustomed to it, you see,' said Jagut, towel-less.

Though supper was delicious, very light—a fish-dish mildly seasoned but with fiercer accompaniments, a pilao and various sorts of wheaten cakes as thin as discs, then fruits—I had no appetite, and Jagut noticed this.

'Don't you like it, then? What should I do, Peter? Tell me straight. I'd said to them *deshi khana*, our Indian dishes. I thought it better far to offer decent Indian food than their mockery of western-style. You used to love *deshi khana*.'

'Still do. Wait till tomorrow, and you'll see. It's only that tonight. . . . I'm tired, I suppose.'

'Early to bed with you, then. Finished? Not even a persimmon? No, no, no, Peter! Wait! Let Rameshwar bring you toothpicks. Shall we sit next door to drink our tea? I call it my "formal drawing-room".'

We went next door and Rameshwar followed with a little silver porcupine, its quills all toothpicks, and I sat there in a big armchair pick-picking. Jagut on a sofa opposite was back-lit by a big blown-up camel's-stomach lamp, its texture much like parchment, a strange object much favoured by the sahibs and memsahibs long ago. Two other oil-lamps lit the big dark quiet room, though 'lit' is not the word: they cast their yellow circles on the table-tops they stood on. Bookcases line one wall; photographs in their crested frames are grouped on writing-desk and small occasional tables. Indian potentates, they appeared to be, quite distinct from the very Nepalese character of the royal progress marching round the walls of my Victorian annexe upstairs. 'Oh look!' I said, of a silver-framed young man in polo-kit a yard from my right shoulder. 'Jai!'

'Yes, Jai. Wasn't your father his guardian during the minority?'

I nodded. 'If it had not been for that I wonder if you and I would ever have met, even. Let alone be "family-members".'

My father was a school-master, of a rather special sort. For more than twenty years he was Principal of the Rajkumar College, one of four such colleges in India for the sons of ruling princes. For the last few years of his service the Government of India appointed him as guardian to the Maharajah of Jaipur, Jai, to his friends, then still a minor and the British still very much in India.

'I never met your father,' Jagut said. 'But I've heard that he was a good man. Jai later spoke of him as *guru*.'

In India a man's *guru* is revered forever more, as well as loved (if lovable), and it does appear that my father was a good and loving man. I was thinking of him now—dead long ago, of course.

To my great regret I hardly knew him; I was at school in England, his home leaves infrequent in those steamship days; and just as he was ready to retire and coming 'home' for good, my time was ripe to sail out east myself—not school-mastering in my case, but as a 'mercantile-assistant' in a merchant-shipper's office in Bombay.

Bombay. I hated it, that smelly sopping city. It seemed like exile.

But quite soon after I arrived there I was to learn that by virtue of my father's special relationship with the young Maharaja of Jaipur (*guru* and *chela*, the strong enduring bond), I was in automatic relationship with him as well; we were *guru-bhai*, brothers under the same *guru*, my father. For my father's sake this prince befriended me, inviting me to stay and so on. In fact my first hot-weather local leave in India was spent in his huge summer household up in 'Ooty'—Ootacamund, 'Queen of the Blue Mountains' in Indian tourist jargon. Jai's brother-in-law, the Maharaja of Jodhpur, maintained an 'Ooty' palace too. Each summer in that faraway period the two princely households would flee the red-hot plains of their native Rajasthan for the cool of seven-thousand-foot mountains in south India. Two private trains would chuff and chug the three-day journey southwards, causing havoc to the normal public train services. The two rulers would each be in his private day-coach, or his private night-coach, their ladies (strictly *purdah*) would be in special pullmans of their own with guardian eunuchs painted on the doors at either end, and real eunuchs attending them inside, their liaison with the outside world. The two 'Ooty' properties shared a common boundary, so what more natural than that the two households should be in constant interchange? It was in the Jodhpur 'Ooty' palace that I first met Narpat—Rao Raja Narpat Singh of Jodhpur whose father—always referred to as 'Sir P.'—had been a great personal favourite of Queen Victoria's. Narpat was the first member I met of what was going to be for me 'the family'. He was some years older than me, his children somewhat younger. At the time I write of he was Minister-in-Waiting to the Jodhpur ruler, a job that kept him so busy that I scarcely got to know him that summer. Less than a year later, however, he wasn't busy in the least—he had been exiled from Jodhpur State.

Exile had always been an occupational hazard in the service of the old-time Indian states. Someone would covet someone else's power, position, property, and so on: words whispered frequently and venomously enough into the ruler's lazy ear might end by being believed, and acted on. This was to happen in poor Narpat's case. Narpat was out, lock, stock and barrel. Someone else was in.

Exile was readily reversible, however, and when in due course the Jodhpur maharaja realised what he should have known full well from the beginning—that it was Narpat he could trust—he quickly reinstated him.

Till that happened, all the same, Narpat had to sit out his exile somewhere. He chose Bombay. And it was there I got to know him and the family. A Rajput nobleman himself, he had married a Nepalese princess, half-sister to Jagut and Co. What easier and more natural than that the Nepalese brothers and sisters and nephews and nieces should come visiting to Bombay as well? Bombay, that smelly sopping city was transformed for me, India was transformed for me—Bombay, Jodhpur (with Narpat triumphantly where he belonged again), Fairlawn Palace, Soon Saan. . . .

In India the family is the only in-group. Not all the family-members are necessarily intimately close: it is the fact of in-ness that here matters. In-ness is absolute, not measurable by degrees. The closest family-members were for me Jagut and Narpat (and his children when they grew up and the age-gap shrank to nothing); Mussoorie, living in Kathmandu now, might then have been as close had he not been in the early stages of his retreat into a life of the spirit which removed him from us, even when he was no further off than behind the sofa, standing on his head in the tiger-pose. This pose he would maintain for hours, his legs folded into a sort of retractable undercarriage, a neat fat fleshy bow that rested on his rump. He was very serious about all this, and in an unguarded moment had let fall that he was well on the way to mastering the reversal of the peristalsis of the lower bowel. He never let us see him practising this useful feat, but it was supposed that he sat in some holy river (or the sea, when visiting Bombay) and that the idea was to draw up water, a sort of spiritual enema. We others found it very funny and it became the subject of a big tease, and Mussoorie simply didn't care a button. Still, all this did tend to make him a creature somewhat apart from us, and being a vegetarian widened the gap as well. He would come to table with us to eat his soft bland foods while we were wolfing meats. 'Carnivores!' he'd say; and of him Jagut would announce, 'Mussoorie, he's true Veg.'

This was 'the family' that let me in, or let me think so, anyway.

49

These were the people I could count upon for warmth and loving-kindness—and I needed both. Narpat in exile from Jodhpur, the Nepalese contingent in exile from Nepal (though fully integrated now, as Indians), with me in what till then had seemed my exile in Bombay.

Narpat is only lately dead, alas, and I am back too late to see him. I didn't want to talk about it yet, and said nothing of all this, just sat there in the semi-darkness thinking it, till Jagut roused me. 'You're half-asleep. Why don't you nip up straight to bed?'

'I think perhaps I shall. . . .'

'Off with you, then! And you'll feel like a two-year-old by morning.'

3

I woke once only in the night, roused by a strangled sort of noise from the back verandah. It must have frightened me, and in waking I too may have made some sudden frightening noise myself. In any case when I peered between the bedhead-rails and beyond them through the big low open window, a silhouette outside had raised itself from the verandah-floor and was peering in at me. Seeing me seeing it, it dropped back quickly out of sight. This would have alarmed me even more, had not another head popped up beside the first to do a hurried peep and mutter something softly, then drop back as well, and the soft muttering continued. So I could conclude with some relief that these were simply members of the household sleeping there, and that the strangled noise that woke me had been one of these two peerers throttled by a nightmare, not by thugs. It had slipped my mind that any floor is 'bedroom'; you spread your quilt and roll yourself up in it, others will have rolled themselves in theirs nearby, so everyone is safe. The Nepalese, most Indians too, habitually pull their quilts or *chaddars* or whatever it may be right over their heads for sleeping. I suppose this makes it safer still, and gives each one a sense of privacy in public. Apart from that it offers them protection from the night air, which is so notoriously filled with noxious vapours.

As I pulled my raw-silk coverlet back over me and settled down to sleep, the raging of the river filled my ears again. A lovely sound, the sleepless river a hundred feet below us where it rages in a tight S-bend about the eastern base of this high rocky eminence we perch on.

My last-remembered thought was this: from now on, for as long as I am here, the river will never be out of ear-shot.

Lying in bed at first light of my first morning I watch the furniture take shape again and think of yesterday, and I tell myself we really managed rather well. Nevertheless we've had a shock, the two of us: a two-way shock.

A tree grows bigger and more beautiful: man only older. We should all grow older for our friends as each grows older for himself, at a saunter so deceptive that not even the most critical of shaving-mirrors reflects what's going on—and on and on. So yesterday all those drawn-out middle years of ours—ahead of us when last we met, behind us now—what could they do but telescope themselves into the split-second of confrontation? Our minds can brace themselves against all kinds of shock, simply by taking thought. Mine had, of course: surely Jagut's must have too. But our eyes can't think; however carefully we brief them, our eyes can only see. And what was there to see? Two old, old friends? Alas, two sudden old, old strangers.

4

Whatever the condition of my mind at dusk last night, or even half
an hour ago, it is more at peace this rosy dawn with the sun now
driving horizontal shafts of radiance across the back verandah and
in through my bedroom, lighting up its undersides. Then out it
goes past tea-corner to the open air again. I can pile the pillows up
against the bedhead, lean back on them, and contemplate the
starting of today with tempered hope.

How will it go?

For Jagut? The pattern of his day is already set, I'm sure, with
every minute filled. He's on his own home ground; it makes it
easier for him than it's going to be for me, both bidden guest and
interloper. How will it go for me, then? In working out my programme I must be careful not to interfere with his, more than I
absolutely must by being here at all. Does he conduct his Soon-
Saan business from tea-corner? I should, if I were he. There is
probably quite a lot of paper-work: pay-rolls, accounts, the com-
missariat (he used to run a kitchen for the men and I suppose he
does so still, why else two cooks?). Then there will be hopelessly
confusing Government-returns that someone must fill in—who else
but him? He has to organise the harvesting, the transport and the
marketing of all his produce, fruits and grains and so on, all at
their various seasons. And he will be busy writing reminders ever
angrier to the suppliers of the car on order these last eighteen
months.

All this could fill his mornings, till it's time for lunch. A siesta
after it? And tea-time earmarked for general supervision and
attending to the peasants' *arzis*? I have remembered the vernacular
for petitions of the sort that he was dealing with at tea-time

yesterday: *arzi*. With one thing and another all this kept him nicely on the run, though it may have partly been evasive action too—evading the embarrassment of me. His dispensary must take up time as well, but I quite forgot to ask about it.

So far I've had no chance to note which is his favourite of the two small divans in tea-corner. There will obviously be moments every day when we'll be sitting there together. I must watch to see which divan I should choose.

Perhaps it's best to stay below this morning, wandering around. I can keep an eye on his routine, all at a decent distance. Sight-lines work both ways: if he can see me on the cobbled apron-stage or up there in the village or by the lily-pools, I can see him sitting on his chosen divan in tea-corner.

Should I try watching birds while I am here—at least till I am better used to being here? Or do I really mean till Jagut's better used to me? Has he some good binoculars that I could borrow? I thought I saw some beside a vase or something, on the corner table that divides the divans. There must be lots of birds about. They would keep me out of Jagut's way and fill in time. There's lots of that on hand as well. I've not just come to dinner, to some old-boys' reunion-dinner and then good-bye, good-bye!—what an evening it has been, just like old times! I'm here to stay, for weeks and weeks on end; and it isn't quite like old times yet. In fact at present it may seem to both of us that someone else has come to stay with someone else.

Even with good binoculars, even with a copy of Sálim Ali's good *Book of Indian Birds* (if Jagut has one), to be truthful I could never take to watching them. Instead, just for the present, I shall occupy my idle eyes and mind with watching Jagut's people. There are lots of them around as well, of all sorts. Agricultural workers, a cattle-man or two, three grass-cutters ('not enough'), a gate man, pig-man, the general-store and tea-shop keepers, the tailor I saw cross-legged in his booth (I expect these pay a modest rental, shop and living-quarters, in return for a small but captive clientèle).

The big discarded mill-stones laid across the lower lily-pool suggest a miller and a mill, for which the water-channel must provide the mill-race, upstream somewhere, round the hill-face, I should think. Then there's a group of men whose duties I'm not sure of—I can name them, some of them, already: Tuman Singh and Sarwa, Shambhu, Nanu, Nirmal, Fateh, the ones who toted baggage, brought up towels, hot water—what are their real jobs?

Of course, all husbandry apart, there's plenty to be done in a community obliged by its remoteness to be self-sufficient. House-maintenance and painting, modest carpentry, and even building. I expect I'll find this aspect much as it was before—though developed since those times—with almost everybody called upon for almost anything that's needed. Fishing for the Soon Saan pot down in the fish-filled Jumna, for example: someone must have, yesterday. They'll probably all be requisitioned for the cutting, binding, toting, threshing of the paddy crop when its moment comes. I guess that they must keep the rice for home-consumption (what we ate last night was a long-grain Patna-type. It might even have been the best of all those that I remember names for, Basmati).

On top of this lot there is a crowd of their dependants. Women, children. Perhaps collectively they can be best described as Jagut's henchmen. He was born privileged and knows it, naturally enough; it always looked to me (still does) as if he also knows and just as easily accepts the responsibilities that go with privilege. 'Henchmen', then? I find the overtones too feudal. I'll call them Jagut's people.

But propped up here in bed, still looking out through the fly-screening and across the front verandah, there's not a one of them in sight for me to watch. There's only greenery. Sounds reach my ears—the distant noises of the farmyard stirring into life again, hens clucking softly, duck-quacks brusquer, an occasional moo-mooing, and just now a peacock screech, the first I've heard since being back in India. Is that peacock Jagut's? Or is it screeching its little pin-head off from the freedom of the woods? Nearer-by there's a *frou-frou-frou* and a rhythmical *huh-slap!* . . . *huh-slap!*; and even nearer still a puzzling recurrent smoothed-out sound that slides each time to a minute and final squeak. I can't make head or tail of these, but I can identify with certainty a jingle-jangle of high-frequency, metallic. This has to be jingling of some woman's anklets as she pad-pads past below. I hear chirrups and pipings and I disregard them; I hear human voices too, but don't know whose. Soon Saan is waking up and I am missing most of it, I who am now determined not to miss a thing. I'll get out of bed and sit myself in tea-corner and I'll watch. Perhaps they'll bring me tea.

But I don't get up, because there's a shuffling of someone's feet along the back verandah and I turn my head in time to see a woman pass outside my open window and out of sight again. Mrs Midget. Off to dust and tidy my annexe? But my head is scarcely back once more against the pillows when I hear the same foot-shuffles much accelerated, and I turn to find that Mrs Midget is scooting past my window in the opposite direction—to Jagut's back-verandah door, perhaps? Curious. Why scoot at all in this peaceful wood-brown, leaf-green, very-early-morning world? And half a minute later, even less, there's Jagut tapping on my fly-screens, partly screened by them in fact, but I can make out that he is in a *loongi*, like last night. He wears a Gurkha cap again, that jaunty little cotton thing that's higher to one side than to the other and patterned in small woven lozenges of colour. Round his shoulders in the cool of dawn there is a sort of shawl.

'Jagut? Yes, of course. Come in!'

'So you're awake? I didn't want to wake you. I hope you won't mind this invasion. Thank you. I fear that I'm the harbinger of disturbing news, so early in the morning too. I would have liked to spare you fuss, but we need your help—you'll see why in a moment. I come to report a theft, a very serious theft—of unheard-of seriousness. For Soon Saan, I mean. Little things, oh well, yes, there have been, but . . . not really "theft". We'll be coming to that too in a moment. It was your Mrs Midget that discovered the loss. Only a minute back. May she come in too, please? Come in, Afim! Come on! You too, Sarwa—your Switzer for the duration, Peter. That's what we'll call him: Switzer. And this is Bishnu, whom you won't have seen. Don't be timid, Bishnu—the sahib is asking you to come in too. She's your under-chambermaid, No. 2 room-cleaner and bed-maker, Bishnu. Not *Vishnu*: he's the god; she's only Mrs Midget's assistant, but for all that much concerned in this. Look, Peter. She's wishing you . . .'

Bishnu was sidling in reluctantly and making her *namastes*. I made mine back, from bed. Such a sad pinched face, a hopeless look on it. Plain too. And middle-aged. Even her sari had a mournful air to it.

'First things first,' Jagut resumed. 'The nature of the theft. A candelabrum. Description: a huge great solid-silver thing. Nepalese. A real museum-piece. Single column, four foot high, I'd judge. Just the one fat candle. It's got a snuffer, too, on a silver chain attached. Gone in the night! GONE! From your annexe!'

'From my annexe?'

'From your annexe. Weight? Easily a *maund*. That would be—let me see. Yes. Nearing thirty pounds avoirdupois. As heavy as an

56

overladen suitcase, and far more awkward as a load. Of course it has to be an inside-job. How could a stranger pass that encirclement of pi-dogs? No, this was no stranger. Tip-toe up the backverandah stairs he came, under cover of the dark. Direct to your annexe. You've noticed? The back stairs come up the far side of your annexe. No need to pass the Seven Sleepers on the back verandah—less then seven as a rule, though. An inside-job, then. And listen to this. *Two* more men are reported absent-without-leave this morning! *Two!* Absconded! Together? We are assuming so at present. With our second bike, one riding pillion, I make no doubt. The fact of there being the two of them, and the load too cumbersome for one—not to mention that the haul's worth splitting a dozen ways and more, not chicken-feed, please note—it makes us wonder. With trumpery little objects (this is what I was coming to) our Suspect No. 1 would naturally again be Mr Lightfingers, as I propose to call him.'

'Mr Lightfingers? Oh-h . . . I don't know about him, do I?'

'Not that aspect of him, probably. You *may* have seen him—I don't say that you have or that you haven't. You see I have no intention of identifying him for you by name and face, because he simply can't help it. He's a klepto. But note this, Peter. In this veritable spate of absenteeism—I'm even tempted to call them all absconders—our Mr Resident Lightfingers, our permanent Suspect No. 1 on such occasions, is with us yet. So, if guilty, he has broken into what we are obliged to call "the big time", and he'll have hidden his booty away and must be planning to let the hue and cry die down before he sneaks off to place it with some "fence". But where could there be a "fence" this side of Delhi?'

'In his place wouldn't you just melt it down and sell for weight of silver?'

'Oh my God! Melt it down? That museum-piece? He must not! We must not give him time! Look, too, at this terrible coincidence. The only person on the property who's any good at all at finding lost articles is one of our absconders. No. I'm going to say it: "defectors". Your guide-and-escort of yesterday. Everybody knows that he's no thief. Of course he's glad when things get lost, hoping always to extract some small reward from the grateful owners for finding them again. The grateful owner in this case would be me, at least I most sincerely hope so. Of course his very absence yesterday may seem to clear him of suspicion—on the face of it. Or, after all, has he become a thief? Every thief must have

57

his first time: yesterday an honest man, today a thief. What if he had taken and concealed his prize *before* he left here to await you at Lal Singh's tea-shop? He could have watched old Mrs Midget's movements, Bishnu's too—no, Bishnu! No! We are not speaking against you, really we are not . . . (such a nervous creature). He's constantly in and out of the house on one errand or another. They all are—let me hasten to put your mind at rest: Mr Lightfingers has been warned in no uncertain terms by your Switzer here that if he is seen to advance so much as a toe inside your door he will be beaten to death! It's well known how rich all Whites must be and that your room in consequence will be full of your gold and silver trinkets. I don't see any, by the way.'

'That's all very well, Jagut. But how could my guide and escort or anyone else hope to carry off that huge glittering object from the annexe in the broad light of day? Without the whole world's seeing?'

'I've thought of that, of course. The siesta-hour! When all the world's asleep!'

Jagut paused dramatically. He was doing it with great bravura. Was he perhaps enjoying it a bit? 'Go on,' I said, enjoying it myself.

'Peter. Destiny has cast you for a role in this shattering affair. Your evidence is vital to us.'

'But it's the very first time I even hear of any candelabrum!'

'Think carefully, nevertheless. Was this huge old solid-silver candelabrum still in place in your annexe at 5 p.m. last evening? Can you be sure?'

Could I be sure? I tried to visualise the huge and noticeable thing—but had I noticed it? 'A solid silver candelabrum,' I said aloud, but really for myself, '. . . one fat candle only . . . I simply can't be sure. I'm so sorry. I had only that one quick glance at the annexe, remember. It's like Kim's Game, isn't it? My annexe seemed to be so full of things.'

'Not full of candelabra, Peter.'

'No, that's true . . .'

'Let me put it to you in another way, then. Can you be sure it *wasn't* there?'

'I can't even be sure of that. I'm as bad as Bishnu, I'm afraid.'

'Please, *please* don't say her name or she'll start thinking things at random. Look! She's started! Bishnu! *But no one thinks you did it, Bishnu!* Oh my God, she's working up for tears and I won't have it. Just take no notice of her, Peter: the best chance of stopping her is by ignoring her completely—but do try to keep her name off your lips.'

'I'm so sorry. I didn't realise.'

'No serious harm done. So! Who saw the candelabrum last? We don't know. Mrs Midget only consciously noticed its absence when I sent her in just now to give it a new candle.... Yes, Afim? Speak up, then. Sarwa, *chup raho!* Shut up! Yes, Afim? Let her speak, Sarwa. She's trying her best ... give her time. Quietly now, Afim. There's no hurry. Go on.'

Silence. Then suddenly: 'Not there,' said Afim with an air of great importance.

'Afim means it was not there *now*,' Sarwa said sombrely. 'That is what I tried to say to you, Rana sahib, when you cried out to me in rage "*Chup raho!*" '

'Sarwa!' Jagut said, warningly.

Sarwa looked darkly down, annoyed, but perhaps a little apprehensive at having shown as much. Jagut said to me, 'We are all a little overwrought this morning.' He cleared his throat and turned to Afim once again:

'Now, Afim. Think. Carefully. Heads could fall on your testimony alone!—you can follow all this, I expect, Peter, can't you? So, Afim? Do you mean it isn't there *now*?'

She nodded.

'But Afim ... ! That was the reason why you came running back to me, just *now*! Oh Peter, what's the use? It's not her fault that she was born midget without brain, however gloriously. Full-sister to my major-domo, don't forget. Oh well, never mind. It comes to this: we've no idea, not one of us, if the thing was in its place at tea-time yesterday. Very well. Sarwa! Afim! Bishnu! Listen, all of you. No word to anyone! Understand? Not even to your brother, Afim. It would dement him. And Peter sahib is vowed to silence too (nod to them, Peter—yes, that's right). Above all no word to —— (sorry to have to whisper to Sarwa in your presence; just a name ...).' And he whispered it and added: 'Tell the others later,' and Sarwa nodded back, his dignity restored a little. 'And the moment he gets back,' Jagut said to me, 'we'll put your escort on to sniffing out its hiding-place. The idea will be to lull our Mr Lightfingers to a sense of false security and then (if the evidence directs) we'll pounce. Of course he's consummate liar and actor as well as true-blue klepto but Sarwa's here to watch him

59

for the least suspicious move. And by this evening, latest, your second Switzer-designate will be back again, and he and Sarwa can watch the suspect in shifts.'

'My *second* Switzer?'

'Don't you want two, then? Why not? He's gone on leave to be a bridegroom.... Oh Bishnu, stop it! She's my sewing-woman, really. My spinster sewing-woman. Yes, it's a sad face. And something to be sad about, too. She's got so furtive and frightened lately. Do keep her occupied. Work will help her to put aside her woes. She'll do buttons for you, darnings, anything you want. You see, your guide and escort—I won't name him or she'll twig at once—and oh my God, she *has* twigged.... Or perhaps not, after all.'

Jagut turned back to me to ask in a different kind of voice, 'Have you begun to get our *dramatis personae* sorted out? I expect it's a little early yet. Our new descriptive code-names—Switzers One and Two, and Mrs Midget—they ought to help. Also it means that if convenient or necessary we can speak of them in their presence without poor who's-it here dissolving into tears, or your first Switzer getting suspicious, not knowing what we may be plotting. He *is* suspicious, as a character. But only violent when thwarted. And by the way, these code-names are all right and very useful in their place, but I very much hope you'll be committing their real names to memory as well, so that you can wish them when you meet each day. You are? Already? Good. When a man has practically nothing in the world to call his own except his name, he likes to be known by it and is very hurt if he isn't. And now I know what we can call the poor lady here who's waiting for her next cue for tears! The Fair Maid of Astolat! We can shorten it to "Fair Maid" or something, perhaps just "Maiden", directly we get used to it.'

'What's the Fair Maid of Astolat got to do with it, though?'

'But I *told* you ... ! Or no, I didn't. I had to cut it short because it looked as if she'd twigged. She's been jilted by her lover. Most cruelly jilted.'

'She has a lover?' I took a quick secret look at her. 'This poor tear-stained old thing?'

'*Had* a lover. And since she's to be the Fair Maid of Astolat, her lover is automatically Sir Launcelot, isn't he? And Sir Launcelot is your guide and escort! How's that?'

'Good heavens!'

'Oh yes, I do grant you our Fair Maid is very far from fair—and very far from being "maiden", if it comes to that, though resolutely spinster. But then she had no need of beauty to entangle her Sir Launcelot with. He isn't fussy. Out on this hill-top I expect he's thankful for anything he gets.'

'I was wondering at the time, down there at Lal Singh's. Do you suppose Sir Launcelot defected in order to get some girl?'

'He's got a perfectly good girl here. On the premises.'

'A new one, do you mean?'

'New. And rather pretty too, this time.'

'Under the Fair Maid's very nose? How awful! Do I know the new one? Would I have seen her?'

'You *might* have. But why should you be so interested?'

'Me? What about yourself, then?'

He laughed, then stopped to recompose his face. 'We mustn't let them think that it's a laughing-matter. Let me explain that with me it isn't just nosey-parkering, it's more like duty, really. They come to me with their troubles. Poor Fair Maiden, how she did blab on about Sir Launcelot—though I knew it all from the others too. Not much goes on around here that everybody doesn't know five minutes later. And no, I'm not going to name, nor even describe, the new girl for you—the Fair Maid's supplantress, I mean. We can refer to her as "Jezebel", I think. If you approve. And rest assured, only, that Jezebel exists and that in the drama of Soon Saan she doubles the roles of loving wife and mother with that of Jezebel! Her husband has his guilty reasons for making no objection. The predicament is what I think the French call *"un secret de polichinelle"*. Have I got it right? Good. Moreover Jezebel is reputedly as rapacious in these matters as a harpy, so it's quite on the cards that poor driven Sir Launcelot stayed behind at Lal Singh's simply for a night of perfect peace. But it may have been for a change of partner: people like a nice change—and don't *you* laugh, Peter, for goodness' sake! Your Switzer's getting jumpy. And *don't look!* Now *he* thinks we're talking about *him* all the time. Everybody has the vanity to suppose that everybody else is talking exclusively about him. Excuse me a moment. Yes, Bal Bahadur? What is it? Come in—you won't mind my major-domo's coming in as well, will you, Peter? Sarwa! Open the fly-screens for Bal Bahadur sahib. Yes, that's good. Hook them back and let more light in—no, Peter? Come in please, Bal Bahadur. (How upset he looks! Perhaps our secret's sprung already—I've seldom seen his old impassive face so agitated. I do hope he's not working up to another little fit.) Bal Bahadur, this is Peter sahib whom you'll remember from so long ago. He won't, though, he remembers nothing any more. He's getting old. We all are, I suppose, but he's been getting older.... We call him major-domo but it's little more than a sinecure these days. Others have to do his work ... no, no, Peter—just wish him from your bed. Now Bal Bahadur, what is it?'

'Rana sahib, Rana sahib—our second sow! She's vanished!'

'Oh my God! The plot thickens! Peter! You come all this way, thousands upon thousands of miles—to visit me: I'm very touched, I truly am. Of course I know that it's to see the others too, but still. You come to my Himalayan retreat, for peace and quiet, and no sooner you arrive ... the lightning strikes! Twice! In the self-same place!'

5

Thinking over how I try to pin Jagut down on paper, particularly his voice, how sharp I make it—staccato, urgent, even rasping—perhaps I'm overdoing things. I make him sound so restless, and that isn't it at all: it's the need to be up and doing all the time, when there's never time enough in hand; Bal Bahadur, major-domo, is no longer of much help and everything goes wrong if Jagut doesn't watch out like an eagle. It is true, as well, that our renewed relationship is still a little wobbly on its feet, off-balance.

I realise how hard it is to do him justice. I can apprehend him only through the filter of my eyes and ears and then must reconstruct as faithfully as I can, then edit. I think I get his fluency and speed, and his vocabulary, which sometimes strikes a strange outmoded bell and I hear my father talking. Jagut and Mussoorie and their youthful fellow-princes all learnt their English from Englishmen (though not my father, in their case) at least a generation older than themselves—the turns of phrase already rather dated, the slang, the educated talk of an England before the Kaiser War. And Jagut and Mussoorie were never subsequently to bring their English up to date by contact with younger Englishmen. I can have been of little help because I, like them, was living right outside mainstream evolving English when first I knew them. My English probably still has its Anglo-Indian flavour.

What a business! Of course I see that Jagut had to play it out in deadly seriousness, if only for the sake of discipline, but I find it just as difficult today as ever it used to be before to be certain that he's not laughing his head off inside. Yet the fact remains that in a remote antique community like this, major theft to top the spate of defections is a very serious business. It must have shocked him.

There's no doubt about the genuineness of his feelings for all his people here, and I sense that they respect him. Certainly they must count upon him for livelihood and their security. Perhaps in some odd way they even love him, a compound of love and awe with self-advantage edging in between. He is their lord and father. Are they his children?

There were no children of his marriage. A marriage had been arranged in the proper way, a high-born princess chosen, horoscopes compared, pronounced compatible, settlements, dowries and the rest agreed. And he was to prove a very lucky little boy in their choice of bride for him. She came to him in her eleventh year, when he himself was twelve and still under the guardianship of his elders at Fairlawn Palace away over the mountains from Soon Saan. 'I was so excited when they told me she was actually arriving,' he once told me: 'It was as if I was at last to get an extraordinary and long-promised toy.'

He grew to love her dearly. But she was frail, this little toy-child, and grew frailer still as womanhood was reached; and soon they no longer dared to hope that she could bear the son they wanted so. She died, poor woman. I believe she had been ailing for some years. Poor Jagut, too. He had not taken a second wife while she still lived, and after she was dead did not remarry.

The consequence may now well be that his people here have come to represent for him the children that his marriage never brought him. I hardly think he looks to them for gratitude—only the maddest father looks for that—but to have his good intentions rewarded in this outrageous manner, and in addition to have me here as witness to it all, must add to the indignant shock of it a certain loss of face. Not much, but some. This may explain why he was at such pains to tell me a moment back that my coming here isn't like the visit of some important official '—for tea, with everybody present and correct, clean clothes, best behaviour—whereas you are simply "family". Yet it is our duty to look after you to the best of our resources and ability. And as things are turning out, it can only be "as best we may".'

'As best you may? Jagut! What with my Switzer here, and Mrs Midget, and the Fair Maid of Astolat, plus a second Switzer-designate, I'm wonderfully looked-after!'

'They know nothing about handling the Whites, this lot.'

'But you said you don't think of me as quite "White", anyway.'

'That's true.'

'Then it's all right, isn't it?'

Tea growing cold. I'll get up in a minute.

This morning's great upheaval, sudden, almost seismic in intensity, brings it sharply home to me that Soon Saan must be regarded as a little world entirely to itself. What matters to us here is what happens to us here, with neither time nor thought to spare for what goes on a million light-years distant in other people's worlds. If other worlds must have their famines, pestilences, wars and earthquakes, well then, they have to have them. But let no tremor reach this far.

I am a sort of tremor, though; and I have reached this far. My coming cancels leave so long looked-forward to. No wonder sufferers defect. As for the two unprecedented thefts, that's something else again, but I see now that their outcome has eased our 'situation', mine and Jagut's. Soon Saan is living out an evil moment in its little history—its microcosmic history. In the face of major crises of the kind, we're all in this together, shoulder to shoulder, bold front, four-square! And I am honoured with a walk-on part in it. I no longer feel quite so much the stranger.

Soon Saan may have been knocked practically off-orbit, but the inhabitants (we sworn-in five apart) are still serenely unaware of anything, and I can hear with my own ears that life goes on as if nothing world-shattering had befallen us at all. Soon Saan, having finished with its early-morning yawns and stretchings, slips sweetly into gear again. We're off! I'll play my walk-on part.

Dressing-gown. Disgraceful black cotton-towelling old thing wrapped round me, fraying filaments all pulled to loops, but never mind. I'd like to wear a *loongi*, really. And a shawl. That shawl of Jagut's—he gave me one just like it years ago, but long since lost, of course. I wish I had it still; it would be perfect for wearing here. I think it's called a *khasto*, a traditional Kathmandu affair. His is (mine was) a two-colour cotton hand-blocked print with the pattern showing through a sandwiching of milky muslin, roughly two yards by one. You wind it round you and throw one end back over the left shoulder.

Looking over the front-verandah railings I can immediately interpret all those sounds that teased me so, except the *huh-slap!* . . . *huh-slap!* That seems to have stopped meanwhile. What was it, I

wonder? Oh well, does it matter? Yes, it does, and I know exactly
why it matters, too. The world I've come from was always far
too big, too full of people no one ever knew or wished to, whole
cities, nations, continents of them, all getting in the way of private
life. So I've been content for decades now to let that awful outside
world go spin itself. But Soon Saan, this glorious private planet, is
of a size to grasp and love. Now that I'm suddenly a part of it,
however minor, I'm going to grasp and love it. I haven't seen it all
as yet, and so far only under lighting so sharply horizontal, cre-
puscular, matutinal, that a four-foot Buddha-rock can cast a ten-
foot shadow—but every detail so clear-cut and so immediate, so
dioramatically presented to my all-seeing eye that even if I wanted
to escape involvement, I could not—like Jagut with that poor old
buffalo (will it have lived to greet this rosy dawn or not?). And
anyway I want to be involved in everything that happens here.
Nothing is too small to command my attention: the *frou-frou-frou*
the French might guess was rustling silks, for instance; it comes
from a band of little girls retiring in balletic line across the cobbles,
sweeping-sweeping, *frou-frou-frou*, as they drive the dust before
them and away over the culvert towards the farmyard where dust
quite properly belongs and soon will settle. The leader of these
children is very nearly nubile, thick and rather ugly, but I think
she's going to be a devil with the men, the *jolie* little *laide*.

The recurrent 'smoothed-out' sounds that slither to a squeak are
seen to come from just below me—a man is on his hunkers busy
cleaning chimney-glasses from a dozen oil-lamps that last night's
duties blackened. He uses screws of paper—old copies of *The
Hindustan Times* lie conveniently to hand. He turns his paper
screws inside each chimney, tightening the turn as the lamp-black
disappears and the chimney makes its final squeak of protest, like
children having their noses cleaned out with twists of handker-
chief. This involves me with my childhood rather, but not for long
or exclusively, and out of the corner of my eye I have noted barely-
teenage Deepak passing by, hand in hand with a four-year-old I
take to be a brother. Should I know who fathered them? Not yet,
but I shall enquire. Shambhu I see again and can identify, both
name and jolly-looking face. A member of the pariah-pack is drinking from the water-channel upstream of the culvert, where I see
there is a gap left in the hedge. This must be Soon Saan's water-
hole and that is Kalé at it. Kalé, Bird-Fancier. I know him for his
size and his dark and starey coat. He has a frizzed-up ginger beard

that does not suit his looks. As soon as he has quenched his thirst he stands up stiffly, leans his weight right forward over long front legs so that his back legs stretch out far behind him, foot-pads uppermost. He raises first one back leg and then the other, like someone at his boring exercises. Kalé then yawns until his jaws go click—I know they will have, though too far off to hear it. Now he has snapped his mouth shut; and now he has shivered his whole skin and all at once relaxed. Is this important too? Of course it is. Also it is instructive to reflect that the large ignoble creature was only very recently a runt and bullied by his smallers—all of them bitches too! (I hope I'm here to witness the coming triumph of poor Mingy down in those pig-sties. Now who on earth would have, could have, stolen Jagut's second sow?) I see another member of the pariah-pack as well, a softy bitch. She is in the farmyard area, lying beside a very little girl who is busy thrashing her painlessly with a bunch of twigs she ought to use for sweeping. The other little sweeping-girls are moving out of sight beyond the bullock-carts. This puny imp has ratted on them; but she soon tires of her twig-beating and starts a better game—filling her victim's upturned ear with dust. To ease her task she holds the ear open by its feathery tip in a very intelligent manner. That little puny will go far. The bitch makes no protest; probably she enjoys any sort of personal attention. She is rather beautiful in her common way. Yes, it is Kalé's sister—*half*-sister; I know her for her mushroom-coloured cloak and ivory fur boots. I see now that her behind is wreathed in a boa of ivory-coloured feathers. Not surprising that her brother fancies her, now she comes of age.

Ahhh–h–h...! At last! Here's something I've been hopefully awaiting. The Brahmin lady-cooks are coming into view under the biggest mango-tree and past the mango-stairway. I know exactly why their long unbraided hair is sodden water-weed. 'Old ladies now and only two of them...but of course they still take their daily river-dip.' They are returning from their daily river-dip, just as they have been returning from it every morning of their lives here when the sun has reached this level. I see now how presumptuous it was of me to have felt sorry for the poor old Jumna river down in the plains of Delhi: on the contrary I should congratulate it, because in return for its final grovelling submission to Holy Mother Ganga it forever sucks back virtue from her all the long way up itself. In direct consequence these two Brahmin ladies can take their daily sanctifying dip in Jumna's upper reaches.

There used to be three cooks, that's so; and in a properly-conducted noble Kshatriya establishment they must be Brahmins. Servants? Not at all. More like high-priestesses dispensing blessed food. But I'd got it wrong about Saraswati. Though Brahmin, certainly, she was never one of the three cooks. It all flowed back to me: originally Saraswati had come to the boy Jagut's household as a little girl herself, part of Jagut's child-wife's entourage. And when the latter died, Saraswati had stayed on as housekeeper, 'First Lady of Soon Saan' by now, and ruling with a rod of iron. She loved Jagut, at least I used to think so: perhaps he loved her too. I wondered about this, a little. She was beautiful and strong, intelligent as well, and I fear she may be dead, because there's been no talk of her. There's been no talk of Narpat, either, no talk of Bahadur, one of their full-brothers, who I know is dead. It's too soon still to talk of death, perhaps.

A violent commotion has broken out—honks, quacks and squawkings, wing-beats, rushing wind. They've opened up the poultry-pens and the farmyard fills with fowls, like children helter-skelter out of school. The geese are gathering about the water-hole, the ducks dive straight into the woods, White Leghorns and Sussex Whites and fat Rhode-Islanders forget what they were helter-skeltering about and stop wherever it may be that each one finds herself. Jagut's door has opened and he is coming down the verandah saying, 'Eight o'clock! Breakfast!'

'But you know, Jagut. I don't really eat any.'

'Nonsense. It's all ready waiting for us. Come on down.'

'Dressed like this?'

'Why not.'

Since last night someone has put a great towering silver centre-piece—a Victorian epergne—in the middle of the table. It hides us from each other most effectively. I wonder—is this accident, or is Rameshwar-houseman showing off some of his master's silver-closet treasure? Or could it be design? A comfort, anyway. Soon Saan's history may have unexpectedly thrown us closer, closing up our ranks with me inside them, but our eyes know no short-cuts. They can't be rushed. Let us compose our current faces, each to his separate side of this towering epergne, and wait for everything to grow familiar at its proper pace. There's plenty to distract the mind meanwhile. 'A quick résumé of the news,' says Jagut.

'On the candelabrum-front, nothing you don't already know. As much as any of us knows. Darkness surrounds it still. Eat up your porridge while it's hot. Milk? Sugar? Can you reach it? Help yourself. Now. This Riddle of the Second Sow. An inside-job, this too? It has to be. Who could expect to drive off, carry off, a great reluctant porker without squeals and remonstrations echoing throughout the valley? Who indeed? Alas, only my pigman. And here again I have to grill you, Peter. Actually it's much the same sort of grilling as with the candelabrum, part of a similar process of elimination. Think now, please. How many animals did you see down at the sties yesterday?'

'Let me think, then. Two boars, of course: bully-boar and Mingy. Sows? One only, surely. . . . No?'

'One *only*? Think again.'

'Only one. I'm sure of it.'

'Exactly! And do you know what the pigman's daughter is saying now? It was she who came to Bal Bahadur in tears to announce it: "The second sow has gone in the night—escaped through a little hole in the zareeba-fencing. Ask Rana sahib—ask Rana sahib's *ferangi*"—you're just a Frank to her, you see, Peter; but a Frank whose credulity she hopes to turn to good account. "Ask the *ferangi*, Bal Bahadur sahib! He will tell you that he saw the second sow last evening—with his own eyes he saw!" '

'I didn't see her, though. Did you? But I thought the girl seemed nervous.'

'You noticed that too, did you? She knew full well what was already afoot. What a family, what a family! And see the wily trick? If you could be coaxed into doubt, into thinking that perhaps after all you had seen the second sow—hiding in some dark corner of the inner-sty, for instance—then her father, already departed on his leave, is automatically innocent. *They* made that hole in the zareeba-fencing, to substantiate their tales. And off my pigman went and the second sow with him. Oh swine of a pigman! And to think I gave him special good-conduct leave for the feast, drat him! And feast's the word for it, all right. You mark my words: that poor little pig was loin chops and rolled shoulder long before midnight. Cut up, roasted, eaten! There's your feast for you. No, no, no, not my pigman's feast, he won't have eaten her—though not from scruple, either. He's sold her. And from the proceeds perhaps he's set aside the price of some skinny fowl to feast himself and daughter on—if he comes back in time and doesn't gorge it all down himself. Be sure the selling-price was handsomely depressed, too—to as little as a hundred chips, I dare say. Two, at most. It should be four at least. And to think that every shred of evidence is gobbled up by now. Shred of evidence? Oh my God! The candelabrum! We must act before the criminal has time to melt it and destroy all trace there too. Should I despatch a posse at once, to bring Sir Launcelot back? Under guarantee of unconditional pardon provided he dowses out the hidden treasure? No. I'll give him till the evening. And if you don't mind, Peter, I'll send off your first Switzer, with one of the tougher men as aide, if Sir Launcelot, guide and escort, isn't back of his own volition. He is the type to resist. And it is a feast-day.'

'We certainly are living out our history. I was thinking so just now. We're not just reading other people's in *The Hindustan Times*. Our microcosmic history.'

'Not so much of your "micro", if you please! Tell me where else in the universe they have a demon Mahasu on their very door-step? I'd swop him for a train-smash any day of the week, or a nice bit of radio-active fall-out. And I'd sack that pigman out of hand, make a real example of him, but it would mean having to find two replacements—three!—he himself does the work of two, *and* his daughter helps as well. No. I must wait for somebody to be at fault whom I can do without more readily. And soon. I've simply got to stop the rot. What can the world be coming to? Eat up your eggs and bacon, Peter. Go on, yes, I mean it. We plan to fatten you a bit. You're too thin. They're all commenting on it. We're going to have you fleshy by the time you go to Kathmandu. What would Mussoorie say to see a skeleton arrive from Soon Saan? How long can you stay with us?'

'I was wondering myself . . . Would a fortnight be too long?'

'Be too *long*?'

'*Seem* too long.'

'For the fattening? I'd say a month at least.'

'I didn't mean quite that: I meant do you think you could—well, bear it?'

'What are you talking about? Though there is, of course, the question of the weather. You'd be wise to get to Kathmandu while it's still agreeably warm. It must be nearer five thousand feet above sea-level than four. And the moment you feel winter in the air, come straight back here to us. Our warm weather goes on longer, naturally.'

'That is a point. Our altitude—I mean the triangulation point up behind the village: it's only 2,376.'

'How do you know—so exactly?'

'From the one-inch-to-the-mile map-sheet.'

'Oh, I see. But whatever it is I think you'd better stay a month at least in the first instance. That should leave you with a full month in Kathmandu before their cold begins. And meanwhile we'll be fattening you up nicely. But we'll need your close co-operation, mind.'

'You're much thinner than I am, Jagut. Much.'

'It's my current nature to be skeletal. Don't you like bacon? I thought all Englishmen loved bacon.'

'We do.'

'Then eat it up. It ought by rights to be the flesh of the wild boar which we would have ridden down relentlessly and stuck in the jungles. Wild-boar flesh, how good it is! Some Kshatriyas even say that it's enjoined on us, as a caste. We *must* eat it. But I'm not fussy about caste-matters and content myself at present—and settle my caste-conscience too—with little bacon rashers that come to me in sealed plastic envelopes from some pig-farm outside Delhi. I forget the name. Quite decent, isn't it?'

'Extremely decent.'

'Then eat it up, please. More? I can easily get them to prepare some more.' He paused thoughtfully. 'I wonder who could have cooked it for us this morning, though. . . .'

'By the way, I was delighted to see your two Brahmin ladies coming back from their river-dip just now.'

'Don't be mad, Peter! You're not suggesting that our ladies could touch the bacon-packet, let alone cook the stuff. Meat! They're Brahmins!'

'Of course—I simply wasn't thinking—I was . . .'

'Or shell our eggs!'

'Mustn't they shell eggs either?'

'But of course not. It's tantamount to taking life. We Kshatriyas can take life, in fact we must—being the warrior caste. A warrior wouldn't rise very high in his profession if he was squeamish about a little bit of life. But with the egg once safely shelled by someone else, our ladies do consent to cook it for us—though not fry it, as today, because of bacon-fat. *Ghee* would be all right —in fact it's holy stuff, a product of the cow. All this is why I have to go to the expense of keeping a special eggs-and-bacon cook; he has to be a Rajput, of course.'

'So caste does rather complicate your life, then?'

'Theirs. Not mine. And do you know who he is, the Kshatriya scullion who defected in the night? It's Nirmal! Remember? The one on shampoo-fatigue. And to think that all the time he stood beside me at his task he was planning base defection. What a fiend! Ready for curds now? Or honey? Not just a little to finish off your toast? Very well, I won't force you, your first morning. Now for your aphrodisiac intake. Why! Our *amlas*, naturally! Our star-apple preserve. Let me help you to some—pass your plate round the epergne. That's it. No, no, no, I'm going to give you more. More still! There! Get outside of that. Didn't I tell you down in the orchards that the *amla* is a highly aphrodisiac fruit? Oh yes, a very treasured fruit. And perhaps it is a bit unfair to fill you up like this, then leave you stranded on our hill-top. Never mind. It will be interesting anyway for you to test its potency. Please report. I sell the crop to a contractor. We expect him here today with his men and truck. To start the picking and packing. It was he who was to bring your luggage in for you—if you had come by bike as we expected. He markets it down-country. Mostly *ayurvedic* pharmacists. Those *ayurveds*, they say they all make fortunes. My *amlas* may well be one of the secret ingredients, along with gold and powdered gems, in the famous Royal Yakuti— remember the advertisement?'

' "For rich men and princes only"? I remember.'

'Exactly! Yes, Rameshwar? What is it? Yes, yes, you can clear now. Was it perhaps you, Rameshwar, who prepared our eggs and bacon for us this morning?'

Rameshwar nodded, busying himself with clearing.

'Rameshwar's Kshatriya too, you see. At least . . . well, not very strictly (nor is Nirmal, for that matter)—but shall we say "fictionally"? And it certainly would not be right to expect Rameshwar to scour our soiled cooking-vessels (as defecting Nirmal must). Such menial service is not for Rameshwar. He *is* my major-domo's full-nephew, after all. Oh yes, didn't you realise it? He's Mrs Midget's son. Perhaps by now you will begin to see how absolutely dislocating to our lives—not only to yours—is that verit-able spate of defection. Bacon-cook and vessel-scourer gone; Sir Launcelot; bridegroom; helper-handyman; receptionist—oh yes, I do agree, those with official leave-of-absence shouldn't really be lumped in with true defectors, but they're absent just the same, aren't they? And the polyandrous lady in question's second husband—he's defector, too; though I'm bound to say his going won't affect the household service. He's strictly outdoor labour.'

'By the way. Has that poor buffalo lived to greet the dawning of today?'

'The eight-o'clock bulletin, received while I was dressing, says that it still breathes—with difficulty. A further confidential report should reach us later in the morning. Lunch-time, latest. Something's in the air. The owner's thought to be preparing counterblasts. It's too soon to say more at present. We may have to make another secret recce, though I'd rather not risk it. How will you pass your morning? Don't forget we're going to the temple in the afternoon.'

'I have my plans. And you?'

'Work! Never-ceasing work. Never an idle moment. We look around and see all green and beautiful, but don't imagine that it happens by itself.'

'No, I'm sure not. Incidentally, that giant mango-tree beside the house. Do you sometimes think that. . . . Well, I mean. . . .'

'Do I sometimes think what?'

'Is it—is it a well-intentioned tree?'

'It had jolly well better be! What do you mean exactly?'

'I expect I was only imagining things. Silly of me, but I thought it had rather an odd air. Predatory.'

'*Predatory?* Our dear old giant mango? It's the most docile tree in all Soon Saan!'

'I'm so glad. I'd had a mad sort of fear that the vegetable kingdom might be taking Soon Saan over. All this violent rampaging green.'

'*I've* taken over,' Jagut said.

'Good. I thought it might have been King Veg.'

He looked round the huge epergne, smiling comfortably: 'I'm happy to inform you that it's me.'

6

I feel a bit silly at having so misread the signs, particularly at
having announced my reading of them. By light of day the mango-
tree proves to be all that Jagut claims for it. I have been sitting
in it with my note-books for the past hour at least, and nothing
could be more peaceful nor more convenient; moreover it ad-
mirably solves my problem of keeping out of Jagut's way.

When you are immediately beneath the tree, on the cobbles, you
don't realise what Jagut has been up to, and in the gathering dusk
of yesterday it was all too shadowy for me to see; even from tea-
corner you can't see because the truth is hidden from you by a
masonry arch that finishes the verandah off. The truth, however,
is that far from its being the mango's groping hand and forearm
that seek to hook the upper-floor verandah to itself, it is a little
wooden bridge some four feet long that hooks the mango to the
house without a by- or with-your-leave. The bridge takes off at an
angle from the arch, right into the mango's very crutch. Here a
wooden platform has been laid, with an extension out along an
enormous horizontal bough. Low railings surround it, and a set of
foot-high chairs and table furnish it. The chairs are hewn from
solid blocks of wood with a section left for back-rest. They should
be awful, but instead are very nice to sit in, legs out-stretched.

From here I really do begin to understand a little what's been
going on in Soon Saan since I saw it last. Hard 'never-ceasing'
work, of course. That's obvious. But Jagut has had a slavish ally
too. He must have beckoned with his bold green fingers and the
vegetable kingdom has crawled in to him on hands and knees,
begging to be put to service. How satisfying to possess such
powers! I wonder if the animal kingdom has offered him allegiance

74

too—including, I sincerely hope, its serpent section. Coming along the verandah an hour or so ago, I caught sight of the whip-snake again. It has changed its tree since yesterday. Naturally it is free to do this, but I find it ominous. I'm glad to say I can't see it from where I sit in what I propose to think of not as the mango's very crutch but as a leafy aerial pleasuredome.

From the pleasuredome, then, Soon Saan offers a different aspect of itself, a wider aspect, to include the terraced area beyond the tree: the threshing-floor. The end of the house bounds it to the north and a white-washed cottage (two up, two down) to the south. Bal Bahadur came out of it a little while ago so I think it may be his, as major-domo. I greeted him as he passed below me between the mango-tree and the water-hole but he paid no heed. He still looks stunned by the pig-theft. What will he look like when he learns about the silver candelabrum? Others have passed by as well, and I've been greeting them for practice with their names: Shambhu, 'Fatty', Nanu and so on. Or is it that I'm trying to curry favour with the faithful non-defectors? I foresee that if Jagut feels obliged to uphold discipline by punishing those absent without leave when they get back, it may strike them as being on my account, and they'll remember it against me personally. If that should happen how am I to cut the gracious kindly figure I was planning for myself while I am here? So possibly I am not practising names at all, but injecting prophylactic doses of sweetness and light against the risks ahead. I changed my seat for another still more comfortable and something hidden from me hitherto by the mango's heavy foliage now stood revealed. Two things, in fact. Two poles stuck in the threshing-floor; well yes, I'd noticed their two bases: but now their tops were visible and it is an agreeable surprise to find that each is surmounted by a brass Buddha's head, quite small and unobtrusive; and below each head is a circlet of animal horns, in one case simple goat, and in the other branching and bleached white, a deer of some sort. I wonder what they can be for? They look like Viennese bent-wood hat-racks—celestial hat-racks. Odd but beautiful.

In Soon Saan there are many things that seem both odd and beautiful. The oddness will have faded out within a day or two.

Tuman Singh (tall, thin, quite handsome) with Jagdish straddling one shoulder (round and plump) has just gone by. I made a dashing attempt at a phrase in the Hindi 'continuous-present' tense: 'And how is Jagdish getting on?' He is getting on very well, thank you, it appears.

The geese who used the water-hole before breakfast have given place to cross-bred Jerseys, one of them yesterday's bored heroine, I suppose. Pretty velvet creatures. A blowing noise alternates with sucking when they drink.

To the east of the threshing-floor where the ground drops down vertiginously, there is a parapet backed by spreading trees that philodendrons batten on. Between the trees you can see deep into the valley, a long oblique view of it and of how the hills have flattened out as they draw near the left bank of the river. The temple I am promised for this afternoon is some two hundred yards from the left bank. I can see this from the Government of India survey map-sheet I am looking at. It rates the Archaeological Department's sign for 'temple'. So looking down obliquely through the trees that flank the threshing-floor I can decide that it must be the small white building with others still smaller near it that I can make out under heavy trees not a mile from where I sit—as the crow flies. It is strange that I never went there in the past because I much enjoy temple-visiting—or is this a pleasure I've developed since those days? This temple is evidently dedicated to Durga.

Durga (or Kali) may be thought of as the 'black' aspect of the god Shiva's consort, the 'white' aspect being the goddess Parvati who is the lady normally seen by his side in moments of gracious living. Durga and Parvati, however, are really less consort or wife to Shiva than the female manifestations of his godhead. Durga is the repository of his strength, his power, his energy. She is what is called his *shakti*. The not-so-orthodox among the millions who worship Shiva are said to worship him solely as a necessary male counterpart to goddess Durga the adored (and feared). A perverse element among his worshippers concerns itself with only two of Durga's various spheres of activity—her magical powers and her dominion over all sexual relations. Durga, 'black' goddess of disgracious-living, of the sexual act, of magic and destruction, is to be placated only by blood-sacrifice, preferably human. In 'bazaar' oleographs she is sometimes depicted eating mangled babies. Well, we shall be visiting her this afternoon to offer our respects, though as a matter of fact the ten-day Dussehra festival has nothing at all to do with her or Shiva. It is a Vishnu festival, connected with him in his Rama incarnation: it celebrates Rama's victory over the

Demon Ravana. These multiple identities will always confuse me. But whatever the case I am sure the goddess Durga is ready to use anybody's festival as an excuse for getting worshipped.

If Durga, Shiva's *shakti*, stands for sexuality in all its convoluted splendours, then it is understandable that Shiva himself should be symbolised by his lingam, or phallus, an object of veneration so widespread and popular, and above all so innocent, that formalised models of it in mud or stone and so on are frequently set up along the public highways, to comfort wayfarers. The wayfarer who stops to offer it a prayer or a libation, or sprinkle a little red powder on its head, may well have no thought of sex (as sex) in mind as he makes his meritorious gesture. While I am at it, may I say that it is only now, on looking down towards the lily-pools, I realise what it was I leant against so comfortably as I sat sipping *lassi* on my mushroom in last night's gloaming: a five-foot stone phallus. Lovingly and accurately fashioned by Nature herself. I think, actually, that she may well have fashioned its column and its bulging head in two bits, and that some simple devotee (one of Jagut's people not-coming-empty-handed-home, perhaps) must have found the second element, seen it at once for what it would be if united to the first, borne it reverently home and here united them. All the same I know that I shall feel awkward leaning up against it drinking *lassi*, back from the Grand Tour each evening. It will mean a change of mushroom.

But the goddess Durga and Lord Shiva and his lingam are for this afternoon and now is for now and I return to my note-books, or try to. However the Fair Maid of Astolat has come on scene round the end of the house and has settled herself down on a rickety chair to sew. She is stitching at the muslin cover of Jagut's *khasto*, the shawl he was wearing earlier this morning, twin to the one I used to have myself. The pattern showing through the muslin sandwiching is nostalgically familiar to me. A big design of Jagut's personal armorial bearings, a panoply: stumpy cannon, centre; spears as supporters to each side of it; sword, crossed *kukris*. Very martial. Below it in a formal cartouche are his name and appellations, all in Roman script—JAGUT SHUM SHERE JUNG BAHADUR RANA. The family rated cannon in their day, and it is precisely this aspect of them, or rather of their father, that I have been looking up in my note-books, flagging whatever I have been able to find in published matter and the old Government of India records because I want to ask Jagut about him. I know something

77

about what happened to him in June 1901—the kidnapping in Kathmandu, the exile—but so little about him as a man before or after this, and that little mostly from Sylvain Lévi's *Le Népal*.

In 1898 Lévi, a Sanscrit scholar of high repute, came to Kathmandu on a Sanscrit-inscription-finding mission. There he met Jagut's father (at that time Commander-in-Chief), and what started in a formal meeting soon developed into friendship. It is in Lévi that I find the explanation of the family's frequent easy use of French words and phrases, not slipped-in little show-off bits, but as if this was the way they had always talked at home in childhood. Their father, Lévi tells us, had been fascinated by all things French, not least the language—'O, if I too had the voice of gold!' he once exclaimed when Lévi was reading something out to him in French. He did not speak the language, but he must have picked up phrases and used them to his children. Lévi describes him— short, broad, quick, intelligent, friendly, charming manners and so on—and it accords so closely with mid-nineteenth century published accounts of Jagut's father's father before him, and again so closely with what I know myself of his sons after him (particularly is this the case with Mussoorie) that I like to think of it not as straight family resemblance but something nearer to reincarnation. You are allowed to say this sort of thing in India, though in fact I shan't say it to Jagut. I doubt if Jagut can have managed Lévi in the French and I know of no translation into English. Perhaps, if he likes, I'll type out relevant extracts for him in English.

I never met their father. He had died in Indian exile long before ever I came out to work there. Nor is it strange that I have been able to turn up so few references to him in my reading (except for the central tragedy of his life referred to just now) when you consider how brief and aborted was his chance to make the bold progressive contribution to the history of Nepal that he was clearly planning. He was Maharaja Deb Shum Shere Jung Bahadur Rana, fourth in succession in the line of hereditary prime ministers of Nepal that the great Jung Bahadur had initiated in 1856 under the seal and *sanad* of the Maharajadhiraj (great king) of Nepal of the time. Deb Shum Shere came to power as prime minister on the death of his brother Bhim Shum Shere, oldest of seventeen brothers. This was in March 1901. In June of the same year Maharaja Deb was lured into a trap set by his younger brothers (headed by Chandra Shum Shere, Deb's junior by one year) and sent into exile. This done, Chandra could assume power himself as prime minister.

Perceval Landon's *Nepal* tells us a great deal about Chandra Shum Shere's 'reign' but has little more to say about the deposed and exiled brother than that he was well-educated, spoke excellent English, and that 'although his character was unmarked by the vices that so tempted his relations, it was equally unmarked by strength, judgement or foresight'. (Chandra Shum Shere, the power-usurping brother, being by inference abundantly possessed of these necessary qualities.) Landon writes of a programme of reforms that Chandra had soon set in motion 'with resolution, steadiness and tact', but by the time he died (in 1928) nothing much seems to have got done about anything. There was talk of overhauling the penal-code; the mild form of slavery practised in Nepal was now abolished for the look of things (it was not 'slavery' at all, little more than, for example, the working off of debts by forced labour); *sati*, too, that no one practised any more was now abolished, and I hardly know what reforms Landon could have had in mind. It is true, of course, that it was Chandra who ordered the electrification of Kathmandu city, and this may be thought of as progress, I suppose; but it could have benefited no one except the Ranas in their palaces (and the king kept prisoner in his) for not many citizens could have afforded to get their houses wired for electricity nor even have recognised the need for such new-fangled luxury. Street-lighting would not much affect the citizens because a strictly-enforced curfew kept them all at home throughout the hours of darkness. Chandra introduced another novelty, however: a rope-railway from the foothills bordering India, up and over the mountains and into the Valley of Nepal. This was progress too—but it did not mean that Chandra was relaxing by an iota the policy of Nepal's absolute isolation from the outside world and its evil people—a policy old as the Sah dynasty itself, and long pre-dating the Ranas. Far from it. The rope-railway was strictly for the import of the country's need; grand pianos, billiard-tables, and the like. No passengers, of course. No road was built to link the outside world with Kathmandu,* and such prying visitors from outside as were allowed to enter the country did so only with the express permission of the prime minister himself and

* The fine 80-mile highway that today links Kathmandu with India (the *Tribhuvan Rajpath*) was the gift of the Indian Government after the 1950 Revolution that unseated the Ranas.

few were granted it. The Maharajadhiraj, great king of Nepal, direct descendant of the god Vishnu, not to mention of the Sun in his heavens, could not even leave his palace gates without the prime minister's permission and a strong Rana escort. He had to make do, and did, with women, women, women, booze and mail-order catalogues.

Chandra in his wisdom, strength, judgement and foresight, courageously upheld the *status quo* that upheld his absolute authority, and with it the accord with Britain established in his uncle Jung Bahadur's time: Britain would not interfere in what the Ranas did so long as she was provided with recruits for her Indian Army, Nepal's astonishing Gurkhas.

In briefing his chronicler, Perceval Landon, it was obviously no part of Chandra's purpose to reveal what really led him (with the backing of his younger brothers) to exile Deb their senior, and to elevate himself to the vacated 'throne'. He probably thought that he had acted with great clemency in not assassinating Deb in the traditional way. At the back of all this, however, was Deb's liberalism, a liberalism his younger brothers did not share and entirely out of keeping with his background and the Rana family advantage. Yet it was true liberalism, and on coming to power Deb soon let it be known that he intended to work towards a form of government in which the people should play their part. But the immediate prerequisite was education. The ruling Ranas had their private tutors; the people had no schools at all. Deb Shum Shere set to work. Landon gives it a couple of disparaging lines: 'By a stroke of the pen this thistledown wit [Deb Shum Shere] inaugurated thirty primary schools—a third of which had died out in a few months...' A third of which? All of which. Landon should in honesty have linked for his readers the few months of these schools' existence with the very same few months of Deb Shum Shere's brief moment in power. But with Deb deposed and exiled, how could any of his schools survive him? Chandra knew only too well that education for the people was dangerous, heady stuff.*

Jeremy Bernstein is one of the few writers on Nepal to give Deb something of his due. He writes: 'If Deva (Deb) had been allowed

* In 1918, seventeen years after Chandra had seized power, he opened an English college for the over-privileged. The under-privileged had to await the fall of the Rana régime in 1950 for their needs to be considered. Illiteracy in Nepal was then still 96%.

to rule, the subsequent history of Nepal might well have been entirely different and the country could have been half a century further along in its development.'

Another interruption. Someone arriving at the water-hole to shoo the little cows away. Sarwa, first Switzer, I think it is—from his back-view. A bundle of grubby clothes under his arm.

'Sarwa?'

He looks up. Yes, it is Sarwa. I say nothing, having nothing to say at present, but I bow, and he bows.

Sarwa strips to the waist, which means his shirt comes off. He squats by the water-hole and starts to wet his dirty clothes. Then he soaps them piece by piece, a vigorous performance. I can return to my note-books. No, I can't, because my grass-hopper eye has been taken by someone else arriving. The little nearly-nubile *jolie laide*. She stands below me watching Sarwa, and I think she fancies him. He is jumping on his wash now, working it with vicious feet. The little girl does not watch him for long, however: she has been distracted by something else. A man is coming through the farmyard to the house, and I think he must have noticed this girl, or even caught her eye, because on crossing over the culvert he changes course and comes up to the water-hole. Sarwa and the little girl and I, we are all looking at the newcomer now. His looks are absolutely staggering.

This part of India cannot be said to breed a handsome race, at least not at the peasant level (I mean 'not handsome' in terms of what the West finds handsome). The Indian upper classes are an entirely different matter, this country being still a country where the rich and poor are different forms of life, as in Dickens's London. The locals here are mostly thin and wretched-looking, from what I still remembered and saw again on the road from Dehra Dun: meagre-bodied, faces emptied of emotion. All this may well be partly poverty and malnutrition—though it isn't malnutrition here with Soon Saan's locals. Jagut's hill-Rajputs are better specimens by Western standards, though less good-looking, I should say, than the Rajputs of their native Rajasthan. Sarwa, is he handsome? Hardly. He is simply young and strong and tough. Tuman Singh, then? Yes, just. But the newcomer is extravagantly handsome. An almost classic Aryan head and features, thick black-silk hair, shoulders square under a spotless white *camiz*, deep-chested, strong. His swaggering gait as he crossed the farmyard

81

suggests he perfectly well knows the effect he makes on people. From his white cotton ballooning pantaloons that come in to a band at the ankles (*salwars*—as opposed to Tuman Singh's wide-bottomed *paejama*, for instance), I take this man to be Punjabi, from the 'land of the five rivers', a long way off north-west.

The people round Soon Saan are medium-dark in colour, a greyish, even greenish tinge, a sallow dark: their skins drink in the light and give back nothing—at least that's how I try to explain it to myself. With this newcomer it is not so much his skin-colour (which is fairer than 'ripened wheat', more russet) as its texture and quality. It is radiant with light. Yes, I'm sure that he must be Punjabi—son of Hindu refugees perhaps, from West Pakistan, after the Indo-Pakistan Partition of 1947 and the wholesale cross-migration it involved. In general the further north you go in this sub-continent, the more handsome are the peasants, men and women, judged by Western standards.

Sarwa clearly doesn't like the look of this man at all. His eyes fixed on his wash again, he says, 'Who are you?' in a very surly voice.

'I am Rana sahib's new tenant.'

The new tenant catches sight of me above and greets me with *namastes*. 'If you please, sahib, where is Rana sahib?' I think that he is by-passing Sarwa on purpose, to turn from his scowling face and also to rebuke him. I lean out as far as I dare from the pleasuredome and peer along the upper verandah into tea-corner. I can just see it, and that it is empty.

'Rana sahib must be in his room,' I tell the man politely, 'up-stairs there.'

'Rana sahib is very busy,' surly Sarwa says, still addressing his wash. He stands up, catches at a soapy shirt, cruelly twists its arm and tail and, taking a deep breath, exhales with violence as he bangs the poor thing on the stones—*huh-slap!* ... and then again—*huh-slap!* So now I know what makes that noise. I also know that it is not only when thwarted that Sarwa can be violent: he is violent in his *dhobi*-avatar as well. But of course the new-comer has provoked a lot of this. Little *jolie laide* may think that she's provoked it all, and it could well be true.

'Sahib-ji? Is it permitted to go and see if Rana sahib will receive me? I wish to pay my respects.'

Sarwa cuts in. 'I told you. Rana sahib is very busy.'

I say, 'Yes, I am sure it will be all right. The first door on the verandah.'

Sarwa, listening, thumps his wash as bad butchers hack their meat—with hate. The Punjabi smiles, ignoring Sarwa, and takes his leave of me, a golden beam of smile, white teeth, fringed eyes, is he the Sun or someone? I feel warmed by his rays as I return to my note-books.

But this is my first morning; even without the *clatter-bang* . . . *clatter-banging* that has this instant broken out and fills the air, I doubt if I could concentrate. Who is clatter-banging? What about? I ask Sarwa, who is displeased with me and answers gruffly that it is the call to mid-day dinner (sauce-pans banged with wooden spoons, I think). Anyhow Sarwa has risen from his wash and left it—off he goes across the culvert, skirts the big mango just beyond it and down the path that leads behind the lily-pools towards the ochre-coloured cottage. The men's kitchens must be on the lower floor of it. Others have appeared meantime and all converge now on the cottage.

Soon Saan is left in suspended animation.

I sit alone in the aerial pleasuredome with not a soul in sight. Even the pariah-pack has hastened off towards the cottage, ravening for scraps. I sit on here alone and softly thinking—the spirit of this place, already flowing over me, has started breathing itself into me. Don't they say that horse-lovers bind their horses to them by blowing up their nostrils—that they magic them with breath? Soon Saan is quietly blowing up my nose, spell-binding me, and why should I resist? Then I wonder if the mid-day bulletin about the 'spell-bound' buffalo is in yet. I wonder what we're going to have for lunch. I'm rather hungry: I've scarcely eaten since a railway refreshment-room supper on Delhi station, and that's two nights ago. Yesterday no lunch and only a couple of home-made biscuits for tea. A tiny bite of fish for dinner, too tired to eat; today a couple of rashers of bacon and a couple of fried eggs, some toast, and of course a lot of *amla*-aphrodisiac. Should it be acting yet? I sit waiting for it to act, wondering what it's going to do to me, waiting rather as people sit round waiting for their 'pot' to do its little bit.

Had I been dozing?

Jagut's voice from the upper verandah roused me. He stuck his head into view over the railings. 'Ah yes. There you are. They told me you were in the tree.'

'Yes. What's the time?'

'Beer-time, if you like. Then lunch.'

'Good. What's for lunch?'

'Wait and see.'

'How's your morning gone?' I asked him as I collected my bits together.

'Well. . . . Anyway I'll be with you on the verandah in a moment.'

On leaving the pleasuredome for my room I bowed to the Fair Maid, still on her rickety seat below, still disconsolately sewing. She looked up, like a bird warned by some sixth sense. So I pointed to the *khasto* she was stitching and I mimed 'how nice', in order to take part in her lonely troubled life and to encourage her. Instantly she seized up her sewing as if I'd caught her out in some misdemeanour, and with a look of horror on her face she skimmed round the corner of the house and out of sight behind it. It may be better not to talk to her at all, nor even look her way.

When I came out of my room Jagut was already in tea-corner, on the divan by my door, so I suppose that's his. 'Any news?' I asked him, as I sat beside the beer. I handed him his glass. I had deposited my papers in my room but had brought out something else with me, a sort of *ballon d'essai*, really. It was a reproduction I had had done in London from a contemporary wood-engraving of Nepal's great nineteenth-century figure, Jagut's ancestor, Jung Bahadur. I put him face-down on the divan for the moment, to bide his proper time. I glanced at Jagut.

I could see that he was agog with mid-day news—news far from good as I was now to learn. 'Let's get the worst bit over with,' he started. 'Though it isn't over yet, not by a long chalk.'

According to the latest bulletin the owner of the 'bewitched' buffalo has decided upon a counter-blast to sorcery that has the brilliance of absolute simplicity. It consists simply in making over the spell-bound beast to the lady in question, with the demand for five hundred rupees in settlement. She has already sent back a categorical NO! Of course, as Jagut said, she could never even find such a sum, but this is not the point: even if she could, she certainly would not. So? The Panchayat it has to be. 'Thank God my major-domo's past it now. So dignified and serious, but past it. Not as stable as he was. He used to act as what you would call

84

chairman. So I'm not involved even to the extent that he is to judge the case.'

Calling in the Panchayat is expensive, it appears, even for the aggrieved party, even with judgement in his favour. There is no provision for costs. So before ever the owner took this step, he gave the lady one final chance to settle out of court. Messengers were despatched requiring her to swear before them that she was innocent of their black charges. She was required to swear, moreover, on none other, *none other*, than the great feared-one. Unnamed.

I interrupted here to ask a question: 'Durga-devi, would it be?'

Jagut in a dark voice answered: 'No, not Durga. Someone nearer, more local, shall we say. And to that extent more *terrible*, if you get my meaning.'

Two of the household were 'in-waiting', quite nearby. They must have known what sort of news it was that Jagut had for me. They fixed us with four gimlet eyes.

At this point I regret to say I made a little gaffe, tricked into it by the realisation that I'd got things slighty wrong. 'The great feared-one, Jagut, close at hand . . . ? Would that be Mahasu? But is he Mahasu the Terrible? I've been calling him "the Horrible"—in my head, I mean.'

Mahasu! The staff in-waiting gulped—good Christians would have crossed themselves—but quick as thought Jagut had silenced me. Dead-pan face and voice he told me flatly, 'Never name that name, please—unless in abject praise, of course. No one can overdo the praise of demons.' He then said that if I had to name the name, actually vocalise it (and he couldn't imagine in what circumstances this could be), then the proper attribute was 'the Terrible' and not what I'd said. 'Who on earth or under it would care to be conjured up as "horrible", let alone in the middle of his own territory? "Terrible" is quite a different thing. I shan't say the Hindi for it now, with everybody listening so anxiously, but nobody would mind being "terrible". In fact quite a lot of people probably like being able to strike terror into others. Be that as it may, the lady herself was properly terrified. Which is what the other side intended. Oh but they're shrewd, the other side—they're shrewd all right!'

Jagut now mimed the scene, and of course the others with us got it right away and stood there nodding, urging Jagut on: '"Swear on one so present and so powerful?" she cried, or so the messengers reported. "Never! That I shall never do!" She was afraid to, you see, Peter. She was in no way acknowledging her guilt, not she. Only acknowledging her fear of powers her 'magic' can't control. The other side, of course, construed the wretch's fear as evidence of guilt.' He lowered his voice and spoke out of the side of his mouth: 'Please look very serious, Peter, or you'll deeply offend our audience. Because as you and I sit here drinking down our beer in what seems blessèd peace, a bare half-mile away Nemesis takes charge. The owner and his party will by now be humping that great bulky spell-bound beast from where we saw it (outside their cottage, remember?), dragging it across the open field and pushing it up on to the terracing that fronts the lady's cottage. Such a load, too. How will they manage without tackle? That great steep bank. Here note the brilliance and simplicity. If the poor creature lives, then it is that, her "black arts" parried, she will be presumed to have lifted her own spells—rather than lose not only five hundred rupees but the buffalo too. Can she lift spells at all? Anyone's? We all remember the *Sorcerer's Apprentice*, don't we?'

'And if the poor beast dies?'

'Then it will be said that she's called up demons for the bewitching too powerful to be dismissed again—no one will believe she's innocent. As easy as that! Let the Panchayat pass judgement! It hasn't been convened for ages, now I come to think of it. They'll be demanding a feast as well as fees.'

He took a sip of beer. 'That's the bad news, then. Now for the good. Sir Launcelot is back home again. Sheepish, with flower-offerings.'

'Did you punish him?' I asked—an airy easy voice that begged him for the answer No.

He gave it: 'No. I ought to have but didn't. And in the old unrepentant days of our forefathers in Nepal, I can tell you, nothing short of rolling him down a steep mountainside would have sufficed as punishment.'

'From what I remember of his shape Sir Launcelot might prove too angular to roll far.'

'All trussed up into a ball? Once trussed he'd roll indefinitely. But we live in enlightened times'—he gave a quick smile at this—'and I've simply issued an ultimatum: "Dowse out the silver candelabrum—*or else*!" I haven't said yet what the "or else" would be: we might talk about that later. Moreover he rode all the way home on a flat tyre and it's a write-off. Should I fine Sir

Launcelot for ruining that tyre? I'll think it over. I don't want to
upset him for the moment because his mind must be as calm as
possible—he's busy "dowsing" already—with Sarwa, first Switzer,
keeping our Mr Lightfingers under secret "round-the-clock" surveillance at this critical juncture. It could be Mr Lightfingers'
moment of truth, if he is guilty and betrays it. But let us not pre-
judge the issue. I'm sorry that I've had to detail your Switzer for
these special duties, because it may all take ages. But your second
Switzer should be back by the afternoon bus from Dehra: he's
the Bridegroom. He's been up in Mussoorie marrying one of Sis's
little maids, though he didn't really want to. It was *we* who thought
it tidier. He's been conducting what we may delicately call a
liaison with the little thing for quite some time now, so the
marriage has long since been boringly over-consummated. He won't
want to tarry there a moment longer than he must.'

'Jagut. Do tell me straight. What are the rules here? About
girls?'

'Rules?'

'Unmarried girls. Conventions. Is it like the countryside in old-
time England—the boy would marry the girl if she started a baby?
Or what?'

He thought for a moment. 'It's more *ad hoc* than that. This I
can say, though. No man would think of doing things to a co-
villager's wife.'

'Sir Launcelot is obliged to think of little else, isn't he?'

'You have Jezebel in mind? I'm sorry I ever told you about
that. But there again the circumstances are rather different. Jezebel
has been "arranged".'

'That's very modern.'

'Very. The official emphasis today is on limiting the family to
two babies. Haven't you seen the propaganda posters? It's on
postage-stamps as well: fat happy parents, two fat happy children,
all hand-in-hand and smiling? Jezebel has had her share of babies
and now she says she's out to get her varied share of men. A
hundred men, she claims she's had since her "arrangement". A
hundred? Here at Soon Saan and round about? Is she to be believed?'

'People are awfully inaccurate in their speech: perhaps she
means she's since had a couple of men—as it might be her husband
and Sir Launcelot—a hundred times in the aggregate. How long
ago was her "arrangement", do you know?'

'Must we dot her i's and cross her t's, do you think? But she says she's going to get a hundred more before she's finished—so I think she must mean different men. No, no, no, she hasn't breathed a word to me about it. It's little birds that insist on telling me.'

'What do the little birds themselves think about it all?'

'Things aren't quite the same here in our hills—they aren't *viewed* the same, I mean, as they would be in the plains. Local polyandry gives a special slant to the relationship between the sexes too—even to those who don't practise polyandry. Talking of the plains and being different, incidentally: I've got a new tenant, from down-country. A Punjabi.'

'I've seen him. Very handsome.' I had nonchalantly picked up the engraving of Jung Bahadur and was playing with it. I laid it face-upwards on the divan alongside me. Had Jagut noticed? He was telling me more about his new tenant:

'He was in just now to pay me his respects. We don't get many Punjabis here, but it appears his mother was from these hills or something: and he says he's got a cousin-brother who's quite a notable in one of the hill-villages higher up. Much higher up, I imagine. I don't seem to know him.'

'Has Jezebel seen the new tenant yet, I wonder?'

'I haven't heard.... Anyway our Punjabi invites us both to take tea with him and his family this afternoon. Would you like that? I must go, in any case. After the temple visit.'

'I'd like to come too.'

'What's that you've got there? Beside you.'

'Oh nothing, really,' I said. Sly. 'Just a wood-engraving of your illustrious ancestor. Jung Bahadur. At the time he visited Queen Victoria.' I handed it over to him. 'It appeared in the *Illustrated London News*. Summer 1850.'

'Very interesting,' said Jagut politely, handing it back to me.

'Don't you want it, then? I brought it for you. I thought perhaps you'd like to....'

'He was only a great-uncle, you know.'

'Yes, I know. But even so. . . .'

'Keep it to give to Mussoorie.'

'But I've a spare with me for Mussoorie.'

'Mussoorie's much more interested in all that old stuff than I am. Here's Rameshwar. Lunch. Finished your beer? Bring it down with you. Are you feeling peckish?'

So much for my *ballon d'essai*.

Lunch was a sort of salmi of duck—doubtless some poor Indian Runner who escaped my taxi's wheels last night only to reappear just now more richly spiced than it would have been in Europe, and black as pitch, its tender flesh falling away from the bones in deliciously unctuous slivers. With it was served a plain boiled rice (and it is Basmati: Jagut told me so. And it is from the Rice Bowl down below). Varied vegetables in separate bowls, chutneys, pickles, all home-made; poppadums and so on and of course unleavened wheat cakes in discs. Then a bland and milky sweet. I'd like to know how the cook cooked that duck—exactly. Had she hung it, marinaded it, what? Was it killed days ago? I'd make up to her a bit and see if she would teach me. I had eaten with appetite and pleasure. It was all excellent, even the bland and milky sweet, for I seldom eat a sweet. Now I was blandly, peacefully replete. Perhaps it was the moment, despite the failure of my *ballon d'essai*, to let drop that I'd been reading up Nepal in London (I'd got to tell him some time). And to underline that it was not only Jung Bahadur but also the brief and noble part that his own father had played in his country's history. What sort of man was he? What sort of father had he seemed to them as children? But even this might prove tricky ground to tread with Jagut. Nepal became news, world news, only when their 1950 Revolution broke and the foreign press could throw themselves upon the fallen Ranas—hang, draw and quarter them—with no one to remember the monsters Jung Bahadur had wrested power from in 1846. Outside Nepal who had even heard of, or if they'd heard, remembered, what Maharaja Deb had tried to do for his people some fifty years ahead of time? I am sure that Jagut must have had to swallow far too much about the downfall of his family to have stomach left for more. What if I made a spring-board out of Sylvain Lévi? I did so.

'I was reading Sylvain Lévi for the first time recently. Back in London. Have you read him? Those bits about your father. It's all very evocative.'

'Lévi? Wasn't he a Sanscrit scholar?'

'Yes. Sanscrit inscriptions.'

'It's not really my line, you know. . . .'

'I know, but I meant about your father, more. It's almost like reading about someone I seem to know. I've been flagging the notes I took. Would you like me to type out an English transcript of the passages for you?'

Jagut seemed more interested in the last spoonfuls of his sweet than in Sylvain Lévi. 'Finished?' he asked me. We got up from table and he motioned me to a silver basin and ewer that stand on a tripod against the dining-room wall. In it is a pierced-silver grid like an inverted bowl; the idea is that someone pours water on to your cupped hands for you to wash them, soap them, rinse them, then you gulp some water into your mouth and gargle it and rub at your teeth and gums with a strong first finger (right hand) and then dribble the water out—no hoicking spits—through the silver grid and into the basin. I did so. Then I poured water for Jagut, and he did so. Then as he wiped his lips with the air of someone signing off he said:

'You mustn't bother with those English transcripts, Peter. It would really be too much like hard work.' He paused, looked quizzical, and said, 'And why are you so fascinated by all that ancient history? What are you scribbling at, up there in the tree? Is it about "us", Dom Moraes?'

Dom Moraes? I knew the name; a younger English poet—actually Portuguese East-Indian in origins. Well-regarded, so I'd heard. 'Would that be a son of Frank Moraes whom I remember from Delhi long ago? The well-known journalist? I met him once or twice.'

'That's it. Dom is the son. He wrote a book, with "us" in it—I don't mean "us", the Fairlawn lot: but members of the family all the same. They were his Rana hosts in Kathmandu. Post-Revolution. It was a great shock to them to read what he published about them, when they had done their very best to be hospitable.'

I hadn't read the book and couldn't comment. I thought I'd seen appreciative reviews. I know, of course, the sort of trouble writers run into if they write of real living people. I could guess what might have happened. The book was *Gone Away. An Indian Journal.* I was to read it later on, in Kathmandu. It includes a Nepal chapter 'Living like a Rana'. His comments on his Rana hosts all seem to me innocuous.

'Yes,' Jagut went on. 'I've been warned against harbouring writers. Warned against you, too, Peter.'

'Jagut!'

'Mussoorie wrote to say that he'd been fully alerted too. I have wondered once or twice if I ought to tell you this—or is it really you who should be warning me, like the police formally warning their captive that anything he says may be used in evidence against him? All those lists of names and Soon Saan secret dossiers that you've been memorising, jotting them all down, I bet. Of course they won't be able to read what you write in English, or even if it were in Hindi, or even anything: but they'd force it out of me. "What has Peter sahib written about me?—and me?—and me? Tell! Rana sahib, tell!" I don't care so much about myself, but about father, that would be different. If you're going to speak of him.... Perhaps I'd better see you get it right. History has slandered him, where it remembers him at all. I'll start by showing you some pictures—no, not now. Now a short siesta. And I'll have them wake you up in time for temple visiting.' He looked hard at me and said: 'I do believe you're looking a bit better already. It's our healthy mountain air.'

7

The temple is less than a mile away, as the crow flies, and all the
bird need do is open out his easy wings and volplane down from
the threshing-floor. Would it take him as much as a minute?

For humans it is different, though they too set out from the
threshing-floor, and as we crossed it I asked about the two brass
Buddha-headed hat-racks:

'What are they for, Jagut?'

'Those? Oh, nothing special.'

'I only wondered.'

'That's the major-domo's cottage.'

'I'd guessed that.'

'I'm a bit worried about him. He's been nervy again lately. And
look! Behind his cottage—have you been round here yet? No?
Our mill.'

'So it is—.' And here imagine not a mill in a Western sense of
the word but a little cottage. Nevertheless it has a mill-race shooting into a hole in one side of it, and the channel flowing smoothly
out from under it the other side, safe in its stone conduit.

We were flanking the hill that rises to the south of us—the hill
I think of as the head and neck from which the Soon Saan shoulder
juts out so spectacularly. Round it you follow the water-channel
against the current, and where our village ends (and with it all
these trees and vegetation) you emerge high on the open eastern
face of a ravine at a point where it is just about as deep as it is
narrow. An up-ended equilateral triangle—seventy foot or so—
would fit in nicely. It is called the Bin Nullah.

Nullah, in down-country Anglo-Indian usage, mostly means a
dry water-course, alive perhaps only in the monsoon, the rainy

season. But here in the mountains, even in the dryness of autumn, quite a stream comes flowing down the Bin Nullah on its way to pay tribute to the holy Jumna river. It comes down in an alternation of little cascades and pools of barely-moving water. Some are deep enough to swim in, Jagut says.

Like the full-scale canal and motorable road from Lal Singh's, our little channel and its attendant footpath share a shelf cut into the hill-face and exactly follow the contour to where it taps the main stream further up. Up? Further on, I should have said. With this primitive but highly effective form of small-scale irrigation—it is locally called a *kul*—no locks, no sluices, the channel must be cut at no gradient worth the name or the downhill flow would be too strong to be controllable. However we were evidently leaving it far short of its 'head-works'.

'We cross the *kul* here.' Jagut stepped over it. 'See the public mill down by the water? That's where we ford the *nullah*.'

'We've got to get down to it first, though.'

Yes, I could see the public mill some seventy feet below and I could see a plummeting zig-zag. Was it a track? There was a twin to it beyond the ford but this time zig-zagging up to meet another traversed pathway such as ours. I was thankful for my snake-staff to save me from sudden sits and slithers. I haven't got the proper shoes, either. But somehow down we went.

A built-up terrace fronts the mill a few feet above the water, a pretty place, planted with flowering shrubs. The mill looked closed but Jagut knocked and called out for the miller. No one answered.

'I was forgetting. He left yesterday—for the festival. Never mind. Another time. He expects to be given a sight of you. He's never seen a White close to: he told me so. The fact is that everyone is extremely interested in you. You're the talk of the town. Did you realise it? They're specially anxious to know—well, anyway, all manner of things about you. I see you're wearing shorts today. Good. Though the water's quite shallow here.'

We waded over, knee-deep, carrying our shoes.

'Now for a clamber!'

A near-vertical zig-zag once again, up to a pathway as easy-going as our own had been and, when I'd got my breath back, a little wave of happiness broke over me, as if of youth again, perhaps, and everything was going to be all right. Soon Saan again, the countryside so beautiful, the Jumna flowing so serene down there across our line of vision, the eastern aspect of the house so high and safe on its escarpment that stands rock-solid bang in the axis of the fast-approaching river. Clear to see from here why the river has to genuflect to Jagut lording it on high and go into its respectfully evasive tight S-bend. Even Jagut himself, now striding on in front of me, was coming into focus for me.

Up-river the right-bank hills rise high and sheer from a narrow cultivated strip. They dominate Soon Saan from across the river. But the left bank, and the gentle slope of hillside we were traversing now we'd left the *nullah*, is richly fertile, the cultivation divided into minuscule small-holdings. Strange-shaped plots adjust their boundaries somehow, each to its neighbours. Could any one of them support a family? A hopelessly uneconomic jig-saw puzzle.

'That's Sir Launcelot's ancestral homestead,' Jagut turned to announce of a little cottage straight ahead, a byre beside it. 'We'll skitter past, though, and hope not to be seen—no time today for idle chatter with his parents, what with the temple and the Punjabi tea-party, not to speak of the Grand Tour. And all before dark. So silence—till we're safely past.'

'By the way,' he resumed, when we were past and out of earshot. 'Sarwa's convinced that the Punjabi is a real bad lot—a proper *goonda*, he says. He likes to think that he can tell at a glance.'

'There's one thing you can tell at a glance about him, that Punjabi. He's extravagantly handsome.'

'That's it, of course. And being a foreigner, to boot. Sarwa's hated enemy—on sight.'

'I'm foreign too. Does Sarwa hate me, do you think?'

'Peter. Forgive me: you aren't young and handsome—any more I mean,' he added quickly. 'Nor a potential rival with the girls.'

I laughed. 'Nevertheless he made it clear this morning that he doesn't approve of me at all.'

'How could you expect him to? You'd sided openly with the enemy.'

'Me?'

'Saying the Punjabi could come up to see me, when Sarwa had that moment said I was too busy. I have been told all.'

'I see. . . . I suppose I do like people to be as handsome as possible.'

'Sarwa's sulking, anyway. Perhaps you could pacify him, once we're back from the tea-party. Tell him, for example, how bad the enemy tea was. Tell him at bath-time. It would please him. Look! We can see the temple now,' and in a moment we were leaving the main pathway by a little downhill track towards it.

The Durga-devi temple stands shadowed by its trees, a cube of lime-washed masonry, some ten feet high, wide and deep, with a flattened dome on top and a broad raised pavement stretching out in front of it. Old? Not ancient, I should judge, whatever its foundations. A line of outbuildings flank its further side. Cultivation surrounds it, land piously endowed for the temple's upkeep, Jagut says.

'We've got a new incumbent since last year. I say "we", though I'm no Shivaite, naturally. Yes, a new resident *jogi*.[1] He's Punjabi too. Why this flux of foreigners, I wonder? Nice, though, if over-talkative. They all speak well of him round here, particularly the women. They think him very spiritual. But I do hear that back in the Punjab he used to have a roving eye—though how they know this, I know not. Before he took the veil, of course.'

We were passing under the first big tree of the group that shelters the temple precincts, near enough for me to get a good look at the man who was now coming out of the temple and onto the pavement fronting it.

'Is that your *jogi*, Jagut?'

'Yes, that's him. But *shh-h* now. Best behaviour, social faces. I'll certainly be expected to enter the temple with him, for a bit of *puja*: and I'm sorry to say you'll have to stay outside. I even doubt if it would be proper for you to mount the pavement—*namaste*, *namaste*, Mahatma-baba. We come to pay our respects to Durga-devi on this auspicious day.' Jagut was climbing onto the pavement, I remained below, the *jogi* took a step towards him, then stopped. Jagut had stopped too. A game of protocol, perhaps? Which should advance to greet the other, how far? The prince? The man of God? And I was thinking—our prince is certainly adroit, for Jagut was turning back towards me, to bring me into play, include me in this meeting. So Mahatma-baba had nothing for it really but to come on forward—'And this, Mahatma-baba, is my old old friend Peter sahib from England, come all this way to visit me again.'

Mahatma-baba greeted me with calm urbanity as I did *namastes* at him from below. He is tall, erect and willowy, shoulders square if narrow, fortyish, at a guess. A bit young to have renounced the world for the life of the spirit, however proper withdrawal 'into

the forest' may be considered once a man's worldly responsibilities
have been fulfilled. A bit young, too, for the renunciation of whatever had been his chosen delights of the flesh. What would his
have been? Meat-eating? Alcohol? Sex, naturally.

Tall, erect (if willowy), then. His posture, 'shoulders-back
stomach-in'—this looked parade-ground stuff. He must have been
a soldier. A fine figure of a man, a little Rasputin-ish, but women
don't mind that. A heavy moustache that almost hides the lips, a
heavy beard that hides the breast, and long thick raven locks
brushed back from a hair-line now receding to expose a high
domed brow. Oh yes, the ladies might well like him. He was
wearing a knee-length shift of hand-spun cotton cloth, a tone or
two darker than saffron, pinker, the colour they call *kavi*, which
is proper to ascetics of all sorts. A necklace to the waist of *rudrakshas* seeds, which are as big as nutmegs but much more craggily
indented. *Rudrakshas* seeds would be required wearing for a *jogi*
such as he: they are 'Shiva's tears' (I remembered this but not
what Shiva had been crying about). I would have expected
Mahatma-baba to 'wear the lingam', a miniature of course; in the
ordinary way its container (a little silver tube) is prominently displayed, say fastened in the hair, or round an arm, or else on a cord
about the neck. I saw no sign of it, though perhaps his beard hid
it, or the long sleeve of his shift. What would his caste be, what
had he been born to? I had an idea that a Shivaite *jogi* could
be of any caste, or even none. We stood there, Jagut and the *jogi*
on the pavement, I below them murmuring my responses to his
welcome as best I could, Mahatma-baba's face composed and
grave, his long brown legs quite bare under his shift, no pantaloons or *loongi*. From where I stood, in fact, I could see right up
his skirts, but as it would be easier still (and possibly less obvious)
to do so through the slit side-seams, I took a casual half-pace sideways. Ahh-h! So in fact he wore a *kavi*-coloured loin-cloth, the
same material as his shift. A *langouti*. I had idly wondered if a
Shivaite *jogi* would perhaps be naked underneath. The *langouti*
tied everything in very tightly. Richly endowed, I had not failed
to notice. He had embarked upon an apology for not taking me
into the temple with them and I was thinking, he has an air of
conscious sanctity, of being drugged with secrets, though it may
be *bhang* that he is drugged with, or some other of the hashish
derivatives—those hooded absent eyes. Hashish goes well with
woolly metaphysics.

96

They went into the temple. I looked around a bit. Not much of an attendance for a feast-day, almost no one. I would have expected local people to be dropping in, even if it wasn't Durga-devi's feast. It costs nothing to offer her a moment's worship, acquire a little merit that could come in useful, you never know. Quite near behind me was a three-stepped altar made of stone, with dark discolorations on the lowest step and on the grass in front of it. Dried blood? A collection of little objects of worship dispose themselves about the steps, and surmounting the topmost is a stone figure of a fat man almost Mayan in appearance—would he be a fertility sprite? But if 'fertility' should he not possess the symbol of his great function? All he seemed to be exposing was an outsize, an immense scrotum. How squat and angry he did look! I'd ask Jagut about him when he came out again. In fact Jagut was coming out now and signalling to me to join them where they were clambering off the pavement on the further side. I walked round to them. A second *jogi* had appeared, a smaller, milder, more retiring sort of man. We were grouped in front of three rough cubes of lime-washed masonry that must be graves, sarcophagi. I stared at them, digging back into what I had once read or heard about the Shivaite cults—did they bury their dead, not burn them? Mahatma-baba saw what I was staring at and nodded to me, saying, 'Three of my predecessors.' And Jagut was explaining to me that when *jogis* die they mostly put them in the river—or else they bury them. 'Sitting up,' he added, 'don't they, Mahatma-baba? Sitting up?'

'Yes. Sitting up. But they are sitting in the earth below. These ...'—he indicated the sarcophagi—'... these just mark the place. And of course carry the lingam.'

Of course 'carry the lingam'. I had seen at once that on each sarcophagus there stood erect a large stone lingam. Reverent hands had sculpted them for other reverent hands to spatter with red powders and for lips to whisper supplications to. I am sorry to be speaking of these objects all the time but the Lord Shiva (not to mention Durga-devi) does rather insist upon them, wave them at you, you can't escape them and the devout don't seek to. It wasn't always thus with Shiva and his *shakti* Durga, however; they've had their ups and downs. The gravest of their downs is really at the back of the lingam's meteoric rise to fame and godhead. It comes in one of the Sanscrit holy scriptures, the *Linga-purana*. This is a brief *résumé*.

97

One day the Lord Brahma (Creation) and the Lord Vishnu (Preserver) accompained by the Seven Penitents (who now reside in the heavens, having become the Great Bear) went to Kailasa to pay a visit to the third member of their Trinity, the Lord Shiva (Destruction). Kailasa is Shiva's personal paradise and the visitors surprised him therein busy copulating with Durga. Neither the Lord Shiva nor Durga turned a hair, they simply carried on with their business. At sight of them the gods (and specially Vishnu) burst out laughing. But the Penitents instead of taking it all in good part were deeply shocked and angry; and they loaded shameless Shiva with their insults and their curses: 'Thou art a devil and worse than a devil! Be accursed! Let no virtuous person henceforth have any dealings with thee! And so on. And after pronouncing these curses the Penitents retired in a huff, taking the gods along with them.

Shiva and Durga must have been in such a state of intoxicated abandon that they didn't quite realise who their visitors had been, nor that they had been so cursed. But later, during a lull when they came to their senses for a bit, they questioned their guards and the truth broke over them 'like a thunderclap'. They thereupon both died of mortification, and still in the exact position that the gods and Penitents had surprised them in.

Shiva saw at once what he must do and set about it. First he proclaimed that the act that had so covered them with shame and caused their death should from then on be celebrated throughout mankind. 'My shame has killed me,' he announced, 'but it has also given me a new life—*and a new shape*! It is the shape of my lingam! And I ordain that man shall worship it and make sacrifice to it.' Whereupon he listed the benefits that would accrue to those who model it in mud (though preferably cow-dung), or stone (seven times the benefit), or silver (seven times seven), or gold (seven times seven times seven). 'Nor shall they ever behold the Prince of Darkness! Embrace the worship of my lingam! It is white! It has three eyes and five faces! It is arrayed in a Tiger's-skin ... it disperses our terrors and our fears and grants us the object of all our desires!'

So this explains it to us—the adored, the adorable lingam.

All the time I was thinking of Shiva's disgrace and miraculous rehabilitation Mahatma-baba had been talking, talking, and was now asking Jagut to note the various improvements he had made in the temple precincts, all in the very first year of his incumbency, rather showing-off in fact—till Jagut broke into his spiel to ask to see the Pilgrims' Room. Mahatma-baba did not seem to hear him; he was giving orders to the other *jogi*, and the other shortly left us.

'It's a little room, Peter. I had it built and gave it. For pilgrims. Not many come, I know that, but those who do have need of somewhere to rest in. I wanted to put up some memorial to Saraswati.'

'I was going to ask . . .'

'Yes. She died. Shortly after the war. You remember her, of course. Saraswati the Good. You never knew my poor little wife? No, of course not. She died so very long ago, before we knew each other, even. But Saraswati, yes—we called her First Lady of Soon Saan.'

'So we did. First Lady of Soon Saan.'

So she had died.

'Come,' Jagut said. 'We'll go and look at her little Pilgrims' Room.' He led me off down the line of outbuildings, saying, 'The new road from my boundary walls up to the house—I've named that after her as well. In memory of her. Saraswati Road.'

'Soon Saan must miss her.'

'It's nearly twenty years already.'

Mahatma-baba was following along behind us. He seemed a bit confused. He was saying, 'Yes, Rana sahib, of course, the Pilgrims' Room.' Then louder, because Jagut wasn't listening, or at least not seeming to, 'You see, no pilgrims come—Rana sahib, no pilgrims come, you see, so we have . . . we have . . . .' His voice was tailing off as Jagut turned the corner beyond the last outbuilding.

'I've put a plaque in the wall, Peter. It's all in Hindi script but I'll read it out to you.' And indeed there was the plaque beside a heavy wooden door. The door was padlocked.

'Padlocked, Mahatma-baba? Why padlocked? Have you got the key.'

'As I was explaining, Rana sahib,' Mahatma-baba started. Then a burst of words: 'You see, with never a pilgrim and . . . and not having any store-room and this little room lying empty and unused, we . . . we thought we'd better. . . .'

Jagut said nothing. He didn't even read the inscription out to me. Instead he turned to me, ignoring Mahatma-baba: 'I think we'd better go, Peter. We've still so much ahead of us.'

Mahatma-baba accompanied us to the far corner of the pavement fronting the temple, near where the three-stepped altar stands. Did protocol demand this of him, or embarrassment? Jagut was cold and silent while the *jogi* held us briefly with the business of leave-taking. It was not the time for me to ask about the little 'Mayan' figure who lacked his lingam, nor about sacrifices, but Mahatma-baba played into my hands. 'Only yesterday another sacrifice,' he said, recovering his poise a little. 'Head off at a single blow.' He sketched an airy gesture, as if he, Mahatma-baba, could effortlessly cause his congregation to keep his goddess sated with the blood she's greedy for. 'A fine he-goat,' Mahatma-baba said.

A fine he-goat? Only a goat? I looked at Mahatma-baba. What had he to brag about, might I ask? Only a goat indeed! What she wants is human babies.

As we approached Sir Launcelot's ancestral homestead a man came round the byre, saw us, called in through a door. A younger man and then a child came out. A woman was at the threshold. Father, mother, brother, nephew—Jagut listed Sir Launcelot's family, and there was nothing for it but to stop for introductions and a moment's talk. 'Is this the sahib we've heard about?' they asked with flattering interest—and Jagut said I was. He was himself again by now, and we chatted amiably. They asked for the latest news about the 'bewitched' buffalo and Jagut gave it. Then Sir Launcelot's brother said, 'Look, Rana sahib. Look at our bullock.' A fine fat muscled animal it was, no evil-eyeing there. 'You remember, Rana sahib?'

'Is that the one I . . .'—Jagut did a mime, eyes darting nervously, then face hidden in his hands to the accompaniment of moans, while the others laughed happily. Jagut stopped all that to tell me, laughing now himself, 'It was ailing, that great lusty beast you see there. So I sold it to them cheap. How much, Govind Singh? Rupees two hundred? Cheaper still—one fifty? And they nursed it back to health. Hey, you two rogues, what's it worth today?'

'Rogues, are we, Rana sahib? Ho-ho, ho-ho! Worth? Five hundred? More!' And we were all laughing now, the farmstead rang with it as we turned to leave them.

Neither father nor son had any intention of leaving us, however. They intended to accompany us, would not take No for answer. 'As far as Bin Nullah, Rana sahib; you have to cross the *nullah*.'

'I suppose we'll have to let them, Peter. They probably want to carry us across the ford.'

'*Carry* us across? Can't we wade?'

'It shows a very proper feeling in them. I've told everyone around that you're a noble too—to build you up a bit. They are glad to carry nobles. Back in Kathmandu Maharaja Chandra Shum Shere was always carried everywhere—those huge palaces he built —up the great stairways, down them, across the courtyards. Pick-a-back!'

'But I'd feel silly.'

'These men won't know you're feeling silly. You should try to feel honoured. They are doing us honour; we must accept it as if we were worthy of it.'

So, the break-neck scramble down, the pick-a-back across the *nullah* feeling silly, but honoured too (and rather touched).

They must have been watching for us from the outskirts of the village or from the threshing-floor (we would have been clearly visible as we returned along the further hillside) because Sarwa and Tuman Singh and someone else were coming quickly along the footpath by our *kul* to meet us. Anxious faces, bad news. Very bad. I couldn't hear it properly because I led the Indian file and everyone was jabbering at once, shocked voices, Jagut's amongst them, grave, then suddenly dynamic:

'Send word to the Punjabi that we cannot take tea with him— make our excuses.' Sarwa, just behind me, gave a grunt. I turned to look at him and saw at once the satisfaction in his eyes.

'What is it, Sarwa?'

'Rana sahib is not taking tea with the foreign *goonda*.'

'Yes, yes, I heard that—but why not? What's happened.'

'Oh bad, bad. . . .'

So as soon as the threshing-floor was reached and I could ask Jagut what was going on I did so.

'It's that poor leper-boy. Oh how did I get the priorities so badly wrong? There wasn't time for everything last night, so I took you to inspect the buffalo instead of . . . a buffalo I couldn't do a thing to save, whereas this leper-boy. . . . In any case I've got to try. I *must* dissuade them somehow.'

'But what must you dissuade them *from*?'

Out through the farmyard gates and down the lane, down 'Saraswati Road'. 'It's for the poor boy's sake they're doing it, I grant you, Peter,' Jagut called back to me and I put on speed to catch him up. 'It's customary, too, I know. *But I do not approve!*'

'Approve of what?'

'Don't you know the practice here, then? With lepers? I made sure you'd know. Yes, yes, don't fluster me—I'm coming to it. They are consigning him to the river. This very evening.'

'Jagut!'

'We turn left here.'

Down Saraswati Road and left where we had turned left the previous evening but then on up the wooded hillside. 'They live behind the lady in question, up above her—we'll be seeing her cottage in a minute.'

'Yes, but—*consign* the leper-boy—what do you mean exactly?'

We were hurrying up a narrow track through citrus-orchards and I'm sure it's Jagut's sense of tease and timing that made him keep me dangling on a hook.

'Look, there it is, the lady's cottage—from the back: with the buffalo's owner down beyond. The buffalo still breathed at 3 p.m. by the way. I think I forgot to tell you. We don't seem able to make out from here if they've managed to hump it up in front of her cottage yet. Perhaps from further on. . . .'

'Yes, possibly from further on—but Jagut, do you mean they're actually going to throw him into the river?'

'No, no, not *throw*! "Consign" seems to me the proper word in English.'

'Drown him anyway? How absolutely awful! Can he swim? Do they have to gag and bind him?'

'Of course not! What a horrible idea. He *wants* to go in. He's said to them time and again that life has become too cruel and burdensome for him to bear. They hate doing it—his family all love him, but he insists upon it. There! You can see their cottage now. With that light string-cot in front of it. Oh yes, he's been begging them for ages. Ever since the disease took real hold.'

Jagut was obviously upset. The dramas of the early morning had had a slapstick element he certainly enjoys. You can't be Nepalese, or partly Nepalese, without possessing a keen sense of comedy and of the ridiculous. This was no longer comedy. As we hurried on he told me how in Nepal their way with lepers is somewhat different: with 'rejected' lepers, that was to say, he wasn't sure about loved lepers. A miserable rejected leper would be driven out from the village when the family could no longer bear his awful presence, driven out to die—for who would take him in if his own family had rejected him? So this outcast in the absolute sense would choose a precipice with an unobstructed drop—'Nepal is full of them. Sheer. Not the sloping kind of mountain they rolled offenders down, all trussed into a ball. Sheer.'

The outcast would have scavenged a big bone to take with him. A skull-and-crossbones bone would be the proper thing. And when he'd reached his chosen precipice, assuming always that his courage didn't fail him (and Nepalese courage does not fail), he would open his great thickened lips to let out one last shout, as if to announce to the surviving world the death of his. Then, with this shout still echoing, banging, ricochetting from rock-face to rock-face, he would clamp the bone between his teeth and cast himself into oblivion. I knew that lepers were in any case denied the Hindu funeral rites (no burning-*ghat* for them), but leaping into the abyss alone, somehow this struck me as far more awful than being 'consigned' to the holy Jumna river. I said something of the sort to Jagut: 'At least it would be a comfort to the poor thing, and his family: to know that he'd go floating down to find peace in Mother Ganga's bosom.'

'Oh but he wouldn't!' Jagut exclaimed. 'Oh no, not he! He'd have got caught up in the headworks not half an hour from here.'

'Oh? Headworks are something new.'

'Since your time. Didn't you see our barrage? You must have. Or no, perhaps from Lal Singh's you can't, or don't And then all the way here on the canal-road you'd be pointing the wrong way. Yes indeed, anyone "consigned" this side of our barrage would get properly caught up in it.'

'And that wouldn't be the same thing at all—I do agree.'

As we drew nearer the cottage we were making for two men came out of it. I said, 'They'd seen us coming.'

'But where's the middle brother? It's him I'm counting on. Do they look drunk? Not yet, perhaps.'

'I don't think so. Should they be?'

'Wouldn't you be, if your were going to consign a loved-one? Ah, there's the middle brother coming out. Good. And it's true, they don't look drunk at all.'

On towards the cottage in uneasy silence that Jagut broke to say, 'After all, if you don't mind, it may be better for me to see them on my own. They might be shy of you—a stranger. Not that you're a stranger, naturally.'

'To them I am. I'll wait here. I'll be quite happy. At least I mean I'll. . . .'

Jagut went on alone to meet them. They conducted him into the cottage.

He was a long time in the cottage.

I had felt it more discreet to move a little further off and had found a grassy mound a hundred yards away and now lay back against it, sucking grasses, trying not to think about the leper-boy, or indeed of anything. I blanked my mind—just let in little visual impressions, nothing sinister or sad. I could see a woman near the cottage Jagut said the lady in question lived in. Was that she? She looked quite plain and ordinary, her movements quite un-agitated. Impossible to make out from this angle, either, if the buffalo was laid at her front door or not. That would agitate her, all right. So I judged they hadn't done it yet. Did she know that they were going to? Everybody else did. But without knowing the proper *mantrams* could you move a betwitched object? I'd read somewhere that you couldn't. A real trial of strength, then: their shrewdness against her 'midnight powers' (would they prove black enough?). And the Panchayat would decide, squatting fatly on their hunkers, expensively at that, their fees and feasting—all in some shadowy mango *tope*. *Tope* is Anglo-Indian for grove.

How beautiful the mango *topes*, how beautiful from here the ripening paddy, Jagut's Rice Bowl, how neat its terracing that steps down to the river half a mile below where I was lying. I lay there looking at it. Nearer to hand in this green silent valley, the river faintly audible, its rage subdued by distance, I could see men working in the fields and orchards, and then—to my surprise—not fifty yards away a young girl squatting underneath a hedge, half under it. How long had she been there? It was only now I noticed her. Very young, scarcely in her teens. Perhaps she'd been there all the time, not moving, rather as an animal will 'freeze' when enemies approach down wind. But animals wear sensible protective-colourings, not a bright orange sari. She studiedly did not look my way. Oh well, I'd just lie back and suck lush grasses.

Eventually there was Jagut coming out again with the same three men behind him. What was the verdict? Jagut's gait announced it long before he was near enough for me to read the triumph on his face.

'I've done it!' he called out, coming closer. 'I really think I have. They've given me their solemn promise that they won't consign him after all. Yes, it was the middle brother who swayed the balance. Sundown was the chosen time—quite soon now. They were preparing for it. That's what the string-cot was there for. As litter. The leper-boy could never have walked—he was absolutely paralytic with country spirit. And it wouldn't have been the thing, either, for him to walk. The state he's in I wonder if he would even have been able to make his last shout.' He hesitated. 'Was I wrong to interfere . . . ? But whatever the case it's done now.' Then he deliberately changed the subject. 'Let's take a squint at the buffalo situation, shall we? I'd like to know if the dumping has been successfully carried out.' He checked himself. 'But we can't take a squint, drat it. There she is in person, our lady. See her? You think she looks "witchy"? She must be out watching for the buffalo-cortège. Or else she's watching us, and wondering about the leper-boy. Both, perhaps. What a relief—about the leper-boy, I mean.'

As we moved off I said, 'What do you think that young girl's doing underneath the hedge?'—we would be passing quite near her in a moment.

'Don't wish her,' Jagut whispered at me sharply. 'Take no notice of her—unless she wishes us, of course.'

'But . . .'

'I expect she's waiting for a friend.'

'Isn't she a little young, though?'

'What for?'

'To wait under a hedge for a friend.'

'That is her business,' said Jagut firmly.

We had passed her by, 'unwished', 'unwishing'. What could the answer be to my questions about little hill-girls' morals? What was the convention here? I'd have to bring it up all over again with Jagut.

Too late for the Grand Tour. The workers in the fields were already starting homewards, their tools across their shoulders. 'Someone has found our Test Case No. 2,' Jagut remarked contentedly. A man in the distance could be seen dragging yesterday's great dead branch behind him up the slopes. 'Very satisfactory. I shall compliment him.'

There is quite a sprinkling of cottages on this long and gently sloping hillside, but the only agglomeration of a size to call a village is our own up above. Most of these more or less isolated cottages are of stone, one-storey, nave roof of low pitch, and where the fall of the ground permits it there will be a wedge-shaped semi-cellar underneath for the family's live-stock or for stores. One small building that we passed was different: square, concrete, flat roof. In fact, as Jagut told me, it is a little primary school, closed at present for the festival. I thought of Maharaja Deb and the thirty little schools in the Valley of Nepal, his pilot-scheme those seventy years ago. 'Oh yes,' Jagut was saying, 'all our kids have to attend school. I gave the building for it. And look, Peter. The cottage up there through the trees. That's my new tenant, the Punjabi we were to have taken tea with. That little thing, the girl outside, scouring cooking-vessels—I suppose she's his wife. Pretty, she looks. I think we'll go home by the short-cut again, shall we? It's getting late and it saves us minutes.'

The light was flattening and failing rapidly. Quite soon down by the river the valley would start filling up with shadows, and the shadows would be darkening and broadening and rising, floating out the sunlight on their surface, higher, higher, climbing the mountainsides till nothing would be left of day except a spot-lit Himalayan peak or two to east of us, and the skies burning in the west. And then not even that.

The short-cut again, while there was still just light enough for it, the fifty yards of tunnelled undergrowth, the streamlet's dry and rocky bed, a little standing water.

'That glum girl,' Jagut turned to say to me, 'remember?'

'The "Unlucky House" girl? Yes.'

'Just so. Well, this is exactly where her unlucky sister was bitten by the snake.' He was making rather a show of tap-tapping with his staff, to remind me what our staffs are for, was it? Or to frighten me? It did. 'It's ten days now,' he said. I kept a rigid silence. 'Poor girl, she died of course. Her blood was coagulating before she could get to the dispensary. I'm not supposed to give snake-serums—and it was far too late anyway. She didn't even know what kind of snake had bitten her, moreover. Cobra? Russell's viper? Different serums for each kind; you have to know which.'

I said nothing, but my mind recorded that Nature's serpent section had certainly not come slithering in to offer Jagut its allegiance. But the dispensary was functioning still. I was busy sharpening my eyes for snakes and kept my rigid silence. Coagulating blood, poor girl. Terrible pain, I'd always heard, but death mercifully quick. Jagut was ostentatiously tap-tapping. 'I call the short-cut "Snake Alley",' he informed me. 'They come for a sip of water this dry weather, poor things.' At this I shouted, 'Stop it!' at his back. He burst out into delighted laughter. Devilish Mongol!

Home, and almost dark. The windows, the verandahs, all pricked with lamp-light once again, the smell of wood-smoke, Rameshwar with our mugs of *lassi* waiting by the big stone mushrooms and the lily-pools, and someone handy to take our staffs and shoes. '*Ahh-h* . . .' Jagut was sighing happily as the man pulled off his shoes. 'How good to feel the cobbles under my bare feet. It's like a luxury.'

Under my own now, too. And why should I, alone in all Soon Saan, be awed by a five-foot lingam? No, I'd take the self-same mushroom as I'd had the previous evening, I'd lean back peacefully against the great god Shiva's sacred person.

Lean safe against the Lord and sip your *lassi*!

A man was coming across the cobbles with a tray, someone I didn't recognise, though Jagut did of course: 'What did I tell you? It's the Bridegroom, back on the Dehra bus.' He introduced him: 'Your second Switzer.' The Bridegroom made a deep Rajput bow across his tray. 'He's offering you a wedding sweetmeat. Better accept one.'

I chose the smallest of the lot, a dun-coloured thing about the size of a ping-pong ball, taking my time and trying to look interested rather than dismayed. I knew what to expect of sugared wedding sweetmeats.

Rameshwar had started on the evening's news. No, the two defectors had not returned—nor, again, the bike that they'd defected with. No, the *amla*-contractor had not arrived (nor would my baggage have arrived either, if I had entrusted it to him). The wife of one of the cow-men was insisting that her pains were on her. Her pains? All Soon Saan—except myself—already knew that they couldn't start for weeks yet. Jagut said she simply wanted to extend the legitimate period of her interest and importance— 'because she's an ugly little thing and doesn't get much attention in the ordinary way—even from the cow-man, so it seems. And think, Peter! The car still undelivered—and you'll admit that that's the *mot juste*, too!—and one bike with defectors and our second immobilised for want of a back tyre. . . . I didn't like to

worry you with our domestic problems but the fact is that with
not even a bike left to us for the race to civilisation to try to hire
a car to come and fetch her, we're finished.'

'Can't they just have babies here at home like everybody used
to?'

'No, they cannot! They've gone so grand these days, it's all
hospitals and lady-doctors and a car to carry them. In the days of
my dear old Buick, off they'd go in it, bumpity-bump—that was
before I'd finished Saraswati Road. Many's the babe born in the
back of my dear old Buick on its bumpity mercy-dash. Well no,
I mustn't exaggerate. Only two, to be truthful. Deepak's youngest
brother was a Buick-baby. Wasn't he, Deepak?'—he had repeated
it in Hindi and Deepak nodded. 'Rameshwar, can't the cow-man's
wife hold off a bit, till the *amlas* are harvested?'—but Rameshwar
didn't know. He did know, however, that Sir Launcelot had not
so far managed to dowse out the silver candelabrum, and that the
'bewitched' buffalo's owner and family were having great difficulty
in moving the poor creature. (Ah-ha! What had I said to myself
about moving bewitched objects? But I said nothing to them. Too
late now: I ought to have aired my knowledge before the event.)

Rameshwar said: 'Rana sahib, may Shambu please bring the
new snake. He wishes to show it before it goes up.'

'Tell him to bring it.'

'New snake? Yes, it's the write-off bike-tyre. I told Shambhu,
let's have a change of colours this time: one grows tired of green
and yellow stripes. Ah! Shambhu! Very nice. Though perhaps
bright red is not all that life-like. How well you've done its little
eyes, though. Are they buttons? Where shall we have it put, Peter?
You choose the tree. Those green-and-yellows, you've seen them,
naturally. One of my visitors actually thought that they were real,
imagine!'

The Bridegroom was in attendance on me at tub-time. An
amiable young man, he appears to be. A big guileless bungie face,
square teeth, large mouth and even so a tongue a size too big for
it. He is certainly a sunnier, warmer, character than Sarwa—yet I
like the surly Sarwa. It was he who must have briefed the Bridegroom, because without waiting for me to call out for more hot
water he came quietly into the bathroom through the annexe door
(left thoughtfully unlatched?) with two more steaming buckets. He
took me unawares. I was lolling back to soak. 'The towel, please,'

I said quickly, caught out in a social gaffe a second time—but the Bridegroom isn't Sarwa, no question here of eyes averted, head the other way. He had a good stare and no bones about it. 'The towel!' I repeated in a loud reproving voice. I know this was very hypocritical of me, when an hour or two before I'd had a jolly good stare up Mahatma-baba's skirts—but then the Bridegroom was not to know about this, and they were his rules, not my own, that I was trying to insist on. He held the towel like a curtain for me to hide behind. I wrapped it round me, he topped the tub up, then left quickly with an extraordinary expression on his face. Had my implied rebuke offended him?

When in due course I went back into the bedroom clean and dry and wrapped in the big bath-towel, I found the Bridegroom quite composed again and standing by the bed. On the bed now lay what was clearly a folded *loongi*. Beside it a *khasto* with Jagut's armorial bearings hand-blocked on it. It must be the one that the Fair Maiden had been stitching at that morning. The Bridegroom picked it up and opened it for me to see, smiling. He is a smiler. 'Rana sahib just now gave them to me to bring to you, sahib,' he said.

I was very pleased. Exactly what I needed. I told the Bridegroom so. 'You may go now,' I added. He went. I didn't want to have him watching my prim struggles to get into under-pants without first taking off the towel—oh these other-people's rules! I didn't want to have him watching my attempts to tie a *loongi*, either. So long since I have worn one. Let me see, now—how did it go? Take an end in either hand and. . . . No. Start again. One end held to the right hip, perhaps, and the other . . . how was it? A single piece of cloth, two yards by one or thereabouts. . . . Anyhow this much I did know, firmly—that it's far from being okay, in fact it's very common, to make a knot in it or pin it. So you wrap it round you somehow, then you carefully accordian-pleat the longish length left over in the front and tuck your bunch of pleat-tops into your improvised waist-band, navel-high. There! Something like that, let's say. Next smooth the pleats and flatten them in such a manner that they fall to your toes as gracefully as may be.

With the *khasto* round your shoulders and *loongi* round your waist you now move gracefully out of the room swaying slightly so that the accordion-pleats swing like the dewlap of some sacred Brahminy bull, out to where the whisky's waiting.

Out on the verandah Jagut was waiting too. *'Shabash!'* he said, on seeing me all dressed up like this. 'Bravo!'

'Thank you so much. I'm so pleased to have such things again. I'd long since lost the old ones.'

'More convenient than shirt and trousers, no? For shampoo-hour, I mean.'

'Yes, much.'

A *chota-peg* in one hand, the other arm relinquished to whoever was assigned to me (no one I have a name for), mustard-oil in saucers, willing hands, light work—how peacefully it does pass the time. We scarcely talked. I sipped my *chota-peg*, lazily watching my free hand move the glass in and out of the golden circle that the lamp beside me cast on to the drinks tray. Someone had come up to attend to Jagut's scalp, and someone else for mine.

So much for arms and scalps. Now for the feet. Yes, *khasto* and *loongi* are certainly the proper dress for shampoo-hour, and oh! the restful ritual.

Eventually Jagut broke our silence. 'Do you know what I tell them? It's a saying of an ancient Hindu sage, Chanakya. "More strengthening than rice is meat; more strengthening than meat is *ghee* ..." ' Jagut intoned it sagely, and *ghee* is clarified butter, "More strengthening than *ghee* is oil"—for shampooing into the skin this time, the sage meant,' Jagut explained. 'He doesn't specify mustard-oil but in my experience it's the best by far. It must be well worked in. Lucky our attendants are so patient and untiring. Enough for the moment, though. Shall I dismiss them?' He did so, and they went off, making *namastes* as they left.

'Yes,' said Jagut musingly when they had gone. 'This is the proper shampoo-hour—right after a hot tub with all the pores still open. By the way I hope they are bringing you enough hot water for your tub.'

'Plenty, thank you. The Bridegroom was on duty tonight. He even brought up more without my asking for it.'

'I know,' said Jagut in a far-off voice. 'Sarwa had told him to, and...'—and there he stopped. He was watching me diagonally across tea-corner with an odd sort of hesitation. What was going on?

'You mean Sarwa bothered to tell you he'd told the Bridegroom to?'

'No. It was the Bridegroom who told me Sarwa had told him to. Just now.'

'Why should he have bothered to, I wonder. . . .'

'Well. . .' He hesitated once again. 'I hadn't really meant to tell you this, Peter, but now I think I should because . . . and even so I'm not quite sure. You might huff.'

'Of course I won't huff. Go on. Tell me!'

'You might. Sarwa announced—well, something. And none of the others could believe their ears. They took it for a flight of Sarwa's fancy. So Sarwa was furious with them—it was as good as telling him he was a liar. He came to me about it.'

'Jagut, do please tell me quickly—what is all this? Does it concern *me*, then?'

'Yes—in a way. In fact it only concerns you.'

'Then if you don't tell me at once, I *shall* huff!'

'All right. But don't blame me. It's got nothing to do with me—except that they came to ask me if it really could be true.'

'And was it—*is* it true?'

'I expect so.'

'WHAT IS IT?'

'Patience! I first heard of it just before shampoo-hour yesterday evening. Sarwa came into my room. Now, let me get this straight.' Jagut had started to giggle a bit. 'Yes. Sarwa came hurrying into my room in a condition of shock and without more ado cried out, "Rana sahib, Rana sahib, I couldn't help it, truly I could not!" ' Jagut was trying to mimic Sarwa's gruffness with the note of shock in it, doing it rather well, at that. But now he said in his ordinary voice: 'I think I had better prepare you for this, a little. It concerns your being a White. Perhaps you should give yourself another *chota peg.*'

I did so. 'But, Jagut. They've seen a White before.'

'Yes—*but never in the bath-tub!*' And here he choked on a great gulp of laughter. He recovered. 'I'll have to start again,' he said as he recomposed his face. Then off he went, Sarwa-voice and all: ' "Rana sahib, Rana sahib, I couldn't help it, truly I could not—try to believe me, Rana sahib, though the others call me liar —I didn't look, Rana sahib, simply I *saw*! In the bath-tub, Rana sahib! Peter sahib is white, white, white all over!" '

And again it proved too much for Jagut; he was overcome with laughter till he could pull himself together a little. 'Where was I? Was it the "white, white, white all over"-bit? "Peter sahib is white, white, white all over, except his, his. . . . Rana sahib, I swear that this is true. *Pink! With a red rosy top!*" '

Jagut had frankly given in and was being swayed back and forth by his laughter, and I was laughing too, though with some embarrassment, perhaps.

'All that was yesterday, after tub-time,' Jagut went on, more calmly now. 'Today has been filled with everybody's speculations —is Sarwa's story false? Or is it true? How could it be? I've refused to take sides. Did you sense anything, Peter? Did they stare and speculate? No? Well, that's because they honestly could not believe it. And that's why this evening Sarwa charged the Bridegroom to go and see for himself so that he could confirm it in every Technicolor detail—which he has done just now. Now none dare call Sarwa liar, and all Soon Saan will certainly be agape!'

'I see,' I said—I hope not sourly. 'What would they expect, then? A little purple aubergine?'—and Jagut, rolling sideways on his divan, managed to cry out—'It would certainly be more usual —that we must admit!' And he was off again, rocked with laughter.

After a little he said: 'Come on. Supper-time.'

We got up. A shout from Jagut: 'Peter! Your *loongi*!'

'My *loongi*!'

It was round my ankles. Had I trodden on the accordion-pleated dewlap and tugged the waistband loose? I quickly gathered up the folds.

'A good thing none of our attendants was here to see, anyway,' Jagut said.

'But I *am* wearing under-pants, Jagut.'

'Even so.'

'I'll go into my room and retie it. Join you in the dining-room.'

In the privacy of my bedroom I carefully retied the thing. It isn't all that easy, but that would have to do and I'd improve with practice. How embarrassing . . . but why embarrassing? What did I care what Soon Saan was agape about? And what was that plate of things doing under the oil-lamp on my bedside-table? Oh dear God, a platter of assorted wedding-sweetmeats. Oh this was awful! I counted them. Twelve. Kind, generous Bridegroom, but what was I to do? In a flash I knew what I must do. I would 'consign' them, one or two each day. Into the palace-pedestal, the blue, the gold on white, I would consign them one by one, down the long long-drop to the waters of holy Jumna river grumbling below. I 'consigned' the first and largest of them and went down to supper.

8

Dawn has just come up again in its pinks and golds, up over the mountains, sending its horizontal rays in across the back-verandah windowsill and through the rails of the bedhead, waking me. My sixth dawn? Seventh, even?

For about a week, anyway, ever since Sarwa's revelations electrified the air and made of me Soon Saan's unwilling wonder, I have been acutely sensitive to stares. At my approach men, women, even children, have seemed to stand back staring covertly. Sometimes when I've been in the pleasuredome they'd stop below it, then glance obliquely upwards, whispering. What sort of gracious kindly figure am I cutting now? At first I thought of asking Jagut for advice, perhaps of begging him to have it put about that they should venerate me, not take me for a freak. They venerate the Lord Shiva, don't they?—'white', with its 'three eyes and five faces' indeed! And all arrayed in a Tiger's skin! If that's not a freaky sort of object, tell me what is! I have finished up by saying nothing, and Soon Saan's stares are gradually lessening. From my third evening in the bath-tub I have nicely fool-proofed my technique. The Switzer on tub-duty taps softly at the door (I've bolted it), I call out 'Wait!', get out and wrap myself in towels, unbolt and call 'Come in!' He comes in, and with dignity we disregard each other.

I think, actually, that both my Switzers may feel remorse at having caused me the humiliations of the past week. They are being particularly good and attentive—not that the Bridegroom ever wasn't, but Sarwa for a time thought he had cause to be surly. But he seems to have forgiven me for siding with the enemy Punjabi. Did Jagut have a little word with him? Or is it that Sarwa finds it easier to forget the incident now that the enemy is reported to have gone off somewhere days ago and not returned? More than one evening bulletin has mentioned this, how his nearby neighbours wander casually past his cottage when they see his little wife outside it scouring cooking-vessels or at some other task. They innocently stop to pass the time of day and try to pump her (where's he gone to—why?). But she speaks to no one, not even to women neighbours, she acknowledges their greetings and no more, then turns back to her task. 'Nine days he's gone, the "loafer",' Sarwa says, using an English word that Hindi turns into the gravest sort of insult. 'May Naga bite him dead,' says Sarwa— Naga being the cobra, Vishnu's hooded holy terror.

There has been something else by way of news as well. It has upset us all, without touching us all that closely. A little girl is missing from her home some way up-river. She's been missing for days already and her distracted parents have been asking everywhere for miles around—Soon Saan included—if anyone has seen her. Killed by a leopard? Did the jackals get her? Drowned? In any case, no trace. Soon Saan fathers tell the mothers, 'Watch the children well. Keep them all close.'

Now that I put my mind to it I realise that I've been here well above a week: the Dussehra festival alone was ten days long. Divali, Feast of Lamps, is rapidly approaching.

It is feasts that regulate the local calendar. Being movable, these Hindu feasts, they move us with them. For example, Jagut tells me that he celebrates his birthday on the third day after the Lord Krishna has celebrated his own; and although this always falls around September by our Western reckoning, it shuttles freely back and forth in the Hindu calendar. I learn in addition that Jagut's sign of the zodiac is Gemini, which we in the West think of as falling between the last week of May and the last week of June, nowhere within hailing distance of September. Our situation here is seen to be irregular.

So when I say feasts 'regulate' the passage of our time, it isn't quite the verb for it. You might suppose that our daily copy of *The Hindustan Times* would serve to keep us in some sort of rhythmical association with the outside world and its reckonings, its days of the week, its dates and so on. Nothing of the sort. The paper's arrival is so erratic, certainly not daily, not even necessarily in date-order, that it's no help at all for that. As a matter of fact I don't even read as much as its date-line, and for me its only useful function is to provide little screws of paper for cleaning our blackened lamp-chimneys each morning. I can hear their squeaks below me as I lie here placidly awaiting Rameshwar with my early-morning 'bed-tea'. I can hear the *frou-frou-frou* as well, and the other muted morning noises as Soon Saan slips serenely into gear again. I note that Kalé's pretty sister has already left my front-verandah door-mat. She has been sleeping on it for the last few nights; it is probably her private territory, and my arrival drove her from it. Since she's back to it, it means that she's accepting me, though we have not spoken yet. Kalé himself sleeps on a wood-and-wicker chair outside the spare room next to mine. (I must inspect that other room one day.) Kalé hasn't started fawning yet, either. Perhaps when Divali comes I'll relax a little with them, because Divali offers us not only 'Cow-Day' and 'Bull-Day' but a 'Dog-Day' too. I much look forward to 'Dog-Day', to seeing Kalé & Co all garlanded with flowers and being made much of. That might be the appropriate moment to extend a god-like hand, let it get kissed—let it get sniffed at, rather—dog-spit being abominable defilement. If I were a Brahmin and so much as a drop of dog-spit should fall upon my clothing even, I would have to jump fully-dressed into the nearest holy water—fortunately quite near and deep. I would expect cow-dribble to be accounted quite all right—her other products are, indeed all five of them are purificants. But pretty as Jagut's cross-bred Jerseys may be, I can't say they hold my interest for long. They are part of our lives, though, and it would upset me if one fine morning they failed to turn up at the water-hole to take over from the geese.

Whatever this morning's day and date, there has now been time enough for Mussoorie to have received the letter I sent him 'Cleft-stick Express' from here, and for his reply from Kathmandu to reach me. It is agreed that I am to fly up there from Delhi by Royal Nepal Airlines as soon after the Divali festival as they can give me a booking. Mussoorie evidently can't accommodate a house-guest, so I am to go to a hotel called 'Green'—neat but not gaudy, he says, and cheap. That's good. Another thing that's good about it is that it is in the middle of the old city of Kathmandu, very near the Hanuman Dhoka, the old city-palace complex where so much family-history was acted out. I know from photographs and travellers' descriptions that the Hanuman Dhoka is spectacularly beautiful, seventeenth and eighteenth centuries, and in part nine storeys high, the highest elements being in the indigenous pagoda-style, like Jagut's midget island-temple in the lily-pool. Somewhere in the vicinity of Hanuman Dhoka there is a building that they called 'the Kōt'. Assuming it still stands, it does so in a big courtyard of its own; and even if it does not form part of the palace-complex, it must be very near. The only town-plan of Kathmandu that I have been able to lay my hands on does not mark it, but I know what it is going to look like—if it still stands—because Landon's book includes a plate of it. It is an altogether unspectacular affair in plastered masonry rather in the Anglo-Indian urban manner of the 1830's and '40's, except for its characteristically Nepalese pantiled roof with deep projecting eaves. They used this place for assemblies of the Council and the Army High Command (civil and military affairs were barely distinguishable) and I hardly think that it would merit more than a glance in passing but for what happened there on the night of 14–15 September 1846 between the hours of shortly after ten—when the news first broke—and dawn. A certain Gagan Singh had been shot through the lit window of his *puja*-room while at his prayers.

Exactly what did happen? Survivors had their different tales to tell and some were downright lies, but there was no concealing of the outcome. Two major facts could hardly be disputed. First that at a given moment in the night the queen had suddenly appointed a new prime minister and it was Jung Bahadur. This was a fact the sun could demonstrate at dawn by shining bright and golden on him in the courtyard of the Kōt—Prime Minister General Jung Bahadur, twenty-nine that year, his six full-brothers ranged beside him (the youngest of them Jagut's grand-father, Dhir Shum Shere). The second demonstrable fact the sun shone down on, perhaps more sombrely, was an enormous mound of still-warm corpses collected in the courtyard of the Kōt. They were all piled up together, higgledy-piggledy—'with no reference to rank'. Except for Jung Bahadur, his brothers, bodyguard and faction—and of course excepting too the royal family and Brahmins whose lives were sacrosanct—almost everyone of any consequence in all Nepal was somewhere in that mound of carcases.

Padma Jung Bahadur (who was to be born in 1857, third of Jung Bahadur's 'listed' sons and biographer of his father), says that only fifty-five names of the dead have been preserved, but that the numbers should be many times more 'as the list could not contain the names of obscure or petty men whose death was not worthy of being recorded'. The lowest figure I have read is one hundred and thirty, the highest a dizzy four-hundred plus.

Every book about Nepal since 1846 contains some version of how the Kōt Massacre came about and who did what. All writers since 1880 have paraphrased the Oldfield version (Residency Surgeon 1850–63), with its marks of authenticity. Oldfield, till our day, was alone among the tellers of the story who had access to an official British Residency document written over the name of C. Thorseby, Resident, and classified as secret. Perhaps he had no right to use it and this may be why his text makes no acknowledgement of his source. This secret document is open to inspection now; I have a transcript of it and I know that Oldfield used it. He lifts verbatim passages from it, much as his own plagiarists in their turn lifted most of what they knew from his version, and as often as not without acknowledgement. I shall delay my version, however, until I'm in the proper place for telling it—in Kathmandu—because I want to check a little theory on the spot. But whatever the detailed truth may be, this much is certain—that the Rana dynasty was born that night; that within six weeks the queen was exiled to Benares by her new Prime Minister Jung Bahadur who later deposed the king and put the latter's eldest son upon the throne, but with this difference—that from that day, for a hundred years to come, the kings were to be reduced to abject puppets. Meanwhile Jung Bahadur was to be the absolute and only power in the land until the day he died, in 1877. He was to use his power with clemency; he ruled the country well according to his time and lights; he loved the British (good!) and was loved by them, with mutual benefits; and he is credited with fathering a hundred sons. He died of natural causes—a feat not one of his predecessors had managed to achieve.

Is it deceitful of me that I haven't said a word about this massacre to Jagut, nor even anything about Great-Uncle Jung Bahadur in more general terms—apart from that solitary occasion when I brought the wood-engraving out and the presentation so misfired? I shall not speak of it, I think, however much I long to ask him how the story has been handed down within the family (the 'Fairlawn lot', I mean). Jagut may be touchy on the subject; perhaps he disapproves, or thinks he ought to. Or else he thinks that Whites like me can't fail to disapprove, and that might be intolerable to him (how dare I disapprove!), whereas in fact I know and understand as well as he does that in given times and places the alternative to getting killed is killing. It was like that in Nepal. A man—and his family or faction—was in power, or else was out of it; alliances and coalitions could never work for any time at all. In the words of Joshi and Rose, 'an 'equilibrium was only achievable through the destruction of the hostile group on as broad a base as possible. So the political process was soaked in blood.' Everybody found this quite normal: you were obliged to massacre the opposition, and wisest to finish them all off in one great bloody go, every man-jack of them. That should keep them quiet for at least a generation, till their youngest sons grew into manhood. It stood to reason. It was to stand to reason well into the twentieth century, for that matter. But as often as the Ranas' enemies organised a Rana-massacre, the Ranas proved to be a jump ahead and did the massacring themselves. Will Mussoorie be readier to talk about all this than Jagut? We shall see.

The Royal Nepal Airlines reservation three days after Divali is made now, and it brings Kathmandu much closer—Mussoorie, too. Perhaps I feel a twinge of apprehension about him, but nothing to what I felt on my arrival here at Jagut's. This must be because the threads I have to gather up with Mussoorie are relatively few and simple, as I never knew him in the sense that I knew Jagut, say, or others of the family, like Narpat and the rest. He's a lapsed ascetic now (so Jagut tells me); his spiritual retreat is over, more or less. I'm much relieved. That brings him closer too. Also I'm sure I know exactly what he's going to look like—'father' in those royal-progress photographs in my annexe. It could well be that I wouldn't recognise Mussoorie in a street full of other Nepalese, but I'll take good care that our first meeting isn't in a street. I'll ask him round to my hotel, and since he cannot have the least idea of what I've come to look like since those days, he can identify me by my name and room-number cross-checked by the management. I am promised bright Nepali sunshine every day, and nights one-blanket cool. I think I'll stay a month or so, and then come back to Soon Saan for a bit before the real cold sets in at this altitude. And I'll leave before Jagut's pack-up for the plains; I should not care to see that going on. Although I know that Soon Saan only hibernates during Jagut's removal to his winter quarters,

I don't want to think that life could even seem to withdraw itself from here.

Meanwhile life continues at Soon Saan and everything has dropped so easily, neatly, into place that it seems to me I might have lived here always; and although 'now' is now, as usual, at the same time it is also 'then', those years before the war when first I knew the family. My distant Indian past and now my present have been comfortably adjusting themselves into a personal time-space continuum and I truly do not know when I have been more consciously content. After the *clatter-banging* for the mid-day dinner sent them all scurrying yesterday and left me quite alone up in the pleasuredome, I announced it to the air out loud: 'I am consciously content!'—to test the sound of it. It sounded wonderful. Moreover I can now look Jagut in his present face and see him just exactly as I've always known he is.

The first overt sign that this might be growing true of me for him was the disappearance of the towering silver centre-piece that for a while shielded us from each other at the dinner-table. One breakfast it had gone. Certainly it took up too much room and wasn't pretty in the least, but it had served a useful purpose, even if it made it difficult for Jagut to spoon refills of food from what I think of as the 'mother-dishes' into the little bowls on my *thali*. The *thali* is the tray—in this case silver—in front of each of us. On it we carefully compose mouthfuls of this and that from our various little bowls, then pop the mouthful in, folded in a flap of *chappati* or whatever type of unleavened bread is being served. All this is done with the first two fingers and the thumb of the right hand. Getting the mouthful safely in is helped by a last-second poke with the middle finger. Jagut does it very neatly. I am getting back into the way of it but am clumsy still, and a bit messy. I see Rameshwar eyeing my messy fingers disapprovingly. Let him.

At breakfast, however, we eat in the Western manner, knives, forks, plates, side-plates for hot toast and butter, honey and the rest. At this particular breakfast with the silver centre-piece removed, Jagut explained its going on the grounds that it's so ugly. 'So it's back in the silver-room. It's only fit for Buckingham Palace, anyway.' He paused. 'It isn't really a silver-room—that was at Fairlawn. Here it's just a couple of great wooden chests in a godown off our lady-cooks' quarters. They are its guardians.' He was examining my plate. 'Eat up your bacon!' he ordered me.

'I am eating it up!'

'You're starting to plump up a bit—they're all remarking on it: but there's some way to go yet, and what with the time-limit set now for fattening you for market, I'm going to be more severe than ever. You've got to do me credit. Nirmal!' A face appeared in the service-hatch. 'Prepare more bacon.' Then, to me, 'Did you know? Our scullion-cum-bacon-cook was back some days ago. De-defected, as you might say. Along with our second bike. And the helper-handyman with him. Both very contrite. Didn't I give them a pi-jaw, though! How they hate that!'

I dutifully ate the bacon on my plate and when Rameshwar brought me Nirmal's second batch attacked that too.

'That's the way,' said Jagut.

'Those two?' I asked him. 'You no longer think they made off with the candelabrum, then?'

'Of course not! No one did! Don't say you haven't seen it! It's back where it belongs—in your annexe.'

'No. I suppose I haven't been in there lately. But Jagut...'

'Some kind person had taken it to give it a good cleaning—to lighten Mrs Midget's work, I dare say. It took Sir Launcelot hours, but he dowsed it out at last, at dawn next day.'

'Yes, but...'

'The Case of the Missing Candelabrum is now closed—definitively.'

'Oh, I see—,' I said, but I didn't see.

'Ready for your aphrodisiac?'

'To be honest I don't think it is—*at all*. And I don't really like its taste. I'd much rather have some honey, please.'

'What! *Not aphrodisiac?* My *amlas?* I won't hear a word against them. Don't you let the *amla*-contractor hear you speak like that when he gets here. But perhaps there's not been time enough as yet—you know, to build up a proper concentration in you. Once that's done you'll be all right, and then it's only a question of a booster every so often. You must have been terribly run down. Let me give you a decent helping. There! Did I tell you? The Riddle of the Second Sow is solved as well. She's back! She'd made that hole in the zareeba herself and wandered off. And she was making such a noise, rooting and munching and grunting in the guava orchards, that the pig-man's daughter heard and at once recaptured her. Good, isn't it? Except that poor Mingy has his three tormentors once again. I wish he'd jolly well hurry up and stop being a runt.'

Yes, of course, all this is very good and satisfactory. Our second sow is home again and no one sold or ate her; the silver candelabrum is safely in its place again and no one stole and melted it; all our defectors are back again—had there been only three? It seemed like dozens at the time. Even the buffalo-lady's junior husband who'd abandoned her and run off in a fit of tantrums (though he didn't count for us), he's back again, we hear. I expect he counts for the wife he shares with his brother, accustomed as she is to two bedfellows, turn and turn about—one at a time only being considered proper in our local polyandrous society, I'm assured.

Anyway, all's for the best again in the best of all possible worlds, and yet . . . and yet. . . . I confess to a twinge of deprivation. It's as if nothing at all had ever happened to us—though none can make a retro-operative snatch and take away from us the tingling excitement of the day Soon Saan was practically knocked off orbit.

In point of fact we are not really quite back to square one nor ever can be, because the buffalo has died at last. A great relief. We had been growing heartily sick of its appearances in each evening's bulletin 'still breathing—just'. The night the jackals all came shrieking in we pricked our ears and guessed at it; the morning that the vultures lumbered down like bald-head helicopters we knew—because people went to see. By the time they'd been to see, however, the carcase was a skeleton, picked clean. Who can now be certain that its death was not from natural causes? What will the owner do? It should be obvious to him now that the lady will never settle out of court—which is what he was still urging her to do, 'save both of us the fees!'

There are those who see another hand behind it all—a heavy, horny hand—a male hand. This rumour hints at darker things to come, if we're not careful. The reference is, of course, to Mahasu the Terrible, though people are as always careful not to name the name. Actually I have started thinking of him as 'the Horrible' once more. 'The Terrible' might be Ivan or anyone at all, an all-in wrestler, for instance. But Mahasu isn't anyone: he's Someone. And it is widely thought that he should be propitiated—but who's to buy the goat? A second rumour has it that the lady herself has put about the Mahasu theory—to take the heat off her. But when approached and pumped a bit, she snaps her mouth tight shut and will not speak. So this makes a second little set of sealed lips around here lately to add to those of the Punjabi tenant's wife. Each lady for her good reason.

So much for our News in Brief, then. Now for something that I have recorded at greater length. It relates to the night the *amla*-contractor finally arrived.

After supper that evening, when we went next door for night-cap tea, I was surprised to find the big shadowy low-ceilinged room flooded with a white-hot brilliance that gave it a very startled air, as if caught napping. A petrol-vapour lamp had been put on a small table a yard from the sofa, and stood there sizzling and spluttering. Between it and the sofa was a second small table, to carry a palace-size photograph-album. Tooled leather, gold-embossed.

'You were asking about father,' Jagut said. 'I've had one of his albums brought out—from the period he was in power. You *are* interested, no? Not just inquisitiveness? Or being polite?'

'Very interested indeed.'

'All right. We'll both sit on the sofa, shall we?' He sat down, his fingers on the cover of the album. 'I don't suppose you even know what father looked like, do you? Wait, Peter, wait! Rameshwar's bringing you the tooth-picks!'

'Oh! Thank you. I expect your father to look like Mussoorie when first I knew the family. I'm sure I've identified him in the photographs upstairs.'

'That would just about be it.' He was flicking over the heavy paste-board pages, one enormous fading photograph to each page, each in its decorative mount. 'I hate this hot noisy lamp,' he said. 'But we wouldn't see much without it. Here. This is the one I wanted. Father in ceremonial procession. Shortly after he became prime minister.'

'Yes,' I said, staring at 'father'. 'I guessed right.' There were two ladies with father in the *howdah* of the gigantic elephant that led the procession. 'That must be your mother beside him, no?'

'Yes. Father and mother. It's the state visit to Patan. A beautiful little town, very close to Kathmandu. Temples, palaces. Seventeenth-century and much earlier. Founded sixth century A.D., I think. It's famous.'

I had read about it, seen pictures, so I knew how beautiful it is, though in this photograph little is seen of its beauty, only the narrow medieval street the elephants and foot-attendants are advancing out of, no palaces or temples. The leading elephant with its three glittering passengers nearly fills the frame.

The procession has halted, no doubt for this official photograph. Are their Highnesses, their Presences, ready? They are graciously ready. Nepal is ready. A great hush, the holding of the breath. Off comes the lens-cap with a flourishing one-two-three!—and back again it goes, slapped accurately home. Nepal exhales again. Father is Nepal. *L'État c'est* father! Kings don't count.

Father looks marvellous. Head high and shoulders back, he sits there rigid in his generalissimo's uniform, one small rounded hand on sword-hilt, the other resting on his knee. The paradise-plumes of his head-dress stream backwards from a jewelled boss like the splendid airborne tail they once had been. From his head-dress (which itself seems vaguely bird-shaped, a nesting bird) as also across his breast and round his neck, depend, are pinned, are slung the wearer's weight in polished emeralds as big as lollipops, also ropes of pearls, of course, and diamonds, not to speak of the spiky stars of this or that jewel-encrusted order on his bosom and elsewhere. Father is an astonishing figure of magnificence. Very Mongol war-lord in appearance, stocky, strong. He has the Mongol's epicanthic fold to the eye, and the limp feathery moustache characteristic of the Mongol races. This lack of beard must be a dominant gene, I imagine. Even in Jagut's case, his general air almost as much Rajput as it is Nepalese, tweezers are what he used to use, rather than a razor. Gurkha soldiers quite commonly wear their tweezers on a cord around the neck.

So there he sits, His Highness the Prime Minister, Maharaja Deb Shum Shere Jung Bahadur Rana, fourth in dynastic line.

'Short'—Sylvain Lévi writes of him. This doesn't show in the seated pose, though you can sense his stockiness. Lévi's 'broad' shows, and I can believe him when he calls him 'intelligent ... quick'—for these seem to show too, in the alertness of the eyes and general expression. I can see it here before me, too, in Jagut, the energy. Father was kind and liberal—we know this from his actions, but I wonder if Jagut knows what Lévi wrote about those little rounded hands—perhaps he doesn't; he certainly has said nothing about it, and I shall not bring the matter up with him. *'Avec cette petite main'*, writes Lévi, 'Deb Shum Shere with his two older brothers killed his good old uncle* for making the

* Prime Minister Sir Rana Udip Shum Shere.

123

mistake of showing excessive favour to the sons of the late Sir Jung Bahadur'—the idea being a pre-emptive bid to wrest the succession to the prime ministership from Jung Bahadur's sons and to secure it for themselves, his nephews, the seventeen sons of Jung Bahadur's youngest, favourite brother, Dhir Shum Shere.

Like Pearl Harbor and other pre-emptive bids we easily remember, this one too was absolutely successful, but Sylvain Lévi, writing in 1905, probably had no means of knowing that in fact Deb Shum Shere was not even present at the assassination: Maharaja Chandra Shum Shere was later to let fall this unimportant detail, while readily admitting to his own presence in the room and his complicity. Chandra indeed said it was quite irrelevant which of the brothers actually did the killing of their Uncle Rana Udip—they were all seventeen of them at one in recognising that the good old man must go. So he went. Sixteen years later, as already recorded, Chandra was deciding that his own elder brother must go in his turn, though for different reasons. So Deb 'went' too, though only into exile. But I did not speak of this—there is much that I haven't spoken of. I was content to say to Jagut: 'I think that father's absolutely magnificent.'

'What do you think of mother, then?'

Mother beside him in the howdah, a beautiful small creature, probably a bird. Hen-bird of Paradise? A very small one with puffed-up feathers. Mother is so swathed in gossamer that nothing is really visible of her at all, except her face. She is certainly laden with jewellery, but it barely shows, it is all swallowed up in the gossamer except for huge pearl drops for earrings and a huge diamond star fixed in the front of the tight-fitting little page-boy pill-box toque she wears. Under the toque her fringe of shining jet-black hair is pommaded flat to her forehead. A flattened curl in front of each ear coils backwards, underneath the lobe. But no, I was wrong. It was not a toque at all. Could it be hair dressed in a tight, shining cylinder? A wig, perhaps, or something? I asked Jagut about it.

'No, no. Not a wig. It's mother's own hair: or at the most a plait or two added of her own—they were far too uppish, snobbish, squeamish, to wear hair from lesser beings. I wonder if you noticed mother's "Coronation Group"—galaxy of all the Rana ladies in the land dressed up in crinoline-style frocks (but pyjama bottoms) with the same up-braided hair on which they wore tiaras, or bejewelled butterflies and so on? I know it's wrong to say "coronation" but the Ranas were so powerful that the ceremony was performed with no less splendour than that of kings in those days.'

Mother looks very, very young—though I knew that she had already borne her husband the first two, or three perhaps, of her six children (not yet Jagut or Bahadur or Mussoorie: these three are to be the last). So in this picture she is probably fifteen, sixteen. Round face, big calm eyes, great dignity for someone scarcely out of childhood as we count it. Her skin is the richest, finest, tightest-fitting satin. 'I must say, Jagut,' I told him, 'she's an absolute beauty! Hieratic!' And he was pleased, I think, to have his mother so sincerely praised.

'Yet, I wonder if they really enjoyed all this pomp,' he said. 'Father was such a simple man at heart—though it's true he loved those tiger-shoots on elephant-back, and that cannot honestly be thought of as "the simple life". Did you know that all elephants in Nepal are the prime minister's perk? Were, I mean. Does your queen still claim all British swans as perk?'

'I believe so—technically.'

'How nice for Her Majesty.' He looked at the photograph again. 'All this. Mark you, Peter, I'm not trying to dazzle you with all the grandeur—or am I, perhaps? A bit. To give you an idea of what was taken from him when he was driven into exile. They took his birthright: and, to him still more important, they took the power he held at last—the power to raise his country up out of the middle ages.' He sat silent for a moment. Then: 'How we children loved him! How we loved mother, too. And Fairlawn. Never having known Nepal, to us Fairlawn was "home", not exile. Oh yes, we were very lucky in our parents. Look at them sitting there, Peter!'

Jagut was pointing at the photograph again.

'See that girl sitting behind father and mother in the *howdah*? Poor little thing. She was to die soon after. King Prithvi Bir Vikram had given her to father—the king had lots of them, naturally, he was a tremendous womaniser. He and father were dynastically related: the king's two queens were Rana princesses, nieces of father's, our cousins. But all that side apart the king and father were bosom pals—father was a great womaniser too. Each would make the other free of his maids and such—not that this girl in the photograph was a maidservant, oh no. She was what we call *talimé*. I think it means "well-versed" or something.'

'It sounds like an Arabic root, no? "Educated"? Social graces rather than erudition, I dare say.'

'Yes, social graces.'

I was examining the girl, thinking my thoughts. Very small and appealing. Not so young as mother, I would say, and despite the gossamer and jewels she lacked all mother's poise and *racée* looks. I said as much to Jagut, who agreed.

'But you'd hardly expect more of this ordinary little girl. However pretty. Mother was daughter of a noblewoman at court of the Thakur clan: the finest Kshatriya blood in all Nepal. Father saw her at court one day and fell head over heels in love—at first sight. So the king arranged it all for him, and mother could come to him with the king's blessing, and father went through some form of marriage-ceremony with her. We Ranas can't marry within our clan—you knew that? We're an exogamous lot. So are the Thakurs. We can marry them. And we can intermarry with the king's own clan too, the Sahs, and we did, each generation. The present king's blood is heavily dosed with ours. None of us could have thought of marrying this little *talimé*, naturally. But look at her: she's very sweet. She adored father, absolutely adored him. But when father saw mother . . .'

'Yes, I see . . . !'

I was a little hesitant, still thinking my own thoughts.

'Poor girl. It was to be different when mother came along.'

'That's rather what I was thinking, but . . . I mean. Well, here in the photograph mother has already come along—and the girl has come along too. Didn't mother mind at all?'

He looked at me and almost burst out laughing. 'Mind? Was she jealous, do you mean? Oh you sahibs and memsahibs! Forgive me, Peter. I don't want to seem offensive, but you've been so close to us and our polygamous society, and for so long, I'd have thought that you, at least, would realise that to us the Whites looked terribly *petit-bourgeois*, even if they did rule our roost at the time. Monogamy and the fatuous pretence at being faithful! Really, think of it! Having each other's memsahibs clandestinely—not so clandestine, either. We all knew. The cheap scenes of jealousy—we knew that too. The sahibs' servants reported it all back, naturally. The princes liked to have the sahibs' little secrets waiting up their sleeves. I suppose we don't normally even think of going for each others' wives—we don't need to, perhaps that's why. We've got plenty of healthy variety available without that. And to be truthful,

Rana men have always seemed to prefer girls of the lower orders to high-born ladies—even if father did make an exception in mother's case. He loved her till she died—she died before him. Still young. He died young too. But, no, no, no, this little *talimé*, of course mother wasn't jealous. What could a badamaharani find to be jealous of in a poor little *talimé*? One of dozens and dozens, hundreds, scampering about the palace. Mother was rather fond of her in fact. Father was too. Why else should they have taken her along with them in the *howdah*? Yet it was sad for the girl. She went into a decline—I think she may be declining already in this photograph. I told you she was to die soon after? Of love for father.... People said it was a spiritual *sati* that she committed.'

Tuman Singh was in the doorway that opens on the front verandah and the cobblestones. He was making little coughings, waiting to be noticed. Jagut noticed him:

'Yes, Tuman?'

'Rana sahib, the *amla*-contractor has arrived.'

'At this hour of night? I heard no truck arriving. Did you, Peter? Must I receive him, do you think—what was that, Tuman? Oh, I see: a breakdown was it. They had to walk the last bit. Perhaps I'd better see him. We may need his co-operation—for the cow-man's wife. What's the latest news about the cow-man's wife, Tuman?'—but it seemed that after keeping everyone on tenterhooks the cow-man's wife is satisfied that it was all a false alarm—for how could she have gone against her stars?

'Stars or no stars,' said Jagut, 'pains or no pains, like it or no, we'll pack her off to civilisation with a note to the lady-doctor when the *amla*-truck goes off again.'

I said: 'I expect she wants to enjoy Divali here.'

'She can't have her cake and eat it. All right, Tuman. Show them in.' He was closing the album now. 'And that's the end of our evening—except that, yes, I think I should tell you that when father married mother there was someone who *was* jealous, all the same. His first, and senior maharani. There was a lot of sulking in the corridors of the palace when that happened, I can assure you. But she died too—father's senior maharani—while he was still only commander-in-chief. How galled she must have been not to last long enough to become father's badamaharani, which would have been her title as senior wife when he came to power as prime minister. And to know as she lay dying that her detested rival the junior wife would take her place.'

'Have you got a picture of father's senior wife? I'd like to see.'

'Yes. Somewhere. I'll look it out. But now for these people—I should tell you that he's rather a pushing man, my *amla*-contractor, I really much prefer to interview such people out of doors so that there can be no question of their trying to grab a chair and sit on it. People get too big for their boots if you don't watch out. And it's very offensive in terms of our caste-system where everyone's position is so nicely graded up and down. I don't stick to the rules myself, as well you know—but I bet the *amla*-contractor has no truck with his own caste-inferiors if they should try it on. Of course it's rather a bore, sometimes, being a latter-day prince. But I think I should require traditional respect of them. Some of them take such fiendish pleasure in showing disrespect. Here they come, Peter.'

Three men were coming in, barefoot, as even the very rudiments of manners would require indoors.

Jagut had risen—not to greet them, most certainly not, but apparently to adjust the angle of the camel's-stomach lamp (though it looked quite straight to me). He turned with a *namaste*, then gestured to the leading man to take his place on a carpet across the room from us. It was the conjuror's 'forced card'. Jagut quietly, authoritatively, forced him to the floor—and the other two, like sheep, were following their bell-wether, down onto the carpet, cross-legged, respectful. 'And don't imagine, Peter,' Jagut turned to me to say, 'don't imagine for an instant that they would like me better if I were to let them behave towards me as my equals. They'd despise me. Nor am I going to introduce them to you.'

Amla-talk. Well, Jagut knew my views on *amlas*. What useful contribution could I hope to make? After a while I thought I'd leave them to it. 'I'm off to bed,' I said. 'See you in the morning.'

9

If Divali is to start the day after tomorrow, then it means that
I've been here three weeks or nearly. The last of the Bridegroom's
wedding sweetmeats was 'consigned' so long ago that all sense of
guilty waste has left me. The *amla*-contractor's truck was duly
repaired and on the road again to do its several trips to the Dehra
rail-head laden with the fruit—taking the cow-man's tiresomely
expectant wife with it on the last of them. She sat there snivelling
in the cab, receiving Jagut's last-minute instructions. He had had to
be a little sharp with her. In vain did she mope and snivel and
plead, and beg to be allowed to stay here over Divali (I was right
on that point, evidently)—off with her, while the truck was here
to take her. She had held us all in thrall too long already—her
pains were on, indeed—they weren't, they were! She had a sister
with her looking grumpy: the sister, too, would miss Divali. Off
with them, armed with the note to the lady-doctor, food and pay-
ment all arranged, to a hospital described as 'twenty-eight miles
distant over tankable tracks'. 'And don't come empty-handed
home!' Jagut adjured her. 'This time a boy-child, mind!' A word
to the driver of the truck: 'Careful, over the bumps.' Jagut was
certainly right about her looks. She is an ugly little thing. How
do such ugly little things get married? Dowries, I suppose. Or a
local rule that if she starts a baby the man must marry her. I still
don't know about this. Jagut comes far from clean.

Peace, perfect peace.

I have recently taken to getting up at first light, well before
Rameshwar brings my tea. I awake by clockwork just as the furniture begins to take on shape again. I wind my *loongi* on (and do
it better now and even in the dark—though very far from neat). I

wrap the *khasto* round my shoulders, step carefully across the black lump curled up on my doormat—Kalé's sister, her doormat. She too will take on shape and colour in a few minutes, mushroom and ivory. Meanwhile she doesn't move. It is light enough outside for me to pick my way quite easily to the mango-tree and sit down in it to watch Soon Saan take on its shape and colours—a much more rewarding spectacle than bedroom furniture. Our world has slept the long night through. It feels refreshed and gentle. The sun impatiently awaits its cue behind the mountains.

Sun-up!

Promptly at seven Rameshwar brings my tea-tray, sets it down on the flat-topped wooden block that serves as table in the pleasure-dome. He is a silent man. But it isn't surliness (like Sarwa's, some-times) nor the Buddha-like passivity of Bal Bahadur, major-domo, whom I don't seem to have seen for a week and more. The inside of his head is much less passive than his face, apparently: Jagut speaks of tranquillisers. No, Rameshwar's silence is the silence of the well-trained houseman. The only time he seems to break it, except for murmuring acknowledgement of Jagut's orders, is as announcer of the evening-news at *lassi*-time. He enjoys that moment, obviously. Perhaps he often longs to break his houseman's silence. This morning I encouraged him to do so. 'Good morning, Rameshwar. Any news today?'

He may be shy, of course. He stood in silence. I waited. The little sweeping girls had started on the cobbles.

'Sahib. . . ,' began Rameshwar. Then he swallowed nervously and said, 'a duck lies headless in the woods and that leaves us with but nine.'

'One of our fat ducks—headless?'

The Bridegroom's voice broke in from down below as he came out from the house, scattering the little sweeping-girls to left and right, calling softly up to me, 'Sahib, sahib . . . a duck lies headless in the woods beyond the lily-pools! That leaves us with but nine. A mongoose killed it.'

'A mongoose?'

'Yes, sahib, a mongoose, and . . .'

'*CHUP!*'—Rameshwar had cut in on him. 'Silence!'

Son of Mrs Midget who is full-sister to the major-domo—it gives him status and authority. The Bridegroom *chup*'d. Rame-shwar could proceed but in fact he didn't. He addressed himself to the Bridegroom haughtily: 'The sahib already knows this news, for I have told him'—and with these chilling words he left the tree.

The Bridegroom stood below, a little crestfallen. I tried to soothe hurt feelings. 'Rameshwar knew nothing about the mongoose, anyway. How do *you* know?' I was wondering what on earth a mongoose—or any other animal—would want with a severed head.

'Sahib, who else but mongoose bites the head and leaves the body? Jackal, the Greedy One? Jackal would eat the lot. It is the work of mongoose. Also, other news, the cow-man's wife has had her baby. The postman brought the news last night.'

'Good. A boy, I hope.'

'A little girl again, sahib.'

'Oh, that's bad. Any more news about the little girl who's missing?'

'No news, sahib. Poor little stolen virgin. Two weeks now. And such a little girl. Nine years only. *Tch-tch*. She will never be heard of more.'

'Virgin? Stolen?' I asked him. Nothing had been said in my hearing about 'stolen'. The little *frou-frou* girls were edging closer on their hunkers, miming brushing-motions with their brooms, eyes wide, ears pricked '. . . virgin . . . stolen . . . nine years only?'

'What else could be, sahib?' enquired the Bridegroom loudly, gathering attention. 'Stolen . . . stolen . . .'—the little girls' lips mouthed it silently, in awe; the lamp-man joined them, a half-cleaned chimney-glass was in his hands. 'Stolen, you say?' he asked the Bridegroom.

The geese were waddling nearer too, though not to hear the news. They were making for the water-hole. Strange that I had not even heard the wild crescendo helter-skelter when they'd opened up the poultry-runs—I'm used to it, I suppose, though I could hear it now, and see it—our frenzied feathered friends dispersing.

'Poor little stolen virgin,' the Bridegroom said much louder than before, retrieving my attention. 'The very day they stole her, sahib, be certain she was on the road to Delhi. In a wooden box.' Little lips moving, the lamp-man's mouth mouthing.

'A wooden box—with holes for air!' the Bridegroom added.

I like the Bridegroom for giving details so precise and full, but was keen to know just how precise his details were. 'Holes for air?' I queried.

'Sahib, what use to anyone if she reach Delhi dead? Drugged, she was. Senseless in her box, her cries stifled.'

'Come now, how can you possibly know all this?'

'It has to be, sahib. What else could be? Sold, she was, by evening of that first day. Count upon it, Peter sahib.'

'What a terrible story you tell me. I hope it isn't true.'

'Sold to the *chakla*,' said the Bridegroom with evident satisfaction.

Sold to the *chakla*! If any of the Bridegroom's tale was true then this was likely to be. The *chakla* is the old-time prostitutes' quarter in every city worth the name. But they have closed the Delhi *chakla* now: no longer do our fallen sisters loll about on crumbling wooden balconies between whiles; it is the centre of politer commerce now. Yet who can really put our sisters out of business? Business will always be as usual, though less visible today; there will always be some rich old amateur of this or that to pay good money for a little virgin. These thoughts were spinning in my head. I did not voice them. Instead I asked the Bridegroom, 'Can all this be true?' Tuman was arriving underneath the tree, Jagdish astride one shoulder.

'Can it be true? Sahib!' The Bridegroom was affronted. 'It *must* be true, for nothing else could be! Unless of course the little child was stolen for some sacrifice.'

'A sacrifice,' the lamp-man breathed.

'In distant hidden jungles,' went on the Bridegroom. 'And in such a case, be sure, sahib, she has gone already. They would have done it quick, not caring to be caught.'

'Well!' I exclaimed.

'In hidden jungles....' Tuman was nodding his agreement, and the thought upset him. Carefree Jagdish on his shoulder was not following this upsetting conversation—had not, even if he could. The little sweeping-girls all could, and had. Tuman excused himself and crossed the culvert, making for the two-storeyed barrack-block where he lives, I think. A strapping girl stood at the bottom of the steps that lead up to it, a baby on her hip and the beginnings of another underneath her bulging sari. A handsome great virago of a girl I'd often seen before. 'Is that Tuman's wife?' I asked the Bridegroom.

'Yes, sahib. And see! He's telling her the news.'

We watched him telling her the Bridegroom's news and saw her open up her eyes and clutch the baby tighter to her. 'See?' the

Bridegroom said, much gratified. 'What time would the sahib like his hot shaving-water?'

'In about half an hour, perhaps?'

'Very good, sahib. In half an hour I bring it.'

'But it's Sarwa's day on duty, no?'

'Sarwa. . . . Ah-h, Sarwa, yes, but. . . .'

The Bridegroom bustled off, and left me thinking—oh that poor little stolen girl. But quite possibly the little thing had long since reappeared, discovered safe and sound, and it was simply that no one had bothered to come to Soon Saan to tell us. It is only bad news, after all, that travels fast as light. I decided to settle for this comfortable belief as Kalé's pretty sister passed the water-hole below, hissed at by geese. Divali two days ahead. All that garlanding to come on 'Dog-day', all those unexpected endearments, would she be taken by surprise? Up came Kalé himself, nosing, wondering. His sister sat down promptly, lolled her tongue out, panting, and I said aloud, 'Ah-ha!—I *see*!' And then I spoke to her, the first words I have ever addressed to her: 'So it is not your fête-day you're preparing for, my lass. It's your second coming-of-age; and that incestuous brother of yours has guessed as much, and I know as much. And only yesterday I was pleading your cause with Rana sahib, your master: and if despite my pleas they lock you up again this time, I'll break your prison open, let you loose to try your luck. Count upon it! *Shoo*, Kalé! Bide your time! Here, Fateh! Fateh! Come here, please. Take Kalé's sister off.' So Fateh took her off, with Kalé following, and Fateh kicked at him, he snarled, then cringed, then flopped down on the cobbles good as gold. Two days from now, I thought: I give them two short days—to Dog-Day! How poetic it will be if they should consummate their union on their own fête-day!

Sarwa was advancing across the threshing-floor, then stopped and stood stock still. His eyes were smouldering. He looked dangerously enraged, in fact, and seemed to be scanning the farmyard across the water-hole. I froze like bird on bough and he did not notice me as he passed below the pleasuredome. He jumped the water-hole. I watched him frighten a great puffy inoffensive fowl, White Sussex.

'*BOO!*' He stamped his feet at her and mimed the twisting of her feathered neck and away she whizzed, squawking, partly air-borne. Sarwa, 'only violent when thwarted' (and at the wash-tub)—had someone thwarted him? He let out a mirthless laugh and made

133

off across the cobbles and round behind the house. At this point there was something else that started happening, in the farmyard, though hidden still from me by mango-foliage. Tuman's head, his wife's, the lamp-man's, the sweeping-children's—Kalé'e too—all heads in sight had swung around to stare across the farmyard. And then I saw it too—a youth came running into my range of vision, across the farmyard he came running, jinked past Tuman shouting at him, trying to restrain him, crossed the culvert, then the cobbles, almost intercepted by the Bridegroom whose clutching arm he cleverly eluded, and up the mango-stairway two steps at a time shouting, 'Rana sahib, Rana sahib!' The Bridegroom was running up behind him, catching at him, and I could hear him knocking urgently on Jagut's door.

We waited.

Two minutes later the youth was stepping down the mango-stairway, a little calmer now, though worried-looking still. The others caught him on the cobbles and at once the jabbers started, their questions, his replies, his eyes forever darting glances across the farmyard, then Jagut's voice came zipping out across the top verandah: 'Peter! Where are you? Aren't you in your room?'

'I'm in the tree,' I called back to him, and leaned out to show myself as he himself leaned out across the railings. 'What's going on?'

'Ah yes, so there you are! You saw that boy—the one down there with them? His poor father's fallen from a tree—they're bringing him in to me. On a litter. They should be here in no time. The boy says he's broken all his bones—they always say that, except we've never had them falling out of trees before. Subedar Singh!' The Bridegroom reacted. I know that that's his name, but don't think of him by it. 'Sterilize the *sui*—They live up by the goat-pens. If he's fallen into all that goats'-do he'd better have an anti-tetanus shot just in case. Remember the Unlucky House? It's the father of that family. So it's his turn now. Poor people. I must move them. I hope he's not as bad as the boy was saying. Peter! Look! I mean—*don't look!* On any account. It's Sarwa. Fighting mad. Crouch! Don't wish him unless he sees and wishes you: in that case please wish him sternly.'

Jagut had hopped back into hiding across the width of the verandah; I had made myself as small as possible in the pleasure-dome. But Sarwa noticed neither of us, nor paid attention to the group beside the mango-stairway. The geese had meanwhile scattered as he broke through their ranks to make off round the lily-pools. Jagut came out of hiding and joined me in the pleasure-dome. 'I'm so glad you use this place. Nice, isn't it? Sarwa? It doesn't happen often, but when it does. . . .'

'What's thwarted him?'

'Poor Sarwa, he has so little sense of "when". Tuman! Go out and meet the litter. Take Fateh with you. Help them in. He's a clumsy old man, you see, Peter, that unlucky father. He may well have fallen awkwardly where another man would take no harm. Here, boy! Run back and help them with your father. Oh my God! Sarwa again. What could he have been doing beyond the lily-pools? Sit back, Peter. They say he was after something earlier, but the girl said no. I think she's locked herself away, so he's out for someone else—this instant! Threatening everyone with terrible things if he doesn't get what he wants. Look! He's gone behind the house.'

'He went behind it before. Who's his prey to be?'

'Oh, *anyone* would do. I wish I were an old-time Rana. I'd quieten him all right.'

'A girl would quiet him—that's what he's aching for. Would Jezebel do, d'you think?'

'Oh no, no, no! Not in his present state of mind.'

'The Fair Maid of Astolat, then? If he's really desperate. It might serve to solace her as well.'

'Really, Peter. You know perfectly well that the Fair Maid's broken heart is dedicated to another.'

'And if the other simply kicks her heart around like a football? Have a word with the Fair Maid, why not?'

'I shall do nothing of the sort,' said Jagut, smirking.

'I don't mean have a word yourself. Send a confidential messenger, like in the *Kama Sutra*. "The daughter of your old nurse", for instance—that's who they mostly seemed to use for *billets doux* in the *Kama Sutra*. Failing that, send Jezebel.'

'What next! But it would be handy if we could get Sarwa out of the way till his blood runs quieter, or he'll certainly expect to give the old man his anti-tetanus jab. Sarwa adores the *sui*: thinks he's the best with it—and he isn't bad, either. But in his present state. . . . I know! I'll give it myself, that's what I'll do. He can't object to that. But he'd snatch the *sui* from the Bride-groom, that he would.'

'Perhaps we could corner him and throw a sack over his head and...'

'Who are *we*?'

'Well, "they", then. It would mean ropes and I imagine he'd fight like mad. Have you a "cooler"?'

'To "cool" him in? There's a store-room with a heavy door and no window. That might do—if we could get him into it.'

'And talking of locking people up, Jagut. Kalé's pretty sister— we were talking, yesterday. She hasn't long to wait now. Kalé's started nosing, not quite certain yet, but nosing.... You did promise you won't lock her up this time, didn't you?'

'Peter, please! Does your mind run on nothing but sex?' He looked me in the eyes and said: 'And you dare to pretend that my *amlas* are no good!' He changed the subject. 'A mongoose has got one of our Indian Runners. Its headless body has been found in the woods beyond the lily-pools.'

I didn't quite like to ask if we could have it salmi'd like that first day's lunch. I'd love to know how that was done. I'd like to learn a lot of other dishes Jagut serves. His chicken *biriani*, for example. His food is admirable, but if ever I go near the kitchen fly-screens the Second Lady of Soon Saan advances, fills the door, her arms akimbo. She'd never even let me in, Untouchable White that I am. My very glance would so defile the cooking-vessels that there'd be no cleansing of them ever again—short, perhaps, of feeding a great crowd of ravenous Brahmins. And I much doubt if the Second Lady would ever consent to our eating a salmi of headless duck—I'm not sure about this, but it might well be not at all proper. In Islam you can't eat any animal that hasn't had its throat cut ritually. In the Kshatriya Hindu world? Oh well, never mind. We'd got nine more where she came from.

'Look Peter! Here comes the litter.'

Jagut was half-way down the mango-stairway, with me following in his wake.

They were setting the litter down outside what Jagut calls 'the guardroom', remembering Fairlawn-Palace days. It isn't really a guardroom, there isn't any guard, except the pariah-pack. It is a small ground-floor room beside the drawing-room, an all-purpose room the duty-staff play draughts in, brew their tea in. 'We use it for dispensary as well,' said Jagut.

'That reminds me. I haven't seen a soul come in for treatment since I got here. The dispensary looked closed—the old one.'

'Yes. It's a store-room now.'

'The "cooler"?'

'The "cooler". We've had some out-patients in, all the same, since you came. So few, though, you might well not notice.'

'They used to keep you busy every morning, remember?'

'Everything's so different now. Free state facilities. Improved communications. The area's not too badly served these days.'

'Sad, in a way.'

'No, no, not sad at all. Not for them. It's good. I couldn't have carried on into the penicillin era.'

'I suppose the magic's all seeped out of aspirin and epsom-salts and that dear old electric-shock machine. . . .'

'Oh, long ago. You think they'd make do with less than penicillin now? And antibiotics? Not they! That's the new magic—it is too; much better than faith. I thought at first I'd try to keep things going, but the cost of it! I'd have had to make them pay—cost-price: and then the business of refrigeration, estimating stock-requirements, deterioration, I couldn't really do it. And I'm not a doctor, anyway. Not qualified to prescribe those sorts of drugs. So what with everything, and my holding here reduced to a paltry forty acres—I told you, no? My income's seriously down and the cost of living soaring. But with accidents, first-aid—this poor old unlucky man here. We do the best we can. I hope it's not a break, that arm of his.'

The elbow stuck out grotesquely. Jagut was leaning over the litter, a light string cot, examining the old man carefully. 'Tuman's our local expert with bones,' he said. 'Tuman? Have a look at this. Dislocated, yes, of course. But broken? Fractured?'

Tuman laid gentle fingers on the joint and passed them slowly up and down the arm, palpating it. 'A dislocation only? Are you sure?' Tuman was sure. 'We'll get that dealt with first, then,' Jagut said. 'Lay him down flat.' They laid him flat. The old man groaned. Tuman slipped his sandals off and sat himself beside the old man's feet, then softly laid his right foot in the old thing's armpit, leaning forward, took the old thing's hand, then looked at Jagut. Jagut nodded, gave a little signal, Tuman stretched his leg, pulled on the arm and—*calump!* He had the arm back in its socket with quite astonishing despatch, and it was only now the old man shrieked, '*Ayee-ee-ee-ee. . . !*'

'Shh-h ... poor old man, it's over now. Lie quiet. Now let's see what else there is.' The old man groaned. 'We let them moan and groan as much as they please, of course. If they want to. They mostly want to. Their relatives expect it of them, even when there's nothing much the matter. Didn't Tuman do it well, by the way? He has a natural instinct. There doesn't seem to be much else wrong here. Turn him over, Tuman. The Bridegroom came forward too. 'Help Tuman,' Jagut told him. 'That's right.'

They turned the old man over carefully. His son, the youth who'd run in with the news, was watching anxiously; also his daughter, the glum girl I'd seen before. 'Unlucky House....'

'Luckier this time than you might expect,' Jagut commented. 'Apart from the dislocation nothing but a bruise or two. And he's grazed his thigh quite badly. But we'll soon fix all that.'

'What could he have been doing in a tree?' I asked him.

'You should ask yourself that question.'

'Oh Jagut, come off it! You aren't really scared about what I may be writing, are you?'

'Time will tell.' He turned to the Bridegroom: 'Give me the *sui*. And Peter. Please keep a sharp look-out for Sarwa. We don't want him in on this. I wonder where he's got to.'

'Perhaps he's found a girl. That should keep him busy long enough.'

'I hope he hasn't found one. But he can't have! What girl in her senses, this side of rape, while he's in that state.'

The Bridegroom had been assembling the syringe meanwhile and now tweezed a needle out of the sterilising-pan. He fitted it and handed it to Jagut.

'Thank you. Now the serum. Swab the skin—yes, here please. There! That's it.' Jagut poised his hands in preparation. Then: JAB!

'*Ayee-ee-ee...!*'

'Shh-h, poor old man. Hear that, Peter? It didn't hurt him in the least, of course. I'm expert.' Jagut was pressing the plunger slowly home. Then he whipped the needle out with a fine professional flourish, saying, 'They don't think it's doing them any good unless they think it hurts. That's that, then. We can leave the Bridegroom to do the rest. Dress those abrasions,' he ordered him. 'And the bruises. Clean him up. Breakfast in a minute, Peter. How the time does fly. Never enough of it. You can shave afterwards—if you really must bother to shave at all. Tuman. Ask Rameshwar if breakfast's ready.' Then to the Bridegroom: 'When you've finished with the old man see that he and his family get something to eat.' He broke off. Then in an entirely different key he said to the Bridegroom, 'We never had them falling out of trees before.'

The Bridegroom echoed Jagut's phrase with wonder: 'We never had them falling out of trees...' and at this point the biggest of the little sweeping-girls, the *jolie* little *laide*, came dashing through the farmyard, face aghast and pointing back behind her, crying 'Rana sahib—see, see! They bring him in to you!'

'Bring in who...?'

'The new tenant—the Punjabi!'

All heads swung round for the second time that morning. A group of three was past the bullock-carts by now, as they brought him in. It was he, most certainly, though identifiable only by his ballooning *salwars*, a type of pantaloon that no one else wears hereabouts. So he was back, and look at his condition! Over a fortnight he'd been gone. He could walk, like someone in a dream, and one of Jagut's men supported him. His little wife was close beside him, frightened and tearful. His face was almost hidden by a blood-soaked bandage—his turban, evidently. Tuman hurried out to meet them. The Bridegroom stopped his swabbing and the old man stopped his groaning to sit up and stare; he had lost the centre of the stage, of course: there was no competing with that bloodied head, the one eye visible puffed-up and livid. The First and Second Ladies of Soon Saan appeared across the threshing-floor, re-purified and placid. They saw the group advancing from the farmyard. They stopped and gasped. Blood! Sarwa was on-scene again from who-knew-where. Blood! It seemed to steady him. He stared, his eyes narrowing. Jagut said sternly:

'Sarwa!'

Sarwa said: 'Look at the *loocher* now, Rana sahib. Where has he been so long? What evil has he been up to?'

'It is he who is the victim, Sarwa!'

'Evil *goonda*!'

'*Chup!*' said Jagut.

Sarwa *chup*'d. The group was half across the culvert.

Fell off his bicycle...? The bloody bandage diagonally across his face left the one livid eye and half his mouth uncovered. We could see now that his upper lip was split, a swollen mess. He didn't speak—perhaps it was too painful. It was his little wife who whispered what she knew to Tuman Singh who then repeated it to us. He had fallen off his bike it seemed. Where? When was this? On the Dehra high road somewhere. Yes, last night. Late. But the poor girl really didn't know a thing, indeed all she could say for certain was that he had reached their cottage not an hour ago in this condition, dazed, wheeling his damaged bicycle. He still seemed dazed. Tuman sat him on a bench outside the guardroom.

'First we must get that bandage off. Tuman. Hot water. Cotton-wool and disinfectants. I'm wondering, Peter,' Jagut said in an aside. 'Concussion? Fractured skull? We'll dress his wounds, of course, we'll do all we can but. ... Careful, Tuman!'

Tuman's careful hands unwound the outer layers of the make-shift muslin bandage. The blood had dried in clots that stuck the layers to each other, and the final layer to the wound itself. Sarwa held the kidney-tray for Tuman. The Bridegroom, in the back-ground of events, looked as if he longed to leave his patient and join in, but I suppose he dared not. Slowly the clotted blood dissolved until the final muslin layer came away to disclose the wound. A nasty gash—a slit, rather than a gash. The man's wife saw and shuddered; she started crying softly. Jagut tried to comfort her:

'We'll get him in to hospital somehow, never fear. Oh drat those damned distributors! Shall I ever get delivery of my new car?'— and the Punjabi was waving No, No, No, shaking his poor head, quite clearly determined not to go to hospital—'But x-rays?' protested Jagut. The man's negations became still more vehement.

'The first essential anyway is to clean his wounds. And then we'll see. But how could it have happened?'

'A truck or something hit him, do you think?' I wondered.

'A truck was it, perhaps?' Jagut asked the man. 'A bus? It knocked you off your bike?'—and the man grunted, nodded vaguely, pointing at his mouth, touching his head, as if explaining that he could not speak.

Had he been thrown head first against some jagged rock, a mile-stone possibly? What could have caused that clean-cut gash? And then the damaged mouth. This golden creature, handsome as the Sun, what did he look like now? Sarwa was looking at him too.

By the time they'd cleaned him up, the gash was seen to be less serious, less deep, than Jagut had feared at first. 'But it will need suturing, all the same. And he'd better have the statutory tetanus-shot.'

The Bridegroom happily jumped up at Jagut's call. 'Rana sahib?'

'Sterilise the *sui* again.'

'*I* will sterilise the *sui*,' said Sarwa firmly and was first into the guardroom.

Jagut looked at me. 'I'm afraid we'll have to let him. But he seems quite sobered up. Triumph has sobered him.'

So the Bridegroom must go back to finish with the poor old unlucky man, and it was Sarwa, surly Sarwa, in triumph now, who gave himself the pleasure of jabbing a long needle into the enemy buttock. It was Jagut, though, who stitched the wound. The man's wife watched astonished as Jagut stitched, and so did I. So neat, such expertise. He was giving her instructions as he did it. 'Let him rest quietly in bed. I'll give you pills to kill the pain so he can sleep.' He turned to me and said: 'We'll simply have to hope for the best. If there's any real head-damage and he starts showing intolerance to light in the next twenty-four hours, we'll *have* to get him to hospital somehow. I'll tell his wife to be watchful.' He beckoned her aside to tell her and I heard him finish up with, 'I'll send round this evening to see how he's getting on.' And then— to Tuman—telling him to detail two men to carry the Punjabi to his cottage on a litter. The Bridegroom in the background said with wonder in his voice: 'We never had them fall off bikes before.'

Later, at breakfast, I let loose another *ballon d'essai*. I said: 'You made a very neat job of sewing him up, I must say, Jagut.'

'Thank you.'

'Did you know that your great-uncle Jung Bahadur was an expert amateur physician?'

'Was he?'

'Yes, indeed he was. Dr Oldfield has quite a lot to say about it in his book.'

'Has he? More bacon, Peter? You've only got a few days left for fattening. And by the way, the cow-man's wife has had her baby. The postman brought the news last night.'

'Yes, so I heard. A girl-baby again.'

'Yes, poor woman. And talking of the postman—there was a letter for you in the post. Did they bring it to you? From Baiji in Jodhpur. I know her writing.'

'Oh good. But no, they didn't bring it to me.'

'Rameshwar. Go up to my room and fetch Peter sahib's letter.'

He brought it to me. I said, 'Do you mind if I have a quick look?'

'Go ahead.' Jagut paused. 'She was terribly cut up by her father's death. Dear Narpat. I sometimes wonder how I can carry on with Narpat dead.'

'I know,' I said.

Narpat, our dearest friend and 'family-member'.

'You heard that Bahadur died, no?'

'Yes, I'd heard.'

Bahadur, one of the full-brothers.

Another pause.

'Strange, wasn't it?' said Jagut thoughtfully. 'Two accident-cases within half an hour of each other. Very strange.'

10

Dawn, noonday, dusk. . . .

The sun came up today oblate-spheroid, a fiery orange, though it settled down quite soon to what I'm more accustomed to—the perfect fiery circle. Larger than I think of it, however, and rising faster too. Time has accelerated these last few days; we've been living in inverted commas, moreover, our awareness quickened, sharpened by the Festival of Lights, Divali.

Each evening little oil-lamps, pottery, of ancient form and coffee-saucer size, have flickered everywhere—in windows, down verandahs, in the pleasuredome, circling the pools and threshing-floor. Soon Saan has worn a magic air. People from the hills around have been coming in to marvel at our illuminations. We, for our part, have paid another formal visit to the temple, to offer our respects to Durga-devi. No harm in that. Not that Divali has anything to do with her, of course. It's Rama bringing his abducted wife back home in triumph from his victory over the Demon Ravana that Dussehra celebrated. In this Rama-avatar of Vishnu's the wife is Sita. While Jagut was in the temple with the *jogi* doing his *puja*, I nipped round to Saraswati's Pilgrims' Room and was able to report to Jagut later that I had found it open, swept and garnished.

'Good,' Jagut said. 'Any sign of pilgrims?'

'No. But even so. . . .'

'Good, even so.'

The *jogi* could be thought of as a chastened priest and Prince Jagut could be gracious with him. Incidentally, that stumpy stone Mayan-looking manikin that tops the sacrificial altar—the one with the immense scrotum—Jagut thinks he's not a fertility godlet at

143

all; he may be an *ex voto* of some sort. 'Someone cured of hydrocele, for example,' suggested Jagut.

Dawn, noonday, dusk—but this time only 'dawn' for me. The Feast of Lights is over now, the tempo has dropped back to something nearer normal and, alas, I leave this morning. At least it would be very much 'alas' if I were not to be returning in a month or so. And there's Kathmandu meantime. Mussoorie, too. ('I can't think why he isn't in the position to put a guest up, Peter. Pack you off to some hotel indeed! He's far better off than I am. Rice mills and God-knows-what else. Not to speak of a new young wife!')

Fateh was sent off yesterday to Dehra Dun by bike and bus to fetch the old station-taxi for me. It should be here soon after breakfast, and breakfast will be ready any moment. Time for me to leave the pleasuredome and get back in to finish off my packing. One more cup of tea, one last look round. Geese at the water-hole, little girls *frou-frou*ing.

If I could conduct an orchestra at all I could by now conduct the Soon Saan Philharmonic, or at least beat time to it. And hum. I know the score by heart, and everybody's parts in it, their exits and their entrances; and when the poultry-pens blared open brassy for this morning's rendering of that mad crescendo passage I picked the fault up in a flash—'Ducks! You're late!'—and only eight of them. We've eaten No. 9. Now for the cross-bred Jerseys. Fat geese, away you waddle! I'm promised one of you for my return.

Sarwa was coming too, all smiles. He'd never smiled like that before. He stopped below me and looked up. Our relationship has gradually and subtly changed. He has attached himself to me—or am I wrong? Has he attached me to himself, as if he owned me? Whichever it may be, it pleases me. 'The sahib has heard the news?' he asked.

'No. Tell me, please.'

'That *loocher*, the Punjabi. He has made off again. And nobody knows where.'

'Loafer': *loocher*; if Hindi borrows 'loafer' from the English, then English borrows *loot* from Hindi—plunder. *Loo(t)cher* is 'plunderer'. What could the poor Punjabi be accused of plundering?

'Who knows what new evil he is up to, sahib.'

'What evil was it last time, then? It's no crime that a bus should knock you off your bike. The crime was that the bus refused to stop.'

'Does sahib believe that story?'

The Punjabi has been visiting us each day to have his dressings changed. He must be very healthy; his wounds have almost healed already. The cut that needed stitches is scarcely visible, but for the stitches themselves that have yet to be taken out. No question, either, of a fractured skull, or it would have manifested itself days since. At least we tell each other so. In fact when last I saw him—on Cow-day, was it?—he was radiant again, and swaggering. Now that his swollen mouth is back to normal he can talk, and does so readily. Yes, it was a bus, he thinks. He can't be sure: 'It struck me from behind, you see, sahib, and didn't stop. *Loochers!*' he said indignantly. I didn't ask him what he had been up to at such an hour and place—some girl, I dare say. They seem easy hereabouts. So when Sarwa asked if I believed his story I reacted:

'Come now, Sarwa!'

I felt I had to make a stand.

'Rana sahib will not believe me, either. Remember my warnings, only, sahib.'

The Bridegroom was arriving down below, carrying a great horned skull, all cleaned up and polished. I knew whose that must be, of course, and he confirmed it: 'Yes, sahib, that lady has offered it so I have brought it for Rana sahib. Should we nail it to the mango-tree—here, perhaps?' He was holding it to the tree now, surveying it, so I leaned out perilously far to have a look myself. This made him suddenly solicitous: 'Sahib, sahib! *Khabardar!* Oh careful, careful! Bad things have been befalling men in trees.'

'The sahib is not a fool—to fall,' said Sarwa.

I said: 'Thank you, Sarwa.' Then, to the Bridegroom: 'I think we should wait for Rana sahib to decide about the skull. He may prefer to mount it on a pole. Or else he may not really take to it at all.' And I eased my way back into the bosom of the pleasure-dome.

'The Panchayat has been called at last, sahib,' the Bridegroom said. 'Be sure, however, that the story of the poor buffalo is not the end.' He added, to the air: 'More bad things must happen first.'

'What makes you think so?'

'Oh yes, sahib. More to come.'

Anyhow nothing bad of any sort has marked Soon Saan's Divali —not a single defection even (we boldly attribute this to the firm handling of the Dussehra spate of them). The old man fallen from the tree is mending, slow but sure. Perhaps he doesn't want to mend too quickly and lose the last glimmer of his limelight. Bal Bahadur major-domo, though invisible, is described as being 'somewhat calmed'. No one has been drunk or violent again and with all our dramas restfully resolved, we are at peace, perfect peace.

I must confess to having left something unsaid. From guilt? A lick of it, I think. Something did mar the perfection of our peace over Divali. Or in any case Kalé's pretty sister's peace, and his.

At dawn on Dog-day she was missing from her doormat when I awoke. I knew at once what they'd been up to—sneaking up to get her without awaking me. But where had they imprisoned her? I wasn't going to ask, nor did I want to have them watch me go round searching. Instead I kept my eyes sharped fast on Kalé. Could he sniff the situation on the breeze? Not yet, but he seemed ill at ease. He moaned a little. But of course the flowers he'd been garlanded with were fretting him. The other members of the pariah-pack were fretful too—though in their case only on account of being so garlanded: Kalé's uneasiness and moanings were not shared by them, all being bitches. But wherever Kalé's poor sister had been hidden away, they had reckoned without me, and Kalé. Between us we'd frustrate their knavish tricks. All he and I need do was bide our time.

Cow-day dawned. The cross-bred Jerseys were parading placidly, their horns now wreathed in flowers and greenery, some with gilded knobs stuck on the tips. That was nice to see; nice also to watch the little bull-calves let loose to buck and gambol round the farmyard. It was less nice to see that they had chained poor whimpering moaning Kalé to a post. He had at last received the message that we'd all been waiting for: his sister was of age again. So when the clatter-banging for the mid-day meal left Soon Saan emptied I seized my chance, unchained him—he was off like lightning, following his nose with me hot on his heels. Straight through the farmyard to the old dispensary: I might have guessed. Squeals, barkings, whines, protesting shouts from Tuman Singh's virago of a wife—I flung wide the prison door and Kalé's sister

146

hurtled out to freedom. Off she hurtled, down into the woods, and Kalé after her.

Over lunch I confessed to what I'd done and Jagut said, 'I knew. They've told me. Never mind. Let Nature take her course.'

Nature took her time. Bull-day dawned. The absent siblings had not reappeared. But at *lassi*-time on Bull-day we were all to know what Nature's course had been. Kalé's head came hang-dog round the corner near the kitchens. Someone called to him. He advanced a tentative half-pace, then stopped and gazed back over his shoulder. Then he stumbled forward awkwardly, uncertainly, and it was now revealed to us that his poor pretty sister was close-coupled up behind him, one of her back legs skied and the other who-knew-where. She made her shamefaced entrance backwards, as best she could, on two precarious front legs.

Shocked for her, Jagut said: 'Poor thing. The Curse of Queen Draupadi has struck again.'

And I said, 'What?'

And he said, 'A curse as ancient as the *Mahabharata* itself.'

In the days of the *Mahabharata* (he told me) when the five Pandava brothers and their shared Queen Draupadi were living out their twelve years 'in the forest' that then dressed the hills and mountains all around us they had a little rule. Whichever brother might be in the hut with Queen Draupadi would leave his sandals at the door. It is always a matter of common good manners to take off one's sandals outside, as we know, but in this case the rule would serve a useful secondary purpose. It was the sign that Queen Draupadi was busy at the moment.

One day a dog came by. Seeing two sandals at the door, he bore them off to worry at, in the way that dogs have evidently always had with slippers, even in pre-history. One of the other brother-husbands, coming home and finding everything all clear, went in and there received a social shock. The shock was such that as soon as the poor dog's sneak-thief part in it had been discovered, it justified Queen Draupadi's blanket curse on dogs forever more— that every now and then, as horrible reminder of their guilt, they must suffer this painful humiliation, immobilised in shame for all to see, till they are considered to have paid their share of the penalty. Their share of it takes hours.

Since paying their share of the penalty and earning their release, the reckless couple have done nothing but make public love over and over again and quite unpenalised. It does not really much disturb the scene; now we are so used to it we neither watch them at it nor ignore them any more; and anyway this morning, my last morning, I've far too many other things to do. Complete the packing, for example, Sarwa in the room to help me. But he cannot fold a shirt, much less the suit that's hung there idling in the cupboard all this time.

I must ask Jagut about tipping. With his permission I have already given Sarwa a pocket-torch he obviously coveted: to the Bridegroom, who had not obviously coveted anything in particular, I have given a good solid workaday knife called a 'Stanley'; it has interchangeable blades in its metal stomach, one of them for pruning. I had offered it vaguely to Jagut, thinking it might be something useful for the Grand Tour, but it didn't seem to please him. Perhaps I was too vague; he affected not to realise that I was offering it to him.

'Sarwa,' I said. 'Please take the big thermos down and fill with iced-water. For the train.'

He took it down. And this reminded me about the little widemouthed thermos that had flustered me the day of my arrival. It must still be in the fridge, its contents long ago gone bad. How very stupid of me! It was a small tin of caviar—sturgeon, fresh, the highest grade, authentic. Let others gobble lump-fish roe and call it caviar. I had bought the tin on Tehran airport when my eastbound flight stopped down to fuel. Iran's sturgeon-fisheries are among the finest in the world and their prices marvellously low. I thought it would remind us of an earlier day when Narpat used to feed us caviar with spoons. I went downstairs and got it from the fridge. Upstairs again, I opened up the tin and sniffed. I tasted a few fat globules. Had it gone bad? In all that time it must have, surely. If there were any doubt it would be best to throw it all away. How sad and stupid! Oh well, down the palace-pedestal it went, my last 'consignment' to the waters of holy Jumna river.

I went down to breakfast. Jagut joined me there. Departure's customary *angst* lay heavy round my shoulders. Our talk was disjointed, desultory—though not this bit:

'Here! Give me your plate—for the last time. Till you get back, I mean. It's jumbo booster-day. What matter if my *amlas* drive you demented now? You'll be in Delhi in a moment and you can run riot.'

148

Sitting in tea-corner some minutes later, waiting for the taxi.

'Never an idle moment,' Jagut said. He was tweezing at his Mongol chin. 'The Bridegroom brought me in that poor buffalo's skull this morning. It was kindly meant.'

'He showed it to me. Rather fine, I thought.'

'It would certainly look handsome. In the right tree. But...'

'But...?'

'On the whole, perhaps not—you never know. Though I don't like to spurn the lady's gift. I'd better keep it, and simply not display it.'

Pause. Then suddenly:

'Listen, Peter!'

I could hear nothing.

'A car.'

I could hear it too, now. Jagut had got the lightning-flash; my ears must wait to hear the sound of distant thunder. Practice, no doubt.

'It must be my taxi. And right on time at that.'

'What if it isn't?'

'*What*—if it isn't? But it must be.'

'We must hide—no, no, not immediately, when it gets closer. Think! If it's someone unexpected whom I can't abide? It's not like neighbours dropping in, down there in Delhi. If someone I don't care for drops in here and sees me—I'm done for! I can't turn the man away, can I, in this back of beyond? But if he doesn't see me, how is he to know my men are lying when they tell him I'm away for days. Out on *shikar*, for instance: sticking wild boar for breakfast-bacon or something noble of the sort?' He was laughing, but he meant it too.

I laughed with him. 'Is that why you were hiding when I got here in the taxi, then?'

'Of course. You see we thought that *you'd* be riding in by bike.'

'Oh yes! Of course.'

'And while we're on to taxis, I've a bone to pick with you. I told you rupees thirty-five and not a *paisa* more from Dehra Dun to here. The taxi-man was boasting all around Soon Saan that you'd given him a hundred.'

'Then he certainly was boasting. I gave him fifty—to include a tip. I'd settled in advance for forty-five.'

'Never mind. That once. Actually when I heard what the taxi-man was saying, I told them that you always paid a hundred. I thought that it would build you up a bit. And also so as not to let the taxi-driver down.'

'May I give him fifty this time too?'

'No. You may give him forty total.'

'All right. And Jagut, look!—that girl crossing the culvert. Is it Jezebel?'

'I'm not even going to look.'

'Oh do please look—and tell me!'

'Even if I looked I wouldn't tell you Yes or No. I don't *quite* trust your note-books.'

'What a long time it takes to get here, the taxi.'

'*If* it's your taxi.'

'I suppose that we can hear it from miles off.'

'Miles and miles, yes.'

'I'll miss all this—I've grown so used to everything. The mango tree, the Grand Tour, shampoo-hour—all sorts of pleasant daily things, not to speak of the excitements.'

'You'll miss the paddy-threshing. It's a time I always love. But you'll miss the dust of it as well.'

'I want to know about tipping, Jagut. I was thinking: separate tips for Sarwa, the Bridegroom, Mrs Midget, the Fair Maid, and Rameshwar. Who else separate? Yes, the Second Lady of Soon Saan.' (Could I still be hoping I could win her over, let me in, to learn?) 'I'd like to see her, actually, to congratulate her on her cooking.'

'Please don't. She's already far too full of herself as it is. And don't tip anyone this time. You can do it all at the end of your return visit—if you want to. I'll tell them so. They're not really used to the idea of tipping, as if they were coolies. Or a taxi-driver or something public.'

'But . . .'

'Do as I say, please. It's so easy to sow the seeds of avarice in them: the idea of getting something for nothing, as a right.' Jagut sat up sharply: 'Listen! It's reached the fork in Saraswati Road where we turned off, that day of the leper-boy. Take cover!'

We took cover in Jagut's room.

But it was only my old stuttering, shuddering taxi, with Fatty beaming up at us when we came out to show ourselves. Quite a little group of us in tea-corner: Jagut, Sarwa, Nirmal, Shambhu, Mrs Midget, me and now Tuman joining us to supervise the toting of my baggage, Fatty with him, proud of being so perfectly on time. Down below us they were unroping a bicycle from the taxi's roof-rack. 'Sir Launcelot could have done the same,' said Jagut, eyeing it. 'That's how I knew that his was pure defection. All forgotten now. The crime expiated. But ... ! What do you think's the matter with our fair maiden? What ever has she got there? Scissors ... ?'

The Fair Maid of Astolat was clambering up the mango-stairway as fast as she was able, one hand managing her sari, the other holding high a great pair of scissors with something caught between the blades. She was shaking with excitement as she hastened down the length of the verandah and the others parted to let her through to us—'Rana sahib! Look, look!'

Oh God, what had she got between her blades, what was it? Oh my God, my God! Could she have—was this her vengeance on a cruel faithless lover—was that Sir Launcelot's manhood she was waving in her scissors, that greenish-brownish thing the size of a limp Vicks inhaler-tube? I looked quickly round for Sir Launcelot —where was he? 'Jagut!' I cried, despite myself, then checked myself, appalled. A tiny forked tongue protruded from the tip of it! Could such things be?

The Fair Maid, being speechless, breathless, overwrought, it was witnesses to her derring-do who had to tell the tale for her. Up the mango-stairs they ran, the nameless helper-handyman, the lamp-man, Sir Launcelot himself (thank God!) and out it came— about the pullet over-bold; the baby snake who'd fallen from its nest—a mere fledgling, judged as snake, but judged as worm, enormous, irresistible; the chase across the threshing-floor, the frenzied peck and gulp, the poor baby half-way down a gullet, backwards, stuck, its startled head waving like an S.O.S. I saw it all: the pullet choking, running, frantic, and the Fair Maid on hand to act, along with the perfect instrument for doing so—*snap-snap!* But no time left for me to savour Soon Saan's first-act curtain, the taxi-man was signalling up to me, and pointing at his watch—'It's time to leave, sahib. ...'

'Jagut! I must go, the train won't wait.' I tried to make my thank-you's.

'Yes, you'd better go,' he said and led the way down mango-staircase. I jumped into the taxi, no time even for the baggage-check that travel-nerves demand of me, check, re-check, once again, just to be sure.

'We'll be waiting for you,' Jagut called, and waved.

Soon Saan The house and cobbled apron-stage. The 'Second Lady of Soon Saan' is seen far left, outside her kitchens. Rameshwar-houseman (centre background) watches a small nephew bringing in a decorative stone for Jagut, whose back view can be seen at the top of the stairway down from tea-corner to the dining-room. The mango-stairway is on the right. The giant mango itself, the pleasuredome and threshing-floor are just beyond the line of vision, to the right.

Tea-Corner Jagut Shum Shere snatches a cup of tea and a home-made biscuit before setting out on the evening's Grand Tour of Soon Saan, having exchanged the cap he wears for the old peaked cap seen waiting on its hook (top left). Unlike the drawing-room downstairs (or my 'annexe'—both are furnished 'palace') tea-corner is in traditional rickety upcountry 'Anglo-Indian' style, even to the waisted wicker-stool, cushioned, with sewn-on cotton cover. My bedroom leads off through the wall, right, just beyond the table in the foreground.

Wood engraving of His Excellency Jung Bahadur Rana on his arrival in
London to visit Queen Victoria, May 1850 (*Illustrated London News*)

Maharaja Deb Shum Shere Jung Bahadur Rana with his three successive senior-wives. The first sits to his right (our left); she died before he came to power in 1901, but not before he married 'Mother' (our far left), who wears the famous *Nau Lakha* necklace. The third lady (our far right) is Princess 'Long-Nose' in European dress of her period. None of these ladies (in so far as they overlapped in time) would have readily consented to sit in the same room as either of the others, much less to being bunched up on a garden seat. The explanation is that the photograph is *montage* (c. 1912 ?) from six negatives of widely separated dates—one for each personage, one for the garden-bench, and the sixth for background, Fairlawn Palace.

PART TWO

11

In Rana times, for the lucky ones who carried permits[1] screened
and authorised by the prime minister, the way into Nepal was
quite a trek. Easy for hillmen, certainly, or for the amateur of
mountains, but for the plainsman it was long and arduous enough,
whether on foot or in the Himalayan equivalent of the palanquin,
the *dandy*—often no more than a hammock slung from a single
fat bamboo with carriers back and front. Not comfortable at all.
Nor can it have been so much more comfortable for the prime
minister's specially-honoured guests for whom, I imagine, he
would have sent out elephants. Yet all these travel-weary visitors
would be buoyed up by a sense of privileged adventure, almost of
pioneering. They were getting somewhere other people never
could. On top of this they had a special bonus—the Sudden View.

At a given moment on Mount Chandnagiri the precipitous old
track would round a bend and there it was—the sudden, high,
wide-angle view that left the traveller gaping. The Valley of Nepal
lay spread out far below him, its foothills building up to mountains
of ten thousand feet, snow-peaks behind them up to twenty-
thousand feet and more, then a narrow horizontal band of them
just like a sound-track pricking at transparent infinities of sky, ice-
blue. The traveller would see all this in one great panoramic sweep
of vision, how huge the Himalayan world is, and how small the
Valley of Nepal, and how totally enclosed.

People say the valley was once an enormous land-locked lake.
They like to think that someone called Manjushri came here with
a sword of a size to split the world in two and the strength to
wield it. Manjushri took up his position on the shores of the great
lake, facing the unbroken mountain range to south of it. He raised

his sword and brought it down with such heroic force that he opened up the narrow cleft we know as Chobar Gorge. In this way he could drain the waters of the lake down through the mountains to the plains of India and leave the lovely smiling fertile Valley of Nepal for men to live in. He went on next to found a city that has gone by various names across the centuries and today is Kathmandu.

The traveller high up on the mountain-traverse, looking down, could pick out Kathmandu at once as centre-piece and capital. Some people say the city is the shape of Manjushri's sword—though others say that it is Durga-devi's sword—but even when the walls still stood to give it shape, I beg leave to doubt that it was sword-shaped in the least, for we know from Dr Oldfield (who saw it 'walled' in 1850) that it measured two miles north to south, and one mile east to west—and that would be no shape for swords. But whatever shape it was, there lay Kathmandu, and its satellites close round it, the smallest of them (Patan) a mere one-hour, two-mile ride on elephants for Maharaja Deb Shum Shere's processional state visit that day in 1901. Swayambhunath, the oldest Buddhist *stupa* in Nepal, would be clear to see and recognise, just west of Kathmandu, where the foothills country starts. Another *stupa* a few miles to north-west completely dominates its bit of rolling countryside: Bodhnath, 'Bodha', the biggest *stupa* in the world. A little south of Bodha a plume of smoke, quite likely more than one, would serve to pinpoint Pashupatinath, temple and burning-*ghats*, part-hidden in its trees. To this day dying men will have themselves conveyed to holy Pashupatinath, 'Benares of Nepal', to be laid out with the others to await their death. They wait there in a sort of hospice that overlooks the funeral-pyres of those already dead whose ashes soon will be consigned to flower-strewn Baghmati river flowing by. Nobody is frightened.

Baghmati river—like the Jumna—has her submissive rendezvous to make, down in the plains of India, her confluence with Holy Mother Ganga: so Baghmati too can suck back virtue from the Holy Mother all the long way home through Chobar Gorge to Pashupatinath.

This high, oblique, wide-angle view is of a melting beauty, so quiet and green, so golden when the paddy ripens (the hills are terraced with it like a contour-map). The silver ribbons of the streams and rivers join each other, twist together, one by one, till all have plaited with the Baghmati, and she is ready for the journey of her life down through the gorge. Confronted by this scene what could any traveller have done but fill his lungs with crystal air and gape?

Things are very different for us, however. Since the 1950 Revolution and the subsequent establishment of Nepal's air-link with the outside world, the getting of a visit-visa has become as effortless as before it was impossible, or almost: and flying in from Delhi is a bare hour's flip. We are spared the rigours of the mountain-trek, but alas denied our 'sudden view' and with it any real sense of getting here. To look between the blinkers of an aircraft-cabin window as we bank and circle in to land is to receive a woefully-diminished version of the truth. Nothing but empty air relates and links us to our little bit of wheeling view, no plunging mountainside beneath our feet to give reality and scale to this huge scene.

We land, we disembark, we might be anywhere. Switzerland, perhaps? Here at four thousand five hundred feet above sea level the mountains don't oppress us because they stand well back behind their foothills—and we're almost half-way up to their ten-thousand feet ourselves in any case. If it is autumn, even early winter, a snow-peak may be visible, but niggardly. The Tibetan border may be only forty miles or so away at its nearest point; Mount Everest not more than a hundred and forty—but they are both invisible from here. We are in the middle of an oval valley, and accept it meekly when they tell us that the valley measures sixteen miles from north to south and twenty east to west. We find it harder to accept when they tell us that the valley, too, is the shape of Manjushri's sword (or is it Durga-devi's?).

All we can see of Kathmandu itself as yet is a tall thin tower like a lighthouse.

Hotel Green, Joodha Road, Kathmandu.

The occupant of Room No. 10 has a fourth-floor (top-floor) single bedroom, rather small. It offers him a roughish private lavatory with shower (fairly-constant hot). The place is simple, clean, with lots of willing slit-eyed room-boys sitting on the staircase or pelting up and down it hissing their 'at-your-service' smiles. For a 'single room with bath' the hotel is cheap by international standards, but the standards are not yet international here. It was not the Guide Michelin that awarded Hotel Green two stars; it was the local tourist authority. Forget about the stars; be gratefully content with friendliness, good manners and the most modest

157

of amenities. Room No. 10, however, does throw in a special bonus of the highest, five-star, value: an unobstructed view across the roof-tops westwards of two of Kathmandu's loveliest old marvels. Not the whole of them, it is true, just their topmost towering pagodas. They are the Nautallé Durbar, meaning nine-storeyed seat of royalty, and beside it, above airy trees, the goddess Taleju Bhavani's temple with its triple pagodas 'projected in the form of the mystic Yantra'—as a tourist hand-out tells us (should the occupant of No. 10 happen to know what sort of object that may be).

In the background of all this, two miles outside the city, there will be Swayambhunath, the Buddhist *stupa* earlier travellers would have seen already for the first time in their all-embracing sudden view. Swayambhunath is raised up on a cone of wooded hill.

Once Kathmandu was wholly homogeneously beautiful. When Dr Oldfield first arrived in 1850 this was so, and it remained so, very nearly, right into the nineteen-thirties. In 1934, however, a disastrous earthquake toppled at least a quarter of the city to the ground. When so large a part of such a little city has been suddenly laid waste the eye has no escape from what happened next.

We may guess that Maharaja Joodha Shum Shere, Rana prime minister at the time of the earthquake, stood contemplating all that devastation. Pointing (with his sword, I think) he may well have said: 'I shall have a fine new road cut straight through *here*, from north to south. So much more logical than those old winding lanes. And another road straight through from east to west.' This is a fair guess, for there they are, these roads like cringing sword-cuts. Maharaja Joodha may then have had a happy thought and voiced it: 'Moreover, where my two new main-streets intersect let a statue of me be put up!'—for there he is, in marble, at the intersection, staring with sightless eyes at the uncontrolled and gimcrack jerry-building that since then has struggled up from all that muck and rubble to flank the sword-cuts. It is not vulgar, it is merely dingy. And dinginess should have had no place in Kathmandu.

By some miracle, all the same, the earthquake spared the royal heart of Kathmandu, much as the Nepalese have nearly always spared their sovereigns' lives, the king being almost god, and sacrosanct. The best of Kathmandu still remains as richly beautiful as ever.

I have been here three days now. The sun has just gone down behind the mountains. At present, through my window, Nautallé Durbar and the temple of Taleju are silhouettes against the orange furnace of the sky. Outside the city, in the foothills, Swayambhunath has lit a mast-head lamp, as the rest of the great *stupa* wraps itself in shadows. But whether Kathmandu is wholly beautiful or not I wish I could have reached it twenty-something years ago. I really wish I could have reached here before the earthquake did its awful damage—though in the despair of my first day (a little less despairing on my second, less again today) I would have settled for getting here at any time at all before the rest of us got here as well. But would the Ranas have let me in?

No, they never would have let me in, nor any of us with no good reason for an 'invitation', why should they have? This was a little private city. But we're 'in' now with a vengeance and although our modest numbers would be swallowed up in London, in tiny Kathmandu we're like a swarm of flies and most of us are Hippy-flies and they look so ill, as well as 'sick'. I'm told they talk a lot of 'doing their thing', yet they don't seem to have a thing to do, unless you count the way they barricade themselves inside their emptied heads, with pot, or go slouching to and from the GPO poste-restante desk to ask if there are any postcards for them in answer to the postcards they've been sending. These postcards whizzing back and forth may well be more alive than those who send or get them. At least they have a destination. But just as Kathmandu itself has evidently got used to having Hippies as other cities have their flies, so I am getting used to them as well. A few days hence and it should be possible to disregard them, as already I can almost disregard the tourist-junk in Joodha Road shop-windows. We share at most a taste for yak's milk cheese.

I dream of days I never knew when we outsiders were limited to an average quota of say four of us a year—and in my dream one of the four is me.

It is dusk again. Three days now, and what ever can have happened to Mussoorie?

12

Tappity-tappity...

Fingers at the door. I was watching Taleju and Hanuman Dhoka fade into nothingness. 'Come in!'

A room-boy.

'Telephone please, sahib—*ssss-uh!-ssss-uh!-ssss*...' hissing, gulping, smiling—how splendidly alive their faces are!

'Thank you.'

Outside at the landing-telephone a second room-boy held the ear-and-mouthpiece out for me.

'Thank you. Yes? Who is it?'

'Is that Peter?'

'Yes...'

'*It's me—at last!*'

'Mussoorie!'

'Yes, but...' A momentary pause. 'Shall I come round? Now? All right, I'm coming right away. And Peter. Something. Please don't address me by my name.'

'But...'

'Well, not in public. Is anybody with you?'

There were the two room-boys standing by. 'No,' I said. 'What should I call you then?'

'I'll explain. Now I've run you to earth at last, stay where you are. I'm on my way.'

Fifteen, twenty minutes later he arrived.

Tappity-tappity at the door and a put-on child's voice squeaking, 'May I come in, please?'

He came in laughing.

'You haven't changed at all,' I said, astonished. 'You're just the same as ever.'

'Not changed a scrap? Hair thinner? Wrinkles here and there? And Jagut? Did you find him changed?'

'Much thinner—far too thin. But so alive and vigorous.'

'Me? Do I look vigorous? And you, Peter,' he went on loyally. 'You're just the same as ever. But where have you been hiding? Are you here incog? I thought you must have told the hotel to deny your presence. They certainly denied you. Twice. But the third time I telephoned they relented and admitted that you were here. Room No. 10. When you didn't hear from me why didn't you telephone? You've got my number, haven't you? Anyway I'm in the book.'

'I did telephone—two or three times.'

'Who answered? My wife? No one told me.'

'Not your wife. Does she speak English?'

'Enough. But she would have told me. It must have been the servants. What did they say? Do you speak Hindi still?'

'Enough. They simply giggled.'

'Then it was our giggling maids. Those little mountain girls— completely *jungli*.' ('*Jungli*' is Anglo-Indian for what it sounds like: 'straight from the jungle'.) 'How did you ask for me?'

'By name, of course. And they went off into such shrieks I supposed I'd got the wrong number.'

'You said "Mussoorie"?'

'Shouldn't I have? What did you mean over the telephone just now? About your name.'

'No one calls me by my name. Not in Nepal.'

'Your friends? What do they call you?'

'I have no friends.'

'Mussoorie! No girl-friends even? I simply don't believe you.'

'There you go, you see! Of course I know I've got to let you call me "Mussoorie"—but please! Not in front of others. Not in Nepal. I'm always very careful not to address unauthorised people, foreigners anyway, by their first names. In case they take advantage. A little while ago an American lady that I know here called me "Mussoorie". I pretended not to hear her. I turned away'—he turned away, aloofly, demonstrating it: '—and then I turned back to ask her—"Did you say something, Mrs So-and-So?" I think she got it.' He beamed with pleasure. His Mongol face is not in the least inscrutable. 'Yes, she got it all right!'

'I don't get it, all the same.'

'It's that everybody here calls me "sir". The prime minister calls me "sir", the commander-in-chief calls me "sir". I call a senior cousin "your excellency"—he was in the diplomatic: ambassador to London in the 'thirties. Retired now. You'll meet him: General Singha Shum Shere. So charming and intelligent, one of Maharaja Chandra Shum Shere's sons. I suppose it is that father was always such a stickler for forms of address. So do please try to understand and don't use my name if anyone's around, though right in the inner family circle it would be all right. Others hearing you, you see, might fall to wondering: "What is this? How is it that Maharajkumar-sahib *allows* this Englishman to call him so? There must be something behind all this."'

'What could be behind it?'

'Oh, I don't know—but I suppose you realise it's been noticed that I've come to see you at your hotel? Everybody watches, wondering "What can MK-sahib be doing here in Hotel Green? Who is this Englishman? Knowing MK-sahib, *calling him by name!* What is this Englishman up to?"'—a change of tone—'But whatever you're up to, Peter, you're here! By the way did Jagut tell you about Dom Moraes? He did? Well. . . . And how are you? How have you passed your time in Kathmandu till I could find you? What are your impressions of our Kathmandu?'

'I think it is one of the most extraordinary and beautiful little cities I've ever seen. I've been spending most of my time in Hanuman Dhoka—the Nautallé Durbar: and looking at the temples. They're wonderful. And they free me from the Hippies' almost-omnipresence, because the Hippies aren't concerned at all with Kathmandu's old marvels.'

'Don't you like our Hippies, then?'

'I don't like too much of anything, I suppose.'

'I think they're colourful. Oh yes, and the hotel—is it all right? They look after you?—I told them to.'

'They do. And it's all exactly right for me.'

The present-day, the flesh-and-blood Mussoorie is more the remembered 'Mussoorie' than I could have believed possible—and in looks he is exactly 'Father' in those photographs, as I'd foreseen. I told him so; it pleased him.

'Father?' he said. 'I wish you could have known him.'

Mussoorie is very very different in shape and looks and temperament from Jagut. He is the real Mongol. Shorter, thicker, perhaps a little fairer in complexion. Yet both are radiations from the same source of light and warmth. They both project themselves quite effortlessly—they come over with a bang, complete. How can I hope to immobilise such volatility on paper? How difficult to do them justice!

'I thought we'd take a little stroll together,' he was saying, 'while the light just lasts. They'll be distributing the evening-papers in a moment. Let's get a move on, or there'll be a terrific queue waiting. Not queue, even: a stampede. Still, I can't do without my evening-papers. Then I'll take you home. I have a little tipple I can offer you.'

Mussoorie led the way downstairs, bowed to by room-boys, bowed to in the lobby by the management—'Maharajkumar-sahib, Maharajkumar-sahib'. ('I'm simply Mr Rana now,' Mussoorie whispered to me. 'Not a prince, like Jagut.') As we left the hotel Mussoorie said: 'Be warned. My house is very small and mean. I'm not rich like Prince Jagut.'

The paper-booth, crowds milling, avid for the evening news, and now a human-chain, hands handing back a copy of I-don't-know-what across the heads of others, Mussoorie taking it, and handing in his turn a coin across the chain and greeting someone in the crowd—in English: 'Good-evening, nephew—come on, Peter, we can go now . . . oh, good-evening, nephew'—another nephew. 'This time I have to stop a moment, Peter. Just a sec''—so I walked on a pace or two and turned in time to see this nephew reach for uncle's hand and lay it to his forehead, head bowed respectfully for leave-taking. Mussoorie caught up with me. 'You noticed that one? He's the "Romeo of Kathmandu".'

'Oh is he? Is he successful? But listen! How can they both be nephews—the first was sixty-something if a day—and Romeo looks sixteen!'

'Why can't they both be nephews? Actually Romeo is eighteen. God, here's another coming! Joodha Road is full of nephews this evening. No time for introductions; not today. Or you'll never get your tipple. Good-evening, nephew—'—(bow, bow back)—'Come on, Peter, let's hop it quick. Do you like walking or shall we take a taxi?'

'Let's walk. It can't be far. I've checked the Thapathali area on the town-plan.'

'We'll walk then. It's only just across the Thandi Khel.'

'Are you near Jung Bahadur's palace?'

'Quite. You know of that?'

'Of course. About the Thandi Khel, too—if you mean the enormous great parade-ground.'

'So! You know about that too?'

'Yes,' I said proudly—though it's a matter of no great pride. Anyone who's read anything about Nepal would know these names and what they stand for.

'Yes. Jagut wrote to me—it seems you're very interested in our history—particularly Jung Bahadur and all that.'

'Very interested indeed: and in your father Maharaja Deb as well. I call it "family-history". And you, you're interested?'

'Yes, yes, of course. I don't think Jagut is—except in father's part in it. He might have been a great man, if they'd let him. Jung Bahadur was a very great man. I've got something nice to show you concerning him. Something unique.'

'Good. What is it?'

'All in good time.'

We had almost reached the end of Joodha Road—the narrow, crowded pavements, crowded shop-fronts narrower still, noise and dinginess, then traffic-lights at a T-junction where the road meets the huge old-time parade-ground, Thandi Khel, as central to the city's life as Central Park is to a New Yorker's or Hyde Park to a Londoner. A traffic block.

'I bet you never dreamt you'd see so many cars in Kathmandu, now did you, Peter? It's getting just like New Delhi. When I first came, after the revolution, there were scarcely any cars at all—and now look! Ten cars in line! All blocked! Next year, you'll see when you come. It will be twenty! Quick! The traffic-lights! Green! *Run!*'

We darted over, to where the grass began, and trees, an avenue.

'Jung Bahadur's palace?' I asked him. 'It should be over there, no? Across the Thandi Khel.'

'Yes ... but it's hidden behind all those trees. My humble cottage also.'

Mussoorie's house is very small but far from being mean. It perches—a little perilously—on the lip of a ravine in what is practically open countryside, though not a mile from Joodha Road, the centre of the city. In the gathering dark I could just make out that a road was under construction down below, along the bed of the ravine, man-made, a cutting wide and deep.

'It's what we call the China Road. Into Tibet. It's from miles and miles up there that you can get a good sight of Everest—at least they tell me so. The Indians gave us Tribhuvan Rajpath into India; and the Chinese give us China Road. When you come by day you'll see great tough Chinese working on it. I'd thought that the Chinese would be little men. These are huge. Like warriors.'

'Perhaps they really are. And perhaps they'll be here always now —maintenance on those Himalayan roads must be a never-ending business. How kind of the Chinese.'

'Peter! Please!'

He fumbled for his key and let us in, then called out for a servant. Two plump little girls like russet butter-balls bounced in, saris flying, cheeks shining, eyes flashing, rather ugly little things but very charming, giggling like mad.

'They giggle all the time, Peter. I'll just tell them who you are.' He told them, they burst out laughing and fled from the big sitting-room that we were standing in. 'They're like little children,' said Mussoorie: 'But they're good little children. They came to me with my wife. She's a new wife. Did you know?'

'Jagut told me. I'm longing to meet her.'

'Not this evening, probably. I haven't warned her you might be coming.' He called the servants back and gave them orders. 'They'll bring us our tipple and whatever there is—nuts or grains or something. Eats. Let's sit. Oh, I was quite forgetting. Important news.' He stopped and made a serious face: 'Do you want to meet a lady who knows you?'

'Knows me? Here in Kathmandu? Who can it be? Not Zena?'

'Zena? Zena Rachevsky? You know Zena? You do? Well! But no, not Zena.'

'If it's not Zena—whom I certainly intend to see—then who?'

'Ah-ha! You want to see her?'

'How can I know if I want to see her? Till I hear who she is. Perhaps I hate her. Is she European?'

'I shan't say. I shall tantalise you. Surprise you.'

'Surprises aren't always all that nice. Is she Nepalese, perhaps, this lady? It can't be one of the sisters because I know where they both are at present. Could it be Dibya, possibly? That would be a wonderful surprise. I thought she was in Jodhpur.'

Dibya is a Rana princess, daughter in his old age of the same Maharaja Joodha Shum Shere who stands immobilised in marble at the Joodha Road intersection, not a hundred yards from Hotel Green. I had not seen her since before the war. I knew of her as a young bride, and very beautiful. The Rana women so often are. I thought of something odd:

'Mussoorie. Listen. Dibya, your first cousin. Who married your sister Indra's eldest boy: your nephew Narendra. She must have been Narendra's . . . Narendra's what?'

'She was Narendra's aunt.'

'She can't have been!'

'Oh yes she could. She *is*.'

'Both wife *and* aunt?'

'Why not?' he asked, seeing nothing strange in this—and thinking back I remembered that John Morris has a lot to say about the Nepalese conception of the family, how they see the immediate family as all the members of the same generation, the word for father applying not only to the actual father, but also to all his brothers; and I remembered that Mr Morris gives an odd-sounding example of the common Nepalese use of seniority-terms in preference to given names, and how a youth would say of someone we would call his uncle 'He's my ninth father', meaning ninth younger brother of his actual father. And the same for mothers and their sisters. So that all whom we regard as cousins are addressed as brothers and sisters. It is certain that Dibya, though younger than her husband, yet belongs to his parents' generation, so I suppose that a Nepalese would think of her as Narendra's 'sixth' (or whatever numbered) mother. Possibly Mussoorie felt that to a foreigner —a White—marrying your sixth aunt would sound more reasonable than your sixth mother. The trouble is, of course, that in a community where the rich enjoy plurality of wives (and mothers) the generations tend to overlap alarmingly: each new wife a husband takes is a constant twelve years old or so, whereas unluckily the husband cannot but grow older in relation to each new wife in turn. A man of sixty-five who married first at twelve or thirteen can easily, fairly easily, have an eldest child of fifty-plus and a whole lot more ranging through the forties, thirties, twenties, till the last of all these siblings is an infant at the breast. Of course Dibya can be Narendra's wife and aunt. Of course Mussoorie's nephews can be any age at all.

'But it isn't Dibya,' Mussoorie said.

'I'm sorry that it isn't. Come on now. Tell me who it is.'

'Ah-ha! That *would* be telling!'

'You're an infuriating tease, Mussoorie!'

'Sh-h! Name me no names. The servants.'

The little girls were back again with tipple and refreshments.

'Anyway, Peter. I'm not going to spoil the surprise. I'll simply organise a confrontation—and watch! Try a sip of this. Bet you can't guess what we distil it from.'

I tried it. 'No, I can't guess. But it's good. And very strong.'

'About 98% alcohol, I dare say. We like such things strong.'

'What is it?'

'It's called *raksi*. From millet seed. And now for the *pièce de résistance*!'

He got up and crossed the room, switched on a picture-light and threw an arm out: 'Look! Jung Bahadur—as a young man. There, above the fire-place. It's by his court-painter, Bhaju Macha. Macha means child. A kid, let's say. He was always called that rather than his real name Bhaju Ratna. He did grandfather Dhir Shum Shere too: and great-uncle Jagut. The year they went with Jung Bahadur to visit Queen Victoria. 1850. I've tried so hard to get possession of grandfather's picture, but I can't. Jung Bahadur is very nice, though, isn't he?'

It is indeed a charming portrait and when, shortly after, Mussoorie excused himself in order to see his wife about something, I got up again to examine it more carefully.

Apart from the wood-engraving that I tried to give to Jagut I had seen a number of pictures of great-uncle Jung Bahadur (one only of his youngest and best-loved brother—the sole brother he could trust: grandfather Dhir Shum Shere) but nothing by this hand.

The picture is meticulously drawn and painted, as if it were an outsize miniature, three foot by three. Bhaju-the-Kid paints Jung Bahadur rather as the Indian miniaturists of the first-half nineteenth century would paint the Honourable Company's young subalterns—romantic, pink and white, and very youthful, their uniforms correct in every elaborated detail. All this in a naively westernised technique, for western sitters. In this portrait Jung Bahadur might be just another English subaltern, romanticised and youthful and milky-white (in fact we know that he was swarthy). Bhaju-the-Kid has elongated him (he was rather short, though slim in youth, and beautifully made). Bhaju draws in the

167

small moustache exactly as he draws in the eye-brows, in pencil flicks. Retroussé nose. The uniform is imaginatively rich: high gold collar and facings to his cutaway red coat of what is probably a broad-cloth, a frilled lawn shirt with jewelled buttons; a cravat of watered-silk, white 'liner' showing. Gold epaulettes descending to the elbows give the impression of a bolero. His hands are small and delicate and ringless. He is armed, of course. A pistol left and right, sword on left hip. His left hand holds a flint-lock with a gold-brocaded shoulder-strap; his right hand holds a watch with hour-hand only. The ear-lobe that is visible under black bobbed hair is pierced, but he wears no ear-ring. There is nothing remotely Mongol in his looks, as Bhaju-the-Kid paints him. He looks eighteen (like nephew Romeo) but if this was painted round about 1850 he was nearing thirty-three. No one looking at the Jung Bahadur of the portrait could readily connect this romantic charming princely youth with the Jung Bahadur of the Kōt Massacre four years before.

Mussoorie came back into the room to find me staring at the portrait. 'So you like it, do you?' and I said 'Enormously'—he was filling up my liqueur-glass with more of his fiery *raksi*. 'Next time you come round you shall try another of our distillations. And you shall meet my wife—and sup with us.'

Mussoorie, alone among the sons and daughters of their particular mother, came to live in Kathmandu after the revolution, when there was no longer a Rana prime minister to fear an exiled Rana's return. He evidently feels himself less Indian, more Nepalese, than is the case with Jagut.

I said: 'I want to hear about Jung Bahadur. "Family-tradition" more: not so much the facts that anyone might know.'

'Well—what shall I tell you about him. . . .' He stopped and then said: 'Look. This evening let's just talk our own "old times" shall we?'

We talked our own 'old times' but it was early still when I got up to go. He might be planning to feed in his wife's apartment. He guided me down the tricky foot-path, now pitch-black, to where the road is met and the occasional street-lamps begin to light the way across the Thandi Khel. 'Thank you so much for the evening,' I said. 'I can find my own way home from here.'

The evening had been so agreeable, so exactly as if no gap of years had separated this from our last meeting—where would it have been? What year? The reunion had proved so much easier

168

for both of us than had been mine with Jagut. In Mussoorie's case there was relatively little shared experience to link us; he and I could pick things up again precisely where circumstances had obliged us to put them down.

On saying good-night he added: 'Wait. I was forgetting. General Kiran Shum Shere wants me to take you to luncheon there to-morrow. He's our first-cousin—but much younger. He was the last commander-in-chief.' I probably looked puzzled, so he said, 'Since the revolution naturally.'

'Yes, of course. I'd love to come.' I'd read that a good many Ranas were far from being opposed to the revolution. 'Do you call him "sir"?'

'No. With him—an intimate—we use first names. I'll be round for you at Hotel Green tomorrow, then. Just before one.'

On the way back to the city I realised that I had quite forgotten something too—to ask Mussoorie where the Kōt lies in relation to Durbar Square. Quite near, I know: but so far I have been unable to find it. I've asked several people passing by: they seemed to want to help but somehow couldn't and they weren't going to let on that they couldn't, either. So they just held me there with anguish in their eyes.

I was wondering now—had the building been demolished? I have seen a big new concrete building going up in a lane not fifty yards from Durbar Square. Possibly this new and absolutely alien construction (that is to break the royal heart of Kathmandu when it is finished. How could Authority have sanctioned it?), possibly this is where the demolished Kōt once stood. I would have another try at finding it tomorrow. Before the general's lunch-party.

Meantime, supper. I dawdled over it in one of the city's modest little restaurants though thinking about 'family-history', not the food. The Kōt Massacre was the thing that made 'the family' supreme and that's quite clear; but Jung Bahadur had been up and coming for a year or two already and it looked to me as if it was a single incident in 1806—an accident of History, you might say, before Jung Bahadur was even born or his parents married—that quite fortuitously determined who his sponsors were to be and what would follow from it.

Now that I was actually in Nepal, not merely reading it all up in the old India Office Library and Records back in London; now, supper finished, looking out upon an emptying and dim-lit almost medieval street, I was a little shocked to catch myself deciding that it was the two hundred years that led up to the 1950-Revolution that are for me 'reality'. The here and now seem scarcely 'real' at all. This little private country and its capital that people used to read about but could never hope to see has fallen smack into the public, the international, domain completely unequipped to face the mid-twentieth century. In her situation what could she do but cave in to the blandishments of foreign envoys 'bearing gifts' with strings attached? In 1951 she had virtually no schools, no teachers, no civil service, no communications. The mountains of Nepal are known to be rich in minerals; in mica, for example. There is possibly uranium as well. But without communications, external, internal, how could they be transported even if they were mined? And how move her immensely valuable timber? Her surplus rice grown in the low-lying borderland with India was surplus and exported to India solely because they lacked the means of moving it into their mountain deficit areas.

The Gurkhas have a saying—'The Merchant brings the Bible and the Bible brings the Bayonets.' But unlike huge neighbouring India (with whom the majority of the Nepalese share a common Hindu heritage) Nepal has escaped the merchant and the bible and the bayonets only to drop into the soft fat hands of Foreign Aid like an orphan into an institution. However skilfully to date she has contrived to avoid becoming hopelessly entangled in the strings and institutionalised, she hates it, yet cannot do without it.

It might have been much better for Nepal if it had suited the British 'merchants'' book to annexe her two hundred years ago—'not insuperably difficult' as John Morris comments. By now—like India, who did not escape the British 'merchants'—she too would have won her independence long since, but armed meanwhile to face the present. Annexed by Britain, Mr Morris goes on to say, her 'most urgent problems would never have arisen ... nearly all are the direct consequence of two hundred years of artificial segregation from the Indian sub-continent.'

I walked back home to Hotel Green and got my note-books out again.

For centuries on end, until autumn 1768, a Hindu dynasty with ancient roots in India and unbroken ties with her had been peaceably ruling the Kingdom of Nepal and its Buddhist inhabitants. The dynasty was known as 'Malla',* and the country that they thought of as Nepal was no more than the little sixteen-by-twenty-mile valley of that name. We are told, in fact, that 'Nepal' is no more than a phonetic variant of 'Newar', the Newars being the Buddhist people who inhabited it.

As if the valley were not already very small to be called a kingdom, the Mallas had had the eccentricity to subdivide it among 'family-members' into four still smaller kingdoms—of Kantipur (Kathmandu today), Bhaktapur (Bhatgaon today), Lalitpur (Patan today) and Kirtipur.

While the Mallas quietly ruled the valley, the forbidding mountains were held by petty chieftains, the principal among them being Hindus who for ancestry claimed high-born Kshatriya Rajput refugees fleeing their native Rajasthan generations earlier, when the Muslim invaders were taking power in India.

Down in India, beyond the barrier of mountains, the Mallas of the eighteenth century had newish neighbours—the Honourable East India Company—who were busy consolidating their northeast Indian territorial conquests. The Mallas were very much aware of the British 'presence', perhaps a little nervous of it, but in the 1750's and 60's the Company did not appear to have fixed their eyes on Nepal—they seemed to be content, indeed, to regard her as a small and unaligned and welcome buffer-state between them and enormous China. The Company were naturally concerned with the continuing tranquillity of Nepal, since it looked as if it might provide an important trade-route into Tartary. A few European monks—Jesuits, Capucines—had passed that way, but never an Englishman, monk or otherwise. All the same rumours of natural riches in those mountains had been reaching the British for some time already by the 1760's.

And then, in 1768, an utterly unsought opportunity was given to the Company to make their first entry into Nepal, and this too at the direct invitation of the Malla kings. In point of fact it was less an invitation than an urgent cry for military help against tribal invasion of the valley from the mountains west of it. The Mallas must have entertained the gravest doubts about the wisdom of thus calling in the British (knowing what was going on in India) but the alternative was their own annihilation.

* Ari Deva, mother of the first Malla king, quite suddenly gave birth to him while at a wrestling-tourney so they called him 'Malla', which meant 'champion prize-fighter'.

The Company responded readily—it was much to their advantage to preserve their peaceful little neighbours in their status-quo, earn their gratitude and in the course of it acquire a first-hand account of the Kingdom of Nepal—the sort of market-cum-intelligence report the Company's officers were so skilled in drawing up. They detailed a certain Captain Kinloch to command the two thousand sepoys that were to save the Malla kings.

It was summer 1768.

Can it really be that the Honourable Company had never even heard what local people knew so well about the territory called 'Terai'? The Terai runs east-west along the Indo-Nepali border, it is the rice-growing country just referred to, a low-lying strip of swampy jungle-land below the approaches to the Himalayas. No local in his senses would have dreamed of crossing it except in winter because throughout the long hot steamy season there raged an epidemic so virulent and deadly that it killed men off like flies. Tiger and elephant and rhinoceros and a certain indigenous tribe of outcasts—these were immune, but humans, no. They called it *ayul* or 'owl', as the British transliterated it once they'd learnt of it. They learnt at the same time that it was caused by the breath of serpents—millions of them, busy poisoning the air, and it was not for years to come that anyone knew better.

The *ayul* easily and quickly decimated Kinloch's forces and Kinloch had nothing for it but to turn back before ever he had reached the foothills, and beat an ignominious retreat.

Meanwhile the Malla kings had already been invaded. A Hindu chieftain, Prithvi Narayan Sah of Gurkha, had swooped down with his warriors from his mountain-fastness (fifty miles west of Kathmandu, perhaps a five or six-day trek in country of the sort), and since the Mallas were no match for him as 'champion-prizefighters' and since the British help they'd begged for never came, Kathmandu had fallen by September 1768 and the three other midget kingdoms followed suit not long after it, in the year or so that followed.

'Kings we may not kill,' said Prithvi Narayan Sah, addressing the three defeated Malla kings (the fourth—of Kathmandu—seems to have died without issue some time before), and invited them to say what he should do with them. Two of them wished only to be allowed to go away 'to die', the one down in Benares, the other in nearby holy Pashupatinath. Their victor happily agreed and packed them off. A vernacular History of Nepal tells us that the third king concerned—the King of Patan—

'. . . thought that all this evil was brought about by Ranjit Malla of Bhatgaon and that there was no use in speaking to anyone. He therefore sat engaged in the worship of God and would not speak. For this reason he was sent to Lakshmipur to be kept in confinement and there he died.'

Prithvi Narayan Sah was himself now king of the undivided valley, first of the Sah dynasty he founded. King Birendra of Nepal today is tenth in direct succession.

Back there in the microcosm of Soon Saan, time's variable pace did disconcert me to begin with but at least I knew that, if we chose to look at it, *The Hindustan Times* could provide us with a rough and ready check on the daily change of date. Here in the Valley of Nepal two hundred years ago the calendar was quite beyond control, because when the Sahs of Gurkha took the valley they trusted to the moon in this matter of the calendar and a sorry mess she made of keeping historic time. Every now and then, indeed, the date jumped perilously forward and 'a month was lost'. This may have had the useful side-effect of allowing crops and seasons to get temporarily in step again, but the Parbatiya History just cited records how awful were the other consequences:

'Again a month was lost in [Rajendra's] reign . . . and a great many people, as well as beasts, birds and fishes, died in consequence.'

There were doubtless other serious cases of month-loss that I haven't read about, but perhaps none of it would have happened at all had the Sahs not tried to cash in not only on the moon but on the sun as well. In taking over from the Mallas lock, stock and barrel, Prithvi Narayan Sah also appropriated to himself the Mallas' proud claim to *Surajbansi*. This is nothing more nor less than direct-line 'sun-descent'. Now 'sun-descent' was the exclusive monopoly of the Sessodia Rajputs of Chittor and Udaipur, the bluest of the bluest blood in all Rajasthan. It still is, and let no one else pretend to it, even if it appears to us outsiders that anybody's claim to it is as likely to be as sound as anybody else's.

Did Suraj-the-Sun, the Sahs' retrospectively appropriated progenitor, resent their impudence, as the moon (we may believe) resented their mistrust of her? However that may be, Suraj-the-Sun cannot be said to have shone down kindly on them. Prithvi Narayan lived only five years in which to enjoy his conquest; his son who then succeeded was dead by c. 1777; and for a hundred long years thereafter each Sah king in turn was a doomed man.

The Sah queens were not doomed with their sons and husbands. Far from it. In fact for some seventy of the coming hundred years we have the spectacle of what we may rightly call Nepal's 'Regiment of Women'—most successful to begin with, where 'success' must be read to mean the victorious prosecution of wars against weaker neighbours east and west; expanding frontiers; loot, tribute-money and the filling of hungry Gurkha soldiers' stomachs that (except for war) must necessarily stay empty. Unfortunately this War-economy of theirs in time must mean encroachment upon regions that the British chose to see as within their rightful spheres of influence. So in 1814 the little war the Gurkhas found themselves involved in was the war the Company declared on them, and disgracefully mishandled, though we muddled through to win it in 1816. The Treaty of Segauli, that we then drew up to regulate the peace, included cession to us of the territories we wanted, along with Gurkha acceptance of a permanent British Resident at the Court of Kathmandu, which was something we had made three earlier abortive efforts to secure. The Parbatiya History tells the story of this two-year war in four short lines, a marvel of compression:

'In [King Girvan's] reign war broke out with the British in Taryani [Terai] but depriving them of wisdom the raja saved his country. Then, calling in the British gentlemen, he made peace with them and allowed them to live near Thambahil.'*

—succinct and, allowing for omissions, true enough. What is also true and has great bearing on the future is that the Gurkha prime minister of the time (a wise diplomatist and statesman, Bhim Sen Thapa—a name we shall remember) emerged from the conflict with the salutary recognition that 'England is a power that crushes thrones like potsherds'; and good Dowager Queen Lalit Tripura Sundari, co-regent with him for nearly thirty years in admirable partnership both in and out of bed, could recognise this too. The

* Anybody wishing to read more than the Parbatiya History reveals about this significant little war will find it fully treated in Pemble.

British, for their part, emerged with little glory but with the keenest recognition of the Gurkhas' astounding qualities as fighting-men, and this has coloured our relations with Nepal down to the present day. By the Treaty of Segauli, the British undertook to honour Nepal's absolute and sovereign independence. Already, I suppose, we had dimly come to realise that what Nepal might most profitably mean to us was not just a little country to annexe and plunder, but an extraordinary private reservoir of fighting man-power for service in the Company's Indian Armies. Already in 1816 Gurkhas were offering themselves for enlistment. We may usefully reflect, perhaps, that Gurkha recruits were and still are a much more readily transportable Nepalese export than such commodities as mineral riches dreamed of but not yet mined.

As a footnote to the Gurkhas' grudging acceptance of a British Resident in Kathmandu at last, they wryly specified exactly where 'in Thambahil' the 'British gentlemen' must live, or, to be more accurate, where they would be held in solitary confinement, cut off absolutely from the life of Kathmandu and its seething palace-politics that the Resident had been specifically sent there to ob-serve. It was an area two miles north of the city so well known for its noxious airs that its local name was 'The Abode of Demons'.

The Company's serious interest in Nepal, her people, institu-tions, natural products, economy and so on had not really started till late in the 1760's. Her history, in so far as anybody on the spot had recorded it then (and for many years to come), was simply royal-family chronicles. To such rudimentary 'court-circulars' as these we could add the excellent if necessarily limited 'Accounts' two British officers (Kirkpatrick and Hamilton) had left us of their brief and otherwise ineffectual visits to the valley in 1793 and 1802 respectively. Add, also, such intelligence as the Company's officers could pick up in their nosy way wherever they could find it down in India. Even when the Kathmandu Residency Records start in 1816, the Resident's despatches could not tell us much, though we can at last be sure of dates. How could he hope to find out more when kept so absolutely incommunicado? It was certainly not the palace's intention that he should see or come to know of anything at all that mattered. The Valley's birds and beasts and fishes, and her flowers: yes, all right; the Resident could get permission to go out sometimes, always under the most vigilant Gurkha escort, to observe the flora and the fauna (shoot the fauna, if he wanted, fish the fishes). He was even allowed to receive learned persons (carefully screened and briefed by the palace, certainly) who could instruct him in the intricacies of the Buddhist faith about which so little was yet known to us.

The blanks and the confusions in the recording of political events don't really bother me because my interest is only in the thin red line of Rana 'family-history' and this is scarcely visible till 1844–5. It is spreading right across the page in 1846. Yet I should have liked a clearer, better-focused view of what did happen between *c.* 1777 and September 1846.

I am looking over what we know of Sah royal-family history pre-1846, pre-Rana, trying to fit its jigsaw bits together so as to get some kind of picture of it. But the jigsaw bits, themselves identical in shape, or nearly, are difficult to distinguish from each other, and interlock to make not just a single picture ('pattern' might be a better word) but one pattern five times over, all dimly discernible as it might be through the milky-muslin casing of a *khasto*-shawl, hand-block printed with its own 'repeat'. The 'repeat' on Rana *khastos* such as Jagut's, and the one he's given me, is simple to interpret: a panoply to represent what he was born to. But the 'repeat' we seem to see on the *khastos* of the Sah kings of the period *c.* 1777–1846 looks like the pattern of their history that repeats itself five times within the seventy years of their 'Regiment of Women', with no more than minor variants. The first fifty years of it, and more, were notably successful (despite two upsets, quickly righted) but it finishes in absolute monstrosity, a truly fitting counterpart to the Ottomans' own 'Regiment of Women' two hundred years or so before. There is no doubt that it was their women that brought both Ottomans and in their turn Sah kings to their knees, and their respective countries with them, to the point where in each case History seems to have produced a *deus-ex-machina*—strong, capable and ruthless—to halt the galloping consumption and take over.

The trouble from the outset with the 'Regiment of Women' in Istanbul was that Roxelana and the women who succeeded her in power were far from being Elizabeths the First of England (educated, trained from childhood and equipped to play the role of Queen). In Istanbul these beautiful young girls had been selected solely for the Imperial bed, entirely untrained for, utterly unaware of, any duties or responsibilities outside of it. So when the sottishness or other weakness of their Lords and Masters opened up the way for them, they naturally seized power for themselves. Except for Roxelana, who unfortunately pre-deceased her Lord and Master, Suleiman the Magnificent, the girls continued, as *Validé sultane* (or dowager), to exercise their power over the boy-sultan sons they could so easily debauch. Absolute power had made Knox's 'Monsters' of them all, corrupting absolutely.

In the case of Kathmandu's 'Regiment of Women', we all too readily forget the long opening decades of wise 'stateswomanship', so as to watch the horror-movie of the final fifteen monstrous years in which greedy peasant-girls take over and the country founders.

Reduced to a synopsis, Kathmandu's 'Regiment of Women' might look like this:

FIVE QUEENS
two: very good
one: nobody
TWO: absolutely evil
rule in succession
as *de-jure* or *de-facto*
REGENTS
throughout
THE LONG MINORITIES
(AND WELL BEYOND)
of
DEBAUCHED & VIOLENT WEAKLING KINGS
★
EACH QUEEN'S PRIME MINISTER CO-REGENT
is, in turn,
ASSASSINATED......

...... except the last—the *deus ex machina*, JUNG BAHADUR, Nepal's Historical Necessity, the new Prime Minister, effectively the Sovereign.

13

Next morning I was in Nautallé Durbar once again, up on the ninth floor immediately below the projecting eaves of the topmost of its four pagodas. As in all traditional Newar constructions whether temple, palace, grand or modest town-house, the pagoda, or else the pantile roof, projects so far beyond the walls that it must be supported by wooden struts that come up at an angle from the wall below. In the ninth floor of Nautallé the window-frames and trellising lean out at the angle of the struts and are attached to them. This is very pretty from the outside, and from inside good enough for looking down, but much less good for the panoramic landscape. Yet I could see the Dharahara well enough —the tall white lighthouse of a tower that is the first identifiable object in Kathmandu from the drive-in. It triumphantly with-stood the earthquake of 1934, I'm glad to say, because Dharahara is the only memorial I know of to Bhim Sen Thapa whom 'the family' had so much to thank for. Bhim Sen's tower lords it over the dingy rebuilt south-east quarter of the city.

Glancing down again my eye was caught and held by a big white horse, roaming in Taleju Bhavani's temple-courtyard. No harness, unattended, simply roaming. What was he up to, all alone? What was I up to, for the matter of that, high in Nautallé?

I had been making an absolutely unsuccessful aerial recon-naissance of the Durbar Square area, trying to spot the Kōt where Jung Bahadur had triumphed all that time ago. I would recognise it instantly (from Landon's plate) if only I could see it, but I couldn't and I had to leave defeated. Down the ladder-staircases, out across the interior courtyard of Nautallé with its plain stone coronation platform, past the 'lion-man' avatar of Lord Vishnu in what looks like black basalt. Here his lions' claws are disembowelling an earthbound devil. Hindu mythology likes to have its gods outtricking tricky demons: he who laughs last does the disembowelling.

Out into the open Durbar Square, past Hanuman the Monkey-God standing on his plinth, all swathed in red cotton cloth, his muzzle peeping out at his adorers circumambulating him. Past the little temples dedicated to Lord Vishnu and Lord Shiva. I would make a more systematic search today, like 'gridding' on a map-sheet.

But the only map—a sketchy town-plan—does not mark the Kōt. Nothing I have read has sited it at all precisely in speaking of what happened there. I passed the new and absolutely alien construction going up nearby and wondered once again if the foundations stood upon the prostrate ghost of the old Kōt I sought. I was keen to get inside to check the Residency's secret document about what happened—check on sight-lines, gradients of stairways. I wanted to stand where Jung Bahadur stood, before the slaughter started. There were certain physical possibilities I much wanted to be sure about. So off I went, as seemingly haphazard as the lanes that wind away from Durbar Square, though anything but aimlessly and never far afield because it had to be quite near. How far is 'near', though?

In time I found myself in a sort of old and private-looking square, a breached crumbling wall beside a water-tank of stone and a pretty private house more like a Newar country-farmstead than something for a city. A pleasant-looking man was at the front door of it. He saw me looking at the house and made a little gesture of enquiry at me.

'Do you speak English?' I asked him.

He nodded.

'I was admiring your house.'

'The house? It is very old house.'

'I see it is. How old? Do you know?'

'A hundred years.'

Always a good round number.

'More, perhaps?' I suggested.

'Yes. Much much more. And this water-tank you see. There are beautiful water-spouts from Majushri's time, but now they lie fifteen feet below the water.'

'How very interesting.'

'Yes. And there was an earthen pot they found: and in it rice, a betel-nut, one *paisa*. But someone emptied out that pot and immediately the water ceased to flow. Only a Tantric exercise could start the flow once more.'

He turned and pointed vaguely: 'And there a king once lived. He had married the daughter of the Emperor of China.'

'Indeed?' I felt he had it upside-down. A Nepalese princess once married the ruler of Tibet and is credited with having introduced Buddhism into that country. Which house did he mean, anyway?

'You mean it was *this* very house the king once lived in?' I asked him, pointing at his own.

'No. Over there.'

'Oh.'

'And in that house'—again a vaguely-pointing finger— 'there once lived a . . .'

But I had broken in: 'Exactly which house, please?'

People pointing know what they are pointing at, the general direction is quite good enough for them.

'That one. There lived a brother of Jung Bahadur. Shall I now show you the house of a great man who was killed by Jung Bahadur? You know Jung Bahadur?'

'Yes, yes . . .'

'The whole world knows him.'

'Yes. Please show me the house? Which brother was it?'

'And also where on certain nights there come three headless horses and three headless riders. Jung Bahadur had killed them too.'

'Who were they? Do you know?'

'The man that Jung Bahadur shot was at prayer in his house.'

'Don't tell me you mean General Gagan Singh! But it was not Jung Bahadur who shot *him*!'

'At his prayers. You know Gagan Singh?'

'Not to say "know". Like Jung Bahadur I know "of" Gagan Singh, of course, if you mean the one who was the lover of the Queen.'

This confused and angered him, so he said sharply: 'You know that Jung Bahadur was lover of *your* queen—when he visited her in London? Her name was Queen Victoria. It was in the bathroom. And she with a child in her stomach too!'

No use protesting. On Jung Bahadur's visit to London, Queen Victoria invested him with the Grand Cross of the Order of the

Bath—and what Nepalese who assumed that this great honour had been awarded in the bathroom would believe that intimacy had not taken place and been royally rewarded in this way? Queens had lovers openly—it was well known. The little palace-girls that used to scamper down the corridors had all the lovers they could find. So instead of protests I now said, puffed with knowledge: 'And do you know who the baby was? And he was born some weeks before Jung Bahadur arrived in London...'

'...a baby in her stomach too!'

'No, sir. It was born on the 1st of May, weeks earlier. And it was Prince Arthur, Duke of Connaught.'

'Who is that duke, please?'

'Connaught. And now please show me General Gagan's house and the window he was shot through.'

'You want? Now? You wish it? Very well. And shall I show you my house too?'

'You mean this pretty house by the tank is not your house?'

'Oh no.'

'But I thought you'd....'

'No,' he interrupted. 'This is the house of a friend.'

'Then why did you...oh well, never mind. Yes, let us visit your house too.'

We set off together, towards Durbar Square and the palace, and at a little distance he stopped and beckoned me to follow as he turned into a semi-circular recess in the high brick wall and started round it clockwise—as men ritually circumambulate red-shrouded Hanuman the Monkey-God in Durbar Square. But I noticed that my guide offered no such respectful touch as I had seen people giving Hanuman in passing round him. In fact my guide had stopped again and was stooping down a little, pointing through a jagged hole in the brickwork of the wall, a garden wall, perhaps: trees drooped their branches over it. 'Look!' he commanded.

'I am looking. I can see an old house—not so old as your friend's but old enough—' (for Gagan Singh to have lived in it in 1846, I meant, but didn't bother to say so). 'Quite a big house, though two floors only. With verandahs.' Yet could it have been Gagan Singh's? His had to have another house close alongside from whose roof the assassin had jumped across to do it. Possibly on the far side of this house? I said: 'So this is where General Gagan Singh was living.'

'This is the house of the traitor who went to London with Jung Bahadur.'

'Not Gagan's then? Gagan Singh certainly did not go to London with him. He was dead already. What traitor do you mean, I wonder.'

He said a name I didn't recognise, though the names of Jung Bahadur's suite are all recorded.

I said: 'I'm sure that name is not on the list of Jung Bahadur's suite.'

He was affronted now and said: 'How can you know, sir?'— but he didn't choose to listen to my answer. Instead he drew me round the shrine and out into the narrow street and pointed to a house a little further down it on the right. 'That is my house,' he said and led me to it. As we went in he said, 'Do you play piano?'

An upright piano in a western-looking room with books and pictures.

'Alas I cannot play piano.'

'Never mind. And this—' —a photograph above the piano— 'This is my dear English friend called Miss Brown who live in Yately, England. You know Yately? Miss Brown was governess to the children of the Commander-in-Chief. She would often call to visit us. When she left she wrote to me. But she no longer writes to me and I think that it is thirty years since her last letter. . . .'

I was sad for him. So much can happen to us all in thirty years.

Our conversation had begun to flag. Probably we had reached saturation-point, each with the other, and that is always the good time to part. What had he wanted of me—except that I should listen to his talk? Neither had proved of much real interest to the other, though I had started off with him so hopefully. He had somehow got me nowhere. Yet just before leaving him I would try him on the Kōt: 'Before I go, sir, do you happen to know exactly where I'll find the Kōt?'

'The Kōt?'

'Yes. Where all those people were massacred.'

'Yes, yes. It is by Durbar Square. You will find it very easily.'

'Thank you so much. It has been a pleasure meeting you.'

He said: 'I am happy to have been able to be of service to you. Come again.'

My friend and guide had put me on my way along the lane he lives in, snaking between houses three-, four-storeys high, and sometimes five, all in red burnt-brick with alternating wooden courses, though some of them are plastered white. Most have those massive elongated Newar window-embrasures in deeply carved and ornamented wood. In the grandest cases the wooden struts that support the pantiled roof would be deeply carved as well, often in the forms of grotesque four-legged reared-up monsters with erections—and there was Kasthamandap straight ahead. This big sixteenth-century open-sided pagoda is said to have given Kathmandu its current name—it is also said to have been built as a doss-house for 'fakirs'. You might expect the Hippies, who are no more religious than most 'fakirs' of our times, to have taken over Kasthamandap for their 'pad', but I'm glad to say they haven't.

Lunch at General Kiran Shum Shere Jung Bahadur's—I expect he's simply General Kiran Rana in the telephone-directory—was a very agreeable affair. On a quick check of the Rana Genealogical Table Landon includes as an appendix to his book together with the Sah table, I had established that he is one of Maharaja Joodha's eleven sons and that consequently Dibya is his sister—though the tables omit all reference to the Rana wives and daughters. In fact it is rare, in published matter, to find a longer reference to the Sah and Rana ladies than a laconic note, for example, that Jung Bahadur was marrying off yet another of his daughters (sometimes numbered, never named) to yet another Sah son, welding the two families even closer together, taking Sah daughters for his sons as well, of course. The exception to this silence about the ladies is when the ladies prove to be exceptionally talented or strong or brilliant, as with two of the dowager-queens regent already noticed.

Mussoorie had brought his new young wife with him—I didn't catch her name, perhaps it wasn't mentioned. A very pretty girl. Is she a little shy? More likely that Mussoorie's English is so perfect that she hesitates to try hers out in front of him. There is another factor, too: that it may still be the fashion here in Kathmandu social circles for the men to do the talking when the company is mixed.

General Kiran's house stands in deep rolling countryside and cultivation not two miles from the city's centre. A country house, wide, white and low, two storeys only; and as we drove up to it I could make out a big striped beach-umbrella and heads of other guests above the parapet of the imposing entrance-porch. It seems

183

that Maharaja Joodha built this property and the elaborate stable-yard beyond the house for General Kiran. The other Joodha-sons would all have had their separate places, doubtless. The date of this one is likely to be the early 'thirties, when Joodha came to power and the almost infinite wealth that went with it. The architectural style, however, is of much earlier date, though thought of, perhaps, as modern in Nepal.

Servants greeted us and escorted us across the big square hall to climb the staircase round the big square staircase-well. Tigers huge and flat with heads like snarling footstools drape the walls, and one among them the longest narrowest skin I'd ever seen. There were other trophies of the chase as well. General Kiran is evidently very much the soldier and country-gentleman.

A big library-table faces the stairhead and on it was a visitors'-book, already open. We were to write our names (Mussoorie, no doubt a constant visitor, did not sign). In signing mine I noticed that the entry immediately above my own, the same date too, was a Madame Harriet de Rachevsky—who could this lady be but Zena's mother who (as I knew, by chance, though I had never met her) started life as a Miss Strauss of New York City? I would meet her now and she would lead me to Zena in her monastery miles outside the city. Just above Madame Rachevsky's name was that of a Mrs Bleumenthal.

General Kiran found me signing. He was very welcoming, altogether easy, much taller than the average Nepali, more Indian-looking. I judged him to be forty or thereabouts, a handsome man and very soldierly. He introduced us to his other guests, and servants brought us cocktails on the open porch and of course Madame Rachevsky was Zena's mother, and of course I would be able to see Zena very soon—she was coming in to town some days ahead. Where had I known her, when? The obvious questions. As one might expect of Zena's mother, she too is handsome, tall and straight.

The buffet-luncheon was a very welcome change from food in the cheaper restaurants. I stood there munching happily and Mussoorie caught my eye and winked.

Display-cabinets line the walls of the large reception-room, presentation silver objects, palace furniture, stuff inherited from Maharaja Joodha, obviously, and of his period—again allowing for the 'fashion' time-lag. Round the walls more tigers, sporting heads and trophies and on a table a great chinese-looking metal tree embellished with small flowers carved from jade and cornelian. Seeing me staring General Kiran said, 'The leaves are from the inner-skin of the rhinoceros. Translucent. It makes good leaves, doesn't it?' I said yes, it did indeed, thinking that a rhino's foot makes a nice plant-tub too—there was a nice one in the window— and that the rhino's horn is aphrodisiac. 'The rhino's dying out,' said General Kiran, 'so we have to protect him these days. Are you a big-game shot?' and I had to tell him no. Then he pointed to the various skins around the walls. 'That one, for instance,' General Kiran was saying: 'It measured ten foot two between pegs—but it had fallen into the river and stiffened badly before we could get it out,' and I wondered if he meant that it would have been longer still, or possibly much wider, if they could have pegged it out in time. Is ten foot two from nose to tail-tip huge, for tiger? I could not show my ignorance by asking what might be a very silly question. I admired the creature, though, and asked about the elongated monster on the staircase wall. He told me it had been a tiger very early in his life—did he even say his first? He had given it to a local taxidermist (where Maharaja Joodha would have sent his trophies to Van Ingen down in India or even Rowland Ward in London). So if this tiger looked a little odd, it was that the local taxidermist had stretched it too much lengthwise at a sorry cost to width, yet it was the General's first and if he too was laughing at it, it was in a loving way. 'See that one, now?' he asked us. 'I shot him with a revolver. He took three bullets.'

'And that bow and arrow in the corner?' I asked hopefully. It looked incongruous but full of purpose and I was right, too. It was waiting there, he told us, against the day when he proposed to kill a tiger with it. And looking at the general I should think that he would gladly even grapple with the King of Cats, and come off best. Had not Jung Bahadur put a leopard to humiliating flight by advancing on him with a sword, and was not Oldfield there to witness and record it? Yes, General Kiran is tough, all right, but of disarming charm and very friendly—but when I was friendly back and patted his shoulder to emphasise whatever I was saying, he winced and withdrew, so I didn't pat again.

'How are you enjoying Kathmandu?' he was now asking Mrs Bleumenthal, who answered that she just loved it. The General moved away to speak to someone else and Mrs Bleumenthal confided in me: 'You can take your glorious east for all I care: I'm flying back tomorrow to what I know and like. New York.' I much admired Mrs Bleumenthal for knowing her mind and speaking it, though I believe I prefer the winter sun to double-glazing and steam-heat. Yet all the same I wished she wasn't leaving; I wanted to hear more of her straight-from-the-sloping-shoulder talk. Madame Rachevsky wasn't leaving, I would be seeing her again: she'd be getting Zena to call me at my hotel to fix a meeting. Zena was at her monastery, not so very far away it seemed; the far side of Bhodnath *stupa*, yes, she was very happy there, and Madame Rachevsky was very happy too and kind General Kiran was renting her a converted coach-house to stay in while she was in Nepal. 'Isn't that just nice?' said Madame Rachevsky.

Mussoorie came up, bringing his little wife. Her English isn't bad at all. 'It is time, I think,' she said. 'Are you ready to leave?' and I said yes, of course: and then to Mussoorie: 'Mussoorie. While it's in my mind. Do tell me where the Kōt is—exactly.'

'Why, it's just off Durbar Square. Kiran!' he called, and General Kiran joined us. 'Peter wants to know exactly where he'll find the Kōt.' And General Kiran answered, as everybody answers—'Just off Durbar Square. He can't miss it.'

'But I *have* missed it, and I *can* miss it! Several times already.'

'Why don't you get the Director of Tourism to have some tourist-officer escort you, then?'

'Oh yes, of course . . .'

'But will they let you in? The Kōt is a barracks now.'

'Oh-h . . .'

We took our leave.

On the way back in the car Mussoorie's wife joined in the talk quite freely, smiling, nodding. She really is much more than simply pretty; she is enchanting, and after all not shy, I think. I thanked them both for bringing me to lunch and asked to be dropped off at the general post-office. As I left them Mussoorie leant out of the window of the car and said: 'In case you're interested, I can still cross my legs behind my neck. Remember?'

Yes, I remembered, and congratulated him on still being able to perform this difficult but highly beneficial exercise.

14

From the Tourist Office to Durbar Square is not above a minute's
walk and, as everyone has all along insisted, the Kōt itself is not
half a minute on beyond the square. A tourist officer kindly took
me there—or, rather, took me to a gate, warning me (as General
Kiran had the day before) that it is now a barracks and we wouldn't
be allowed inside. We weren't. A sentry came up to us and said so.

I had passed this recent-looking gate not once but several times
before without paying it the least attention. A gate, no more. And
now a sentry; the Kōt itself, invisible: buildings completely hide
it from the road. 'It's in there, just the same,' the tourist officer
assured me—but to get inside would certainly require a special
pass. I stood there wondering why ever they should let me have
one. An unknown Englishman asking to see inside a barracks?
What would there be to see? Something must be behind all
this.

I would have to get Mussoorie to help, through Kiran possibly.

I thanked the tourist officer and he left me. To tell the truth he
left me a bit disconsolate, but it might be worth a walk through
the lanes encircling the barracks; I might just get a glimpse that
would enable me to identify the Kōt beyond all question, though
I reluctantly supposed the tourist officer must know. Down the
lane beyond the entrance-gate, turn left—to pass the big new concrete block going up: it would immediately overlook the Kōt
compound in time, and wouldn't even bother to. Left again and
back to Durbar Square, no glimpse of anything resembling the
Kōt, and that was that.

Perhaps today I'd give myself a change from palace-pottering,
Hindu temples, let alone the Kōt. I would prepare myself for sorties

out beyond the city-limits, and what better than a second 'aerial reconnaissance' that same morning, but this time certain of success? I would go to Dharahara, as they call Bhim Sen's high white free-standing tower—one hundred and sixty-five feet, a tourist handout says and promises a panoramic view of the entire valley from the top of it. I would survey the valley as in the bright-lit saucer of an old-time camera obscura, pinpoint my chosen destinations and then, later on, I'd visit them, examine them close-to like detail in a large and crowded canvas examined through a microscope. And now I came to consider the matter, I'd limit everything I did while in the Valley to walking-distance. I would walk alone. Nothing to my purpose lay more than a few miles out of Kathmandu, so I could walk into the scenery that Dharahara dominates, the lovely rolling scenery that up to now I'd only dashed through encapsulated in a car—the drive from the airport, out to Kiran's lunch and back. General Kiran is becoming 'Kiran' now, I notice.

To Dharahara—five minutes flat. But I got to Dharahara to find its doors were shut, with a heavy padlock on the gate in the surrounding railings. The tower, itself, as I could see now that for the first time I was near enough, is ominously lizarded with cracks. The tourist handout's promises were dated 1969: so after all the earthquake must have done grave secret damage that was only later to declare itself. I'd have to ask.

Bhim Sen Thapa, prime minister and co-regent, built his tower in 1832. In 1833 a serious earthquake brought it toppling to the ground. Was it an omen? Bhim Sen rebuilt it and the British Residency dubbed it 'Bhim Sen's folly'. For others it was no memorial to Bhim's folly but to his greatness, and a reminder of the terrifying fate that overtook him.

Bhim Sen, Matabar, Jung Bahadur—they certainly all climbed Dharahara for the view. I wanted very much to climb it too. One day early in the year 1851 Prime Minister Jung Bahadur climbed it with an Englishman, his guest, young Laurence Oliphant, King Surendra's younger full-brother was with them—the one referred to always by a seniority-term 'Mohila sahib' (John Morris more accurately transliterates this term '*Mailo*', meaning 'second child'). These three stood together on the top of Dharahara admiring the panoramic view and looking down into the city itself, and Oliphant tells us how—

'... officers were scampering down streets on ponies, dragging along the horse-boys who were holding on by their tails ...'

—where in England of the time a groom might be holding on by his master's stirrup-leather. Oliphant noticed and recorded details unusual to him; men such as Dr Oldfield writing years after the experience had probably forgotten how strange and pleasurable had been the first impression, but Oldfield's water-colour sketches —naively painstaking—sometimes fill in backgrounds in a way his book quite often fails to. Oldfield, the expert on Nepal, pooh-pooh'd Oliphant's young-man's travel-diary of a book, as can be imagined. Landon condemned it as the work of 'a facile, even literary pen'; Sylvain Lévi judged it rightly as 'a simple collection of anecdotes, sport, Jung, by an amusing reporter'. I like the book for its absence of pretension and because, just as Sylvain Lévi a generation later was to bring Deb Shum Shere to momentary life for us (and no one else does), so Oliphant revives Dhir Shum Shere. It is the living 'family-members' I am after.

Oliphant stayed in Kathmandu a month or so, quite long enough (given his entrée everywhere) to get his local bearings, to hear about and sense the powerful animosities that underlay the scene. So he could confidently complete his 'horse-boy' passage thus:

'—all this Mohila sahib pointed out with great affability. . . . Had he been a man to seize a good opportunity, that was the moment to give Jung Bahadur a push over the low parapet; but the Mohila sahib is a man without decision of character and he allowed the Minister to reach the bottom his own way.'

At the close of Oliphant's Kathmandu visit he went to take leave of Mohila sahib and was invited in and tells us of the sentries that lined the staircase to an upper-floor reception room 'filled with incongruous bric-à-brac'; and of how he looked into a side-room and there saw a telescope set up. He put an eye to it and was surprised to find that it was trained on a house he seemed to recognise; and then he saw that it was Jung Bahadur's palace across Thandi Khel at Thapathali—the palace that today is hidden in a belt of trees, with Mussoorie's little modern house nearby. But that day in 1851 of which Oliphant was to be writing a year later, he could confidently add, with hindsight and a note of indignation, that the Mohila sahib must already have been 'contemplating the vile plot he so soon after nearly succeeded in executing'. The plot was naturally against Jung Bahadur, first of the many that all failed.

A wasted morning—did it matter? No. I would waste still more, and while in this mood of sniffing out 'the family' background I would go back to the Tourist Office to ask them if they could possibly open Dharahara up for me as a special favour; and I would not go by the short route I had taken getting here but by way of Thandi Khel, a longish saunter in the sun.

In recent decades some sorceress must have muttered secret *mantrams* over Thandi Khel and successfully transformed the troops that constantly paraded there in Rana-days into the likenesses of guinea-fowl. Battalions of these sombre birds in feathery back-combed uniforms of speckled grey now strut the long day through to the commands of boys with sticks. They wheel, advance, retire, move to the right in column of route or form a British square, and they keep their serried ranks with such precision that it is quite a joy to watch. Their only disconcerting trick is that every now and then each private soldier-bird will feel impelled to jump—a foot and more, a vertical up-down. I stood there watching fascinated, wishing that the sorceress would suddenly transform them back to troops in scarlet uniforms plus shakos for the rank and file, and for officers cocked hats, gold lace and feathers. Ten minutes would suffice me; moreover she could transform me into Sylvain Lévi (another favourite source), set me on his pony for the evening's canter, and it is 1898 again, as with the roar of a cyclone coming up behind me '...a hundred chargers at full gallop in a cloud of dust describe the arc of a circle', driving off unhappy passers-by with violent blows and shouts—though actually not passers-by at all; they are citizens with boons to crave (for this would be the time and place for it), and they haven't got a hope of being heard. A carriage framed in horse-guards is now thundering up, and behind it yet another human wave. It is the Commander-in-Chief, and he's not going to stop for boon-cravers, but he is going to stop for his friend Sylvain Lévi—and it is Deb Shum Shere—or could it be Mussoorie?—'short, broad, quick, intelligent, charming, friendly....' In the guise of Sylvain Lévi I offer him my evening's greetings, Deb Shum Shere (or Mussoorie) does the same, inviting me 'to caracole beside his carriage'.

My feet are on the ground again and, a little chastened by the failures of my morning, I turn towards the Tourist Office.

'I've just come from Dharahara, Director-sahib. It looks ominously closed. Your handout says what a wonderful view of the Valley you get from the top of it. Perhaps it's open, after all, despite the chains and padlocks.'

'You wish to climb it?'

'Yes, I do, rather.'

'Would it not be very tiring?'

'Well yes, I suppose so. A hundred and sixty-five feet. Worth every step, though.'

'It is closed, I fear. Anyway what would you see from there that you couldn't see otherwise?'

'Oh, just the view.... You couldn't, could you...? Special permission, or something?'

'Alas, impossible. It isn't safe, you see.'

I set off for the milk-and-cheese shop, only to be waylaid by a beggar-imp. I have not yet mentioned these beggar-imps. They must be chosen from among the highest I.Q.'s of the little children of the poor and taught this conversation:

'Gimme!'

'I won't!'

'You must'—the English perfect, but mumbly as when the mouth is full.

'I will not!'

'You will! Gimme now!'

'I shan't! Now go!'

Derisively: 'Go! Go!'

The imp extrudes a great bubble-gum bubble from his mouth, as a camel its oesophagus, though smaller and less messy. He can talk more freely now. He says: 'Frenchman say *"fous-moi le camp!"* German say ...'

'Go, go!'

'HUNGRY! *Paisa, paisa!* Baksheesh!'

'Hungry? *You?* No, no, you very fat. Look!'—I point.

'*Not* very very fat!' the imp shrieks.

'You are very very fat. I can see you're full of food.'

'Give!'

'I shall call the police ...'

'Call them! *Police, police!*'

'Leave me alone.'

'No. I hungry. You, who eat at the Soaltee ...'—Kathmandu's only five-star hotel at the time of my visit—starred by the Tourismo

—and I certainly do not eat there: I can scarcely be said to eat at all in Kathmandu—except Yak's-milk cheese and bread, locked in my hotel-bedroom. 'I certainly do not eat at the Soaltee,' I say to the child, hotly: 'Nor at the Annapurna'—another smart hotel.

'Yes, yes, the Annapurna, *and* the Crystal *and* the Panorama'—a list in descending order of cost—'—*and* the Indra!'—which was probably the nicest, cheap or expensive. 'I don't eat nothing,' screams the imp still louder—he is busy catching eyes at present, inviting passers-by to watch my humiliation—oh these imps! So sleek and cared-for, bright, intelligent, oh monsters!

'I don't eat nothing,' he screams at me again. 'I sleep in Monkey-temple!'

'Then go sleep in it this instant!'

'It is my dinner-time—not bed-time.'—

And I fly into the milk-and-cheese shop and am not followed. Having bought my bit of cheese and butter (bread further down the road) I make a carefree face and peer out left and right. Has my tormentor gone? Oh no, of course he hasn't gone, he's waiting to waylay me and take my cheese from me—or if not this one then some other imp, they share out the foreign visitors between them, always lurking at this Joodha Road intersection, torturing us and laughing us to scorn. The same—or is it some other imp, this time? Identicals.

'Gimme that cheese!'—oh will it never end? But I hang on to my cheese and make a dash for it, because it does seem as if the rule must be that if only you can get across the intersection to where Joodha Road actually begins, beyond it you will be considered to have escaped from Tom Tiddler's Ground and to be 'home'.

I was 'home' with my bit of Yak-cheese, its smell so suspect, its taste so stinkily delicious. The hotel-manager gave me a telephone message—from Mussoorie: 'I'll be round for you tomorrow evening at about seven. I'm going to take you to visit friends and relatives—relatives who are friends, I mean.'

15

In tracing out the thin red line of family-history, at first so faint, yet just discernible behind the Regiment of Women, I need a few more names, and here and there a date. Two names we have had already: good Queen Lalit, born a Thapa, though now Sah by marriage to the king: and her co-regent Bhim Sen, also of the Thapa clan, this clan-name being important. Another personage I want is Bhim Sen's nephew, Matabar Singh Thapa. The fourth is not a personage at all; he is someone altogether unimportant, though of family and clan acceptable enough: Bulner Singh Konwar. It is he who figures in what I called just now the 'accident of history' that quite fortuitously was to open up the way for Jung Bahadur later. I need one more clan-name also. Pande. The Thapas and the Pandes are the two great factions in bloody rivalry for power. A third power, always in the background, is the Brahmins, the Hindu priestly-class.

My first date in 1806. The mad and dangerously violent king who had been deposed and exiled to Benares some years earlier was meanwhile back in triumph in Nepal. His senior queen (this same good Queen Lalit) alas was childless; so before going into exile the king had named a little bastard son as his successor to the throne, legitimising him by the expedient of adoption.

It was the little boy's mother who had innocently brought about the ex-king's downfall. She was his favourite concubine, and nothing wrong in that; the king had abducted and seduced her in the first place, and no one found that strange or reprehensible. But the girl was Brahmin. Brahmin girls are sacred to their Brahmin menfolk. The king in fact had committed unheard-of sacrilege.[1] In 1799 the poor girl killed herself because she had fallen sick of the smallpox and her beauty was destroyed. She feared that she would lose the king's attentions.

The king's reaction to her death was an insane and murderous rage against the Brahmins and certain of the goddesses. The Brahmins had been richly paid to organise the necessary *pujas* for him which would bring the goddesses to spare the poor girl's life. The goddesses had done nothing of the sort, so he stormed the devi-temples, in person struck down the idols or took them out and lined them up to face the firing-squad of his artillery. He dared not kill the Brahmins ('kings', Brahmins, Cows and women 'we may not kill'). So he seized their lands instead, and that was his undoing. The Brahmins rose against him. Deposition. Exile.

But he was back again and more murderous than ever, with his first objective the methodical mass-massacre of an entire generation of the leading Pande family, because it had been his Pande prime minister who exiled him, pushed to it by the Brahmins. So the prime minister was the first victim that the ex-king watched his soldiers hack to death. This done he appointed himself regent for the small boy-king and entered joyfully upon a reign of terror. No man's life was safe from him—except a Brahmin's—and in place of Brahmin lives he once more seized the property they had recovered in his absence. They rose against him for the second time, and they were out to kill.

However, just as none may kill a Brahmin, so Brahmins by their own rules are prohibited from taking life (not even an egg's, as we know from current practice in the kitchens at Soon Saan). So they put the ex-king's younger brother up to killing him for them, with the promise of the throne the moment it was vacant: and here we are in 1806, this younger brother whips a dagger out and stabs the ex-king to death before the startled eyes of all the court assembled in Nautallé Durbar. Thereupon 'a young man of twenty-two' (his age has been recorded) leaps forward and with a great lateral sword-swipe cuts the assassin practically in half.

In gratitude to this obscure young man Queen Lalit, suddenly a widow (and in her heart so glad of it, this fine and loyal woman) showers him with little honours, gives him preferment and the command of some unimportant northern garrison, plus a hereditary title, Kazi, for having so expertly avenged her husband's death. Childless Queen Lalit with Bhim Sen Thapa as her prime minister now assumes the co-regency for the Brahmin girl's small orphan.

Except for this high-spot in Bulner's life, his avenging of the king by the simple chance that it was he and not some other man who had been near enough to do it, we may wonder if any more would ever have been heard of him, had not both the queen and Bhim Sen apparently grown fond of him meanwhile. For in due course Bhim Sen was offering his own niece to Bulner Singh for second wife. The little else we know about him personally would barely cover half a page of print, no more than scraps of homely reminiscence passed on by his son. How, for example, he would take an early-morning purifying dip in the holy Baghmati river that then lapped the city-walls of Kathmandu (no walls to lap today); and this he did 'whatever the weather', then back home for a breakfast of 'tea spiced with nutmeg'. We also know that the great Bhim Sen and his nephew Matabar concerned themselves with the choosing of baby's name when Bhim Sen's niece (Matabar's sister) was delivered of a son to Bulner Singh on 18 June 1817. No fanfares, I imagine: just private family rejoicings. Bulner Singh had made his choice of name, but his grand relatives by marriage overruled him. The baby would be called Jung Bahadur, 'the brave in war'.

Such little bits as these we know from Padma Jung's biography of Jung Bahadur, his father. And this—that Dowager Queen Lalit graciously attended the infant's ear-piercing ceremony and presented him with his first little 'richly-studded' earrings. It was in fact Queen Lalit and Bhim Sen, prime minister (and later Matabar, prime minister in his turn) who would open up the way for Jung Bahadur when he should grow to manhood. These were to be his friends at court, his sponsors.

The next date that I need is an exact one. 1 April 1832. The British Resident recorded it. Good Queen Lalit died that day; the admirable Thapa partnership of nearing thirty years at last was over. Her death was bound to weaken Bhim Sen's hold but it did not show at first. The king was still to be a minor for some time to come; Bhim Sen could continue as regent and prime minister. The army was still solidly behind him and his enemies all knew it. They also knew that throughout the country every post of any significance at all was held down by one or other of Bhim Sen's trusted relatives. It would take time to undermine his fortified position. In 1835, however, the king would come of age and would assume full ruling powers. What was to happen then?

It is time to name this king, because he is to play a central role when main-line family-history really started. He is Rajendra Bir Vikram Sah, fifth in dynastic line, grandson of the Brahmin girl the pox was instrumental in destroying, son of her mild and ineffectual son whom the pox destroyed as well, while he was still a youth. Though ineffectual Rajendra might be too, there was nothing mild about him: it was not his father's gentle habits he had adopted but his assassinated grandfather's mad cruelty and violence. And alas for King Rajendra, he was in addition mean, pusillanimous and weak. A coward. He was free by 1832 of Queen Lalit's firm restraining hand, and by 1835 (in theory at least) was free of Bhim Sen Thapa, but the Regiment of Women was by no means over. A teenage girl had been waiting in the wings for Lalit's death.

If Rajendra would have been perhaps eighteen the year that happened, this little monster, his senior-wife (already mother of his heir-apparent and of a second boy as well) was probably fourteen. And that would be a little young as yet for a really active part in power-politics. But she was a ready learner, and violently partisan, pro-Pande, anti-Thapa, rather in the manner I suppose of some teenage football-fan, though the game was life and death, not football. By 1835 she had acquired complete ascendancy over timorous Rajendra. Her heart's desire, in fact, was to have the wretch deposed (or otherwise disposed of), then see her elder boy put on the throne as king and herself appointed regent for him. And heigh-ho! for a long and profitable minority on the well-tried pattern. If this girl could get her way the Thapa clan was for it. Bhim Sen, while still in power, was hurriedly, sedulously grooming Matabar for succession to the ministry. Bhim was an old man now; but Matabar showed the highest promise. With luck the Thapas could hold on.

But by 1837 the girl had done what she'd set out to do—the first step, anyhow. Bhim Sen was out. They got him on a trumped-up charge, though he contrived to save his life. But he was down for good in 1839 when the same trumped-up charge[2] was brought against him. This time it was dishonour, torture, jail. The old man was driven to suicide with his own *kukri* by the gleeful tales his jailors told him of his womenfolk's public degradation in the streets of Kathmandu. His dismembered corpse was shown around and then denied the Hindu funeral rites. They threw the bits out beside the river for the vultures and the jackals to feast upon.

With Bhim Sen dead and eaten; with Matabar prudently gone

off to 'voluntary exile' down in India; with Jung Bahadur 'lying low', the family, for all we hear of it, might be under deep sedation. Till 1843.

In 1839 the Pande clan was in. The senior-queen, now paramount, could bleed the country white, demanding that the king should order crippling retrenchment in all fields of public expenditure, as much designed to bring him into public odium as to raise the enormous extra sums she needed for her enormously increased requirements. Behind it all was something else as well: the furtherance of a plan that she and her favourite Pande, prime minister by now, had hatched together. They would push the king to proclaim a cruel cut in army pay-rates: the army was already in a sullen mood, stomachs empty, no means of filling them these days, with war denied them. The king's announcement would certainly provoke a mutiny, the army would depose him—and who would then come forward as the army's champions, restore the cuts and right their other wrongs? The senior-queen and her favourite Pande, their saviours! To round it nicely off her elder son would be installed as king, and she and her Pande would become co-regents for the child. The year was 1841.

The first bit happened just as the two had planned it; the king announced the army pay-cuts, the army mutinied. But the rounding-off went wrong. The king was visited for once with skill enough to outwit the scheming pair. Or do I sense another hand, a little one, at work behind the scenes, guiding Rajendra into doing what would save him? In any case he did it. He himself immediately withdrew the cuts, redressed the army's other wrongs (or promised to), so it was the king they were acclaiming with a single voice, instead of the two schemers. But his troubles were not over yet, and never would be.

Already for some time the air in India had been filling up with tales of British difficulties and defeats, in fact with predictions of the Company's imminent collapse. The Gurkha army, so long starved of war (and here we see emerge again a familiar motif of earlier Sah history—war, as an economic necessity), urged the king to take advantage of so happy a situation, and the king said yes, of course, but pleaded with them for patience: he had the men, he told them, but where could he find the money? 'War supports itself,' they answered. It was obvious. Let him only give the word and they would kill the British Resident 'who sees and forestalls all' (at that period he did, too: it was Brian Houghton Hodgson at the Residency) and they would be down invading India, looting rich cities, Lucknow, Benares, and they would make the river Ganges the king's new southern frontier!

The Gurkhas got their war. A miniature invasion of a British-Indian district bordering the Terai. But the rumours had misled them; the Company was not at all collapsing. Troops were sent against the Gurkhas, who withdrew behind their frontiers, and the British Governor-General was sternly warning King Rajendra that the only way real war could be averted was by dismissal of the sabre-rattling Pande ministry.

King Rajendra meekly did as he was told—the Pande clan was out.

While all this was going on in public, someone not really introduced as yet was up to things in private. If the senior-queen was in her fifteenth year in 1832 when Queen Lalit died, the junior-queen would then have been no more than twelve or so, and this really would exclude her from power-politics for several years to come—except for teenage allegiance to whichever team it was, the Thapas or the Pandes. This little junior queen was solidly pro-Thapa, though we don't know this at first; in fact all we seem to know about her is that she had borne the king two sons by the end of the 1830's and that she had begged the British Resident to protect these little boys from the senior-queen's intention to have them killed. She sounds so helpless, poor little threatened mother. Helpless? We shall soon see. By 1841 she was going into action.

The senior-queen died suddenly that year. She was on a journey down to India. Those who preferred to think the best of everybody said that as she crossed the swampy strip of the Terai the dreaded *ayul* got her. Others, depending on the colour of their palace-politics, said that the king or else the junior-queen had had her poisoned.[3] In any case the senior-queen was dead. And now, stepping over her dead rival's body, as we might say, the fiend of fiends can make her first formal entrance. The junior-queen. Her senior had rated no given-name in history; she was simply Rajendra's 'senior-queen'. But this one rates a name. It is Queen Lakshmi Devi, and her heart's desire is to repeat what seems to her the glorious pattern of Sah history, exactly as her dead rival had just failed to do: she would have the king deposed (or otherwise disposed of), kill off the heir-apparent and his younger brother, install her own elder boy as king, and then she would be regent for him during a minority even longer than her rival had been hoping for.

Events dropped nicely into place for her. The heir-apparent whose death she had in mind was growing up: he must have turned thirteen in 1841, quite big enough to have his little whims indulged for him—torture, mass-executions, and preferably of the innocent. Everyone who ever wrote of Jung Bahadur has told of the murderous treatment he received at the heir-apparent's hands when assigned to him as a sort of aide-de-camp before his own rise to power. It is time to name this prince: Surendra Bir Vikram Sah.

Unfortunately the British Residents in Kathmandu, even when recording events they personally witnessed, would seldom abandon the stiff officialese of their despatches, and so seldom if ever convey to us exactly what sort of madmen they must somehow deal with in the Kathmandu of the early 1840's. For this reason I record a scene relating to the period of court mourning for the senior-queen in 1841 as described by one Captain Thomas Smith, Assistant to the Resident in 1841–5—an eye-witness account. Note that riding on horseback or in a carriage or a palanquin was forbidden during periods of court mourning; remember also that royalty does not go outdoors on foot and that Maharaja Chandra Shum Shere (who died only in 1928) would mount his courtiers pick-a-back should he wish to go upstairs or down. Remember also that Gurkhas, even very old ones, are renowned for their weight-carrying capabilities.

The background to the scene Smith witnessed was as follows. The king and the thirteen-year-old heir-apparent had evidently had a raging quarrel earlier that morning, and in consequence of it the heir-apparent had obliged his frightened father to come down with him to the Residency to issue an ultimatum to the British. It had been raining heavily.

'... about twelve o'clock we were informed that the Raja and the Heir-Apparent were outside the residency gates. We went out to meet them and there found the Raja and his son mounted on the backs of two very decrepit old Chiefs. The Heir-Apparent requested the Raja to give us the order to pack up and take our departure for the plains. The Raja refused, whereupon the Heir-Apparent abused him most grossly, and urging his old Chief to close up to the Raja assaulted him. A fight ensued, and after scratching and pulling each other's hair for some time, the son got hold of the father, pulled him over and down they went, Chiefs and all, into a very dirty puddle. The two old "nags" extricating themselves, hobbled away as fast as they could, as did the other followers, from fear. After rolling in the muddy water, up got the two dirty kings, and after some little delay fresh 'nags' were obtained and the Raja and his son were taken home.'

From almost every point of view neither Captain Smith nor his book can be taken as authoritative (as later writers about Nepal have pointed out), but this ridiculous, unimportant yet revealing incident has the smell of accurate reporting. It is almost the only thing I find that gives us some idea of these two lunatics seen in the flesh and blood and action.

With such a king and heir-apparent as these, things reached a point in December 1842 where the chiefs of every faction were driven to unite for the first time in Sah history in order to demand that the lives and property, the basic rights and liberties, of every subject of the crown should have some guarantee. They instanced all their sufferings at the hands of the heir-apparent, they instanced the excessive influence at court of the Sah-family faction, with both the Thapas and the Pandes out of office; and finally the chiefs announced their strange desire—that the king's junior-queen, his sole official queen now, should be invested with full powers as regent, though without the actual deposition of the king or of his heir-apparent. They clearly had no means of knowing what sort of woman they were sponsoring. Good queens-regent were so firmly part of the nostalgic myth—'the Good Old Days'—that their eyes were blinded. A sort of Petition of Rights was drafted, signed and sealed, and in January 1843 the king formally invested his queen with full political powers, promising to include her in all his counsels and 'to act in accordance with her advice'. The queen sat back triumphant. She would soon be calling Matabar Singh Thapa home from 'voluntary exile', and the two of them would get to work upon her heart's desire.

By April 1843 Matabar Singh Thapa was satisfied at last that he could count on the queen's promises of patronage and so could safely come back home again. Young Jung Bahadur was delighted too. In fact he had gone down to India ahead of time so as to escort his uncle up to Kathmandu when the astrologers should name the auspicious day. They named it: triumphal entry, welcoming addresses.

As soon as the rejoicings were all over Matabar had a pious duty to perform: the avenging of his uncle Bhim Sen's tragic end. The queen made all this very easy for him: the Pandes who had been responsible were arrested, charged (with perjuring themselves at Bhim Sen's trial), convicted, then taken to the place of execution just outside the city walls, a small natural amphitheatre from the steep horse-shoe curve of which the citizens could sit and watch. There they were put to death—the second Pande massacre in less than forty years. Yet Matabar had shown his clemency: he had acceded to their last request, that they be beheaded with their own good sharpened *kukris*.

The king was far from pleased with what was going on. He dared not openly oppose the queen's intention to give the ministry to Matabar, but he could, and did, hold the appointment up for months to come by somehow not being in the mood to put his seal to anything. But by December of that year he had finally succumbed to *force majeure*. He gave in to the queen and Matabar was in, prime-minister and commander-in-chief.

I get the impression of a disagreeable man. Ill-tempered, arrogant in bearing, even towards the royal family. Later, in different circumstances, the British Resident was to describe him as 'impetuous ... incautious ... yet for all his faults the best man in Nepal'. Matabar quickly made himself unpopular with the chiefs but was most careful to secure the goodwill of the army that his uncle Bhim Sen had enjoyed in such full measure.

Though Matabar was in, it was a triumvirate he found he had to serve: king, queen and heir-apparent, all three with differing objectives. They made his life intolerable and it was not long before he wanted to resign and go back to the quiet and peace of India. He was persuaded to stay on till someone suitable was found who could replace him. Who indeed could do so, or would risk it?

In October 1844 Matabar still held the ministry, 'officiating' as it was said: Matabar himself was saying it was 'to keep the soldiery quiet'. We do not know what his real intentions were.

This much was clear, at all events: Matabar had been gravely imprudent in having meanwhile pushed his nephew forward so fast and far. By now Colonel Jung was an active 'member of council', and Matabar in private conversation with the British Resident was expressing real concern at Jung's 'increasing influence at court and with the army'. In the hearing of the Assistant Resident (the Captain Smith already mentioned) Matabar spoke openly about how quickly he had scaled the ladder to the topmost rung, adding that 'he would regard himself as highly favoured if he were allowed to come down again in his own time'. He knew quite well, and spoke of it, that not one of his predecessors in the ministry since the days of Prithvi Narayan Sah, first Gurkha king, had managed to escape assassination.

Jung was indeed making swift progress, both in influence and self-confidence. He now dared stand up to his intimidating uncle. Padma Jung gives us a good example of this. It is strangely prophetic—if not in fact untrue, as I suspect (though the first part is all true enough). The queen had taken a new lover, the jumped-up palace menial called Gagan Singh, now of course a general. At the queen's instance this Gagan Singh had recently procured the death (we do not know what for) of one of Matabar's several nephews, cousin to Jung Bahadur; and Jung was remonstrating hotly with his uncle for having let this happen. Thereupon Matabar Singh, 'crimson with rage', rounded on the 'insolent stripling' (Padma's phrase) and shouted out in fury that if the queen should require him to kill his own nephew Jung '—or vice versa', it would be an order that 'neither of them could refuse to carry out'. And when, soon after, Matabar transferred Jung Bahadur to the heir-apparent's staff it was really so as to get him safely out of the way. With luck, even, Jung might fall victim to the mad boy's rages. So many did. This must have crossed Matabar's mind.

Jung seen as Matabar's potential rival would be one thing: Matabar had been incautious and he knew it; but he had been far more dangerously incautious in his handling of the queen. Faced by this awful trio, king, queen and heir-apparent, Matabar had finally decided to support the heir-apparent against the other two: he reasoned that the heir-apparent's violence was easier to control than the hopeless vacillations of the king. As for the queen, by now he had not the least intention of carrying out the promises by which he'd gained the ministry. And she had sensed this; his delaying tactics had proclaimed as much. She was now implacably his enemy. We must suppose that Matabar knew it, though his arrogance and self-importance may have blurred his recognition of the danger he was in. The queen's new lover, Gagan Singh, quite clearly coveted Matabar's power and position, and doubtless counted on the queen, his mistress, to give the ministry to him instead—as soon as it was vacant. On top of this he hated Matabar for the contempt the latter showed him for his lowly origins. This sort of thing is not lightly overlooked when a lucky chance presents itself. By early summer 1845 Matabar Singh Thapa was for the high jump.

On the night of 17 May 1845 he was summoned to attend the queen in her upstairs apartments at the palace. She had been taken sick with a dangerous colic. Though Jung Bahadur and Gagan Singh were with her there, they were both hidden behind a bit of trellising that screened the room's verandah. Jung had a rifle; Gagan 'stood over him' with another. Did Padma, who tells us this, mean to suggest that Gagan was present to see that Jung would carry out the queen's command to kill his uncle?

Matabar came in alone. As he approached the queen with his obeisances Jung fired—twice: once to the head, once to the chest. Gagan may have fired as well.

Matabar staggered forward crying out for mercy—not for himself but 'for his mother and his children'. He was struck down from behind. He fell, his hands outstretched in supplication: an attendant with a sword cut him across the wrists and nearly severed hands from arms. Padma completes the ugly story. As soon as the craven king was told it was all over, he 'crawled out of bed' in some adjoining room and hurried in to see the body. Seeing it, he kicked it in the face. Later he claimed to have killed the man himself—'I put the said traitor Thapa to death with my own hands with gun and sword!' but nobody believed him.

When the Resident heard rumours of Jung's complicity in this assassination he had this to say: 'Poor as is my opinion of Jung's moral character, I do believe him guiltless of this murder.' But he was wrong.

They tied an elephant-rope around the corpse and let it down from a window into the street below. Long before daylight a party of soldiers had taken it to Pashupatinath for the cremation, so Matabar at least was granted the proper funeral rites that Bhim Sen had been denied some six years earlier.

They say a trail of Matabar's blood led from the palace to holy Pashupatinath, all the two-mile length of *Ganga Path*.

16

Out from the city through a long thin drab bazaar called Dil, and padding rather irritably along the dusty verges of the road to Pashupatinath. I had not foreseen long drab bazaars, nor yet being driven off the highway out beyond them by country-buses and the dust-clouds billowing in their slipstream. I had had rolling pasture-land and wandering quietly down the length of *Ganga Path* in mind, a foot-worn, hoof-worn bloodied track it must have been that bright May morning I was thinking of. I liked to think the year could still be 1845. Rajendra's reign. Rajendra, Lakshmi Devi, and Surendra—what a bunch! The Sah-dynasty to date—what ill-starred men, their first two kings untimely dead; the third one mad, driven to abdication, assassinated; the fourth one taken by the pox before he came of age. And now the fifth, Rajendra—mad: his eldest son Surendra madder, more violent and awful still. And I stopped to wonder whether history has been right to call the mad Sahs 'mad'.

Is it mad, or just revengeful, to shoot down goddesses who fail you? Was it mad, or simply wise and self-preserving, to assassinate a complete generation of the Pande clan? Was it mad to take it out of incompetent physicians (as Rajendra did) because they failed to save his infant son from death by poison he himself administered? Was it mad to have administered it in the first place, we may ask. No, there was a perfectly logical reason for administering it, and it was perfectly proper that incompetent physicians should die, though actually the senior of the two physicians here concerned was Brahmin, so his life was necessarily spared and he could escape with no more than being 'burnt on the forehead and cheeks till his brain and jaw were exposed'. The junior physician, being Newar with no god-given protection against the death-penalty, was impaled in King Rajendra's presence and 'his heart extracted while he still lived'. Finally must Prince Surendra be accounted mad because, for example, he had sixteen soldiers cut to pieces by drummer-boy 'untouchables'* and could blame it on Matabar (this was one of the offences the king charged Matabar with in writing to the Governor-General to explain why he had put the man to death). Dr Oldfield had no doubt about Surendra's 'madness' which (as he said) 'the extravagance of his conduct could easily be made to bear out'.

But what is 'mad'? In questioning a psychiatrist friend about all this and trying to describe to him the 'madness' of these kings in terms of what we know they did and evidently relished, he questioned me in turn. Was there, for example, any evidence that they were capable of forming deep, enduring relationships? None, that I had ever read of: rather the reverse. Then what would be the background to their infancy and growing-up? I told him the little that I felt can safely be deduced from what we know: rough luxury; a palace-atmosphere compounded of intrigue, suspicion, poisonings, violence, sudden death. A royal father unpredictable and uncontrolled. The rani-mothers (senior and junior) each at the other's throat when not in turns working on the husband both detested with their bullying and threats. Palace-life—wrote Padma Jung of the early 1840's—'was a sink of iniquity', with 'every form of wickedness from a stolen kiss to the foulest murder . . .' and 'all, from the queen down to the humblest maid, engaged in love-intrigues'. The palace-girls numbered nearly a thousand at this period, half of them on duty for a fortnight, it appears, the other half taking over at the end of it. These girls were

'not only powerful engines of immorality but powerful engines of political preferment. Any girl influential with the rani was sometimes courted and caressed by as many as ten or twelve—'
—here Padma slightly loses his head—'—or twenty suitors, all candidates for promotion.'

What Padma tells us is not just hearsay. He certainly had it from his father Jung Bahadur, who had had first-hand experience of it himself.

Even as long before as 1802, when Dr Hamilton visited

* Only 'untouchables' could be drummer-boys—the drum-heads being leather, and leather itself 'untouchable'.

Kathmandu, he noted that 'ketis—all prostitutes' formed a mounted escort for the outings of the little king. They rode astride, of course, were well dressed, armed with swords. No restraints, he says, were put upon their intrigues (he can only mean sexual). Surely not 'prostitutes', however! These were not public girls, but 'palace-girls'—perhaps the toughest of the 'dozens and dozens, hundreds, scampering about the palace' that Jagut had referred to in speaking of his father's palace in the last days of the nineteenth century.

In the politico-sexual hurly-burly of the palace in the mid-nineteenth century and earlier, I hardly think a rani can have had much time or inclination to feed her infant, fondle it and play with it, 'change it', chatter nonsense to it as good mothers do, nor give it lasting love and let it rest safe in the certainty that she would always be at hand. Would there have been instead some loving nurse to act as mother, as the one unchanged, unchanging mother-figure through the years to puberty that a child so absolutely needs? If so, we would expect a different outcome. But as it is it seems to me that the royal tots were much more like foundlings in some richly-endowed orphanage where they are given everything their hearts could need or crave for, except emotional security and love. I think I see them squatting on their little rumps (as I have seen some in an institution of today), brooding, rock-rock-rocking, their big blank eyes turned inwards, loveless, unloving, lost in their lonely rock-rock masturbatory escape—the up-and-coming raw material of delinquency.

On reconsideration, therefore, I suspect that these kings were sacrosanct delinquents. They knew exactly what they were doing and exactly why. Deprived of love as infants, they grew up incapable of loving, incapable of forming any sort of human relationship other than one based in hatred and aggression. The term for them today is 'psychopath', and as things stand at present it seems that psychiatry cannot reach them, nothing can be done for them. They are not 'mad', however, as they would have been considered in Dr Oldfield's day.

A mile or so of highway yet to come, country-buses, dusty verges, and then the ground had dropped away, down on the right a sloping pathway to the temple of Pashupati, who is Shiva, 'Lord of all Living Creatures'. Trees begin here, a grove of them, not just enough of them to line a highway. The exuberance and green of trees is regularly found on hallowed ground—possibly because no one dares come plundering for firewood.

The temple precincts (non-Hindus excluded) were visible through the trees a minute later, grouped round the gleaming two-tier pagoda of Pashupati's temple. His great brass *nandi*—Shiva's 'vehicle', the bull—would be sitting placidly on folded legs in front of it and looking in.

I wonder if this *nandi* was amongst the others that the stricken population of the Valley lugged out to combat Sitala, goddess of small-pox, back in 1816. It was not only young King Girvan that she gave the pox to: she handed it out wholesale and there were countless deaths. Hindus classify small-pox as a skin-disease (or used to) and those who die of skin-diseases are denied the funeral rites: so the corpses of Sitala-devi's victims that year were not burnt, but buried—near the Baghmati river—with the result that—

'the effluvia from the dead bodies spread abroad, the water was poisoned and vultures and wild beasts that fed on the corpses died in numbers. All the *nandis* having been brought out, a plentiful rain fell and washed away the corpses...'

—the Parbatiya history says so, and presumably Sitala-devi left disgruntled. The *nandi* down at Pashupatinath is the most venerable in all Nepal, so they must have lugged him out.

I was very keen to see him. From here he was hidden by the buildings that surround the temple. Perhaps from across the river I'd get a sight of him, from higher ground.

A small Tibetan boy attached himself to me, a quiet-mannered ten-year-old with surprisingly good basic English. Doubtless the child of refugees who had fled before the Chinese invasion of Tibet. I let him lead me down towards a bridge—if it were not he, it would be another little guide. There's no escape. We stood together for a moment on the wide stone bridge. This would be the nearest I could hope to get to the people performing their ablutions down in the flower-strewn river. The steps that run the length of the stone burning-*ghat* continue well below the water-level, so pilgrims can regulate the depth to suit themselves. A thigh-deep woman at her rituals stood just below us, dipping, ducking, her sodden clothing clinging tightly to her body, outlining breasts and buttocks. A small procession had appeared from round a corner, with a body on a litter. An old man. His head, already skull-like, remained uncovered, and his shroud did little to conceal the outline of a terribly

emaciated body wrapped inside it. They were chanting as they set
the litter down. Beyond them people were attending to a funeral-
pyre. I wondered if this man had been patiently awaiting death in
the hospice I had heard about. I asked the small Tibetan to point
the building out to me. He did so. It stands right above the *ghat*
at water-level, a two-storeyed simple building, nineteenth century.
Two curved stone jetties stick out into the river. These, I imagined,
would be the private burning-*ghats*, one for the Sahs, the other
for the Ranas, and the boy confirmed it. So that was where they
must have cremated Jung Bahadur, first of the line called Rana.
Matabar's bloodied body would have been cremated on the quay
itself—not being 'Rana', and the Rana-*ghat* not built yet. But when
the Ranas fell in 1950 public animosity at once directed itself
against the little Rana-*ghat* with cries of 'privilege, privilege!' demanding that thenceforth no Rana should be cremated on it.

Quite a crowd of men and women had arrived meanwhile and
was stepping down into the river, scooping up mouthfuls of the
holy water, swilling out their mouths with it. The Tibetan child
beckoned me to follow him, up between the left-bank shrines, up
steps that peter out where the grove begins again, up through
trees. ('Give me your hand. Don't slip! Here! Take my hand.')

Supported by this charming child I clambered up the carpeting
of slippery and gnarled old roots and listened while he told me
that his father earns his livelihood by toting in the firewood for the
funeral-pyres, but that his mother cannot work because—he mimed
'leg-off' yet limped it two-legged lame. Yes, he went to school:
sixth class. Then he set about explaining the Shivaite world to me,
the lingam and the *yoni*, and *nandi*, Shiva's bull (even from here
alas invisible)—and the Tantric mysteries of the *yantra*.

'Shall I now take you to Guheshwari temple—you like? To see
where the holy *yantra* fell.'

'But will they let me in?'

'They will not let you in.'

'Some other day, perhaps.'

I had read about the temple of Guheshwari—how it is projected
in the form of the mystic triangle that signifies the female organ of
procreation—the *yantra*. I can add this too: that Shiva, in his
Nataraja avatar, 'Lord of the Dance', was dancing through the
heavens with his consort Parvati upon his shoulders (not Durga
this time), when Lord Vishnu appeared, feeling spiteful. Vishnu
threw his discus at them. It struck Parvati and she instantly fell

apart in five pieces, of which her 'secret part' came to the ground where Guheshwari now stands.

We stood there looking down between the boles of trees at the holy river-scene below, pilgrims, flower-heads red and orange floating quietly with the gentle current, the waters olive-green. Just upstream of Pashupatinath, Baghmati river slithers through a narrow cleft all garlanded with tumbling foliage.

We clambered down again ('Don't slip! Don't slip!') and reached the left-bank *ghat* and lingered, simply watching. The emaciated corpse was on its pyre now; they were igniting it. It took at once—no doubt the logs and kindling had been heavily anointed with holy *ghee*. The flames roared upwards and a heat-haze shimmered violently above. What a splendid way to go, with the conches blowing! I had a vivid sense of taking part—and to think that all this beautiful serenity, this lovely life we shouldn't cling to, is at the mercy of an incestuous fiend they buried here at Pashupatinath. 'And Birupaksha?' I asked the child. 'Can you show me where they buried him?'

He nodded. He knew. Good. The child knew everything.

'There,' he said, pointing across the river.

'You mean the little shrine—to left of the temple steps?'

'Yes, yes. Birupaksha, he who made wife of his mother—in the darkness, not knowing.'

I stared across the narrow river, trying to pierce the dark inside the doorless opening to the shrine but I could make nothing out. Thinking of darkness reminded me that I had heard nothing before about the 'darkness' that prevented the Incestuous Fiend from recognising that it was his mother. I had had the clear impression that he knew what he was doing, and that that was why they punished him with burial alive in the vertical position. Presumably he has been repenting ever since and this explains why he is permitted to rise up from the earth again, though very slowly. Those who are allowed close enough to see report that already the tip of his incestuous member is visible above the earth, and this means that he is about half-way to his release. I wonder if he knows, as everyone around here knows only too well, that when he rises high enough to free his feet, the moment he steps clear of his earthy tomb, the world is to burst like an atomic bomb, destroying him and the rest of us along with him.

Back across the bridge the child stood watching as I fumbled in my pocket, then said 'thank you' without looking at what I gave him. We were under the projection of a small pagoda-shrine. I had paid him off, but he kindly offered me a bonus. 'Look!' he said, pointing upwards at the base of a carved and painted strut, a roof-support. 'See! Man and lady! Jiggy-jiggy!'—and there they were, this happy carved and painted couple, blithely executing the jig called *Utpidîtaka* mentioned by the Hindu sex-sage Suvarnanabha. This attitude (a commentator on the sage's text explains that we may call it the 'super-pressive' attitude) is very difficult, 'but exquisitely enjoyable to strong partners'.

Home to Hotel Green. *Ganga Path*, stifled by dust-clouds billowing in the wake of country-buses, thinking again of Matabar's bloody trail. But even on that distant early-summer morning, the scuff of peasants' feet would have covered up all trace within an hour or two.

17

Summer 1845.

The air of Kathmandu was zizzing with intrigue. It gave the Resident a busy time of it. In the ordinary rhythm of the Residency's life there was so little to be done, officially. The Resident must fill his time as best he could, with reading, hobbies, gardening, perhaps. By now the Abode of Demons was 'a well-tree'd park' that guests would comment on, comparing it with the treeless landscape we see in Dr Oldfield's water-colour sketches of a few years later. Sometimes the Resident would ride out into the open tawny countryside, and even with his lynx-eyed Gurkha escort watching him it would seem like an escape from prison for a few hours at least. Perhaps as late as 1845 the peasants were still encouraged to tease and trouble him as he rode by.

The present incumbent was Henry Lawrence—later to be Sir Henry Lawrence of the Punjab and a great administrator. For his first year and more in Kathmandu he must bear a burden even worse than boredom: his Assistant-Resident was detestable from all accounts, a rude aggressive trouble-maker. It was the Captain Smith whose description of the king and heir-apparent tearing at each other's hair and rolling in the mud I have quoted from. Yet I confess to being glad to find a 'bounder' and a 'cad' in the Residency *dramatis personae* to offset the succession of British Officers and Gentlemen whose impeccable behaviour shows up the orgies at the palace in such palatable contrast. How terrible for Lawrence to have to share his 'awful isolation' with somebody like Smith.[1]

Lawrence got the better of Captain Smith in the end, but only after endless letters to India, importunate and pleading; details of Smith's laziness and lying habits, of his rudeness, incompatibility 'in our very little circle'; his debts, his bullying of the placid Residency Surgeon of the time ('even at my own table' as Lawrence bitterly complained).

As soon as Smith's dishonourable recall to India was settled we find Lawrence packing him off hot-foot. Down to the Indian plains with him! Mid-August 1844: the dreaded *ayul* epidemic at its seasonal peak in the crossing of the Terai! But the Captain Thomas Smiths of our up-ended world survive, it seems. Lévi says Smith faced court-martial on rejoining his regiment, but I have not followed up Smith's dossier to check what the charges could have been. Conduct Unbecoming an Officer and Gentleman, perhaps. Bad-penny Smith turns up once again to write his book about 'Nepaul' and publish it in London in 1852. 'A monument of showing-off,' as Lévi was later to say of it ,'of ignorance, plagiarism and error.' With his ignominious departure from the Residency scene, peace could descend again, a leaden pall, on Henry Lawrence and his staff in the Abode of Demons. At least till Matabar Singh Thapa came to grief the following May.

May 1845.
Who was to be the next prime minister?
Now Lawrence had his work cut out: despatches filled with speculation about Nepal's immediate future. By 24 May—six days after Matabar had been assassinated—Jung Bahadur was 'at present doing that duty' and, moreover, giving his assurance to the Resident that 'the king was very anxious to confirm him in the post'. Jung added that despite the pressure he was holding off, and the Resident was passing it all down to India with the comment that 'it would be no surprise if Jung Bahadur proved to be the next victim. . . . After all'—the Resident concluded his despatch—'it is only a question of time between certain families in Nepal—so much blood has been shed during the last half-century and there is so much to avenge that sooner or later each individual must look to judicial murder or assassination as his probable fate.' Yet the Resident admitted that of all the Chiefs, Jung was decidedly the best qualified to command the army. 'He is active, intelligent, and possesses many soldierly qualities, but it is impossible that any party can trust him.'

So who indeed would be the next prime minister?
It made not the slightest difference to the king's five million

poverty-stricken subjects—the *Bhawan Lakh*, as they were called, the fifty-two lakhs (or 5,200,000) of the country's estimated population at the time. The administration of the *Bhawan Lakh* was merely a matter of ensuring that the tax-collectors did their job to the last drop of blood. Once the taxes were collected, enough must first be counted off to keep the army sweet; and the rest of all the revenue was palace spending-money, less the immense sums that stuck to powerfully sticky fingers on the way.

In 1845 the choice of minister would only be of consequence to the man bold enough to accept the job, and—as Lawrence was telling India—'there are not likely to be many aspirants for this dangerous office'.

Dangerous, yes, but not the least exacting. In a situation where almost nobody could read or write in any script or tongue, all boring paper-work and fuss was automatically avoided, and the only basically important thing was for the minister and his faction to keep always one step ahead of *coups-d'état*.

As summer slipped away and autumn came, then winter, and the new year stretched ahead, three men had been emerging as the real 'short-list' contenders for the pinnacle of power: prime minister and commander-in-chief of the army. One was a certain Abhiman Singh, a man of lowly caste, so it was said: a King's Man, with two regiments at his command. The second was of caste still lower, General Gagan Singh, the Queen's Man, her menial lover, anxious now 'like all the others, to strike up friendship with the Resident'. Gagan Singh had won himself seven regiments, by the queen's favour.

The third contender, obviously, was Jung Bahadur.

It was during Brian Hodgson's term of office at the Residency, I think, that men in power, or seeking it (though always with the palace's permission) had started visiting the Resident 'to pick up my sentiments' as Lawrence was to say of this practice in his day. The failure of the Gurkha miniature invasion of British-Indian territory a few years earlier had finally won respect, however grudging, for the power of the British Presence: it could be useful, even, to those who gained its friendly patronage. So both Jung and Gagan sought the Resident's ever-open ear.

Jung had by this time accepted three regiments and the high command that went with them—'those dangerous honours'—but still played a waiting-game both cool and careful. Lawrence was not quite so sure now about Jung's possible complicity in Matabar's assassination—'—if indeed he is altogether guiltless' was how he put it.

In general, however, Lawrence had reached a clear conclusion:

> 'Such men ... as Jung Bahadar and Gagan Singh will not hesitate to grasp all honours whatever may be the consequence. Each will say that a man has only one life and may as well die a general as a captain.'

Henry Lawrence left Nepal on transfer back to India early in the new year 1846. His successor at the Residency had been named, but the *ayul* season had already started before the new man could set off from India to take up his appointment. Smith's successor as Assistant-Resident had long since reached Nepal and, as far as I can work it out, was already due for (honourable) transfer back to India by early 1846. His name was Captain Ottley, and his going was delayed by something, and the *ayul* season effectively upset his plans. A letter dated March 1846 from Lawrence, now in India, ordered him to remain on at the Residency (though unofficially) 'till middle November next, when the Teraee [*sic*] is again open'. Good Captain Ottley, we may notice, was not to run the risk of the *ayul* that Lawrence had so readily exposed bad Captain Smith to. And this explains how Captain Ottley came to be at the Residency, quite unofficially, on the night of 14–15 September 1846 when the course of Himalayan history was abruptly changed.

18

'About ten o'clock on the night of Monday the 14th September 1846, General Gagan Singh was shot in a chamber of his house while in the performance of his devotions.*'

Captain Wazir Singh, the dead man's eldest son, at once hurried to the palace to tell the queen. This much was clear at once: the murderer had been waiting on a nearby roof, or else had jumped the narrow gap to Gagan's roof, choosing the general's known hour of prayer and picking him off through the lamp-lit window of his *puja*-room. Who could miss?

He found the queen in her apartments—where the previous summer she had superintended the murdering of Matabar Singh. His death had caused her no tears. Gagan Singh's was very different. 'The Maharani wept bitterly . . . and hastened to the General's house on foot . . .'—a queen on foot? Unheard of! Captain Wazir Singh accompanied her, together with four of her women attendants, one of them being her *Kotha Mucha*, Sword of State and Shield-bearer.

The queen broke down when she was shown her dead lover's body. Indeed she appears to have been in such distress of mind that for the moment she could not go through with the ritual she had come there to perform, but after an interval she placed the Ganges water, holy basil and gold in the mouth of the corpse as custom required. She was under control once more; it cannot have been often that this woman broke down. It humanises her a little. And next we are told that she turned to her lover's weeping

* Unless otherwise stated all quotations in Chapters 18 and 19 are from the Kathmandu Residency's secret Kōt Massacre document of the 18 March 1847.

215

widows (three of them) and forbade them to commit *sati* on their husband's funeral pyre. Possibly in the woman's liberated world of mid-nineteenth century Kathmandu a faithful Hindu widow's self-immolation was less encouraged and applauded than once it had been.

From the three widows she turned to Gagan Singh's three sons and told them to see to the details of their father's funeral rites— of which the expenses would be defrayed by the State. She must have lingered on there miserably for a while because the Residency text continues thus:

'—afterwards, with her hair dishevelled and weeping aloud she took the Sword of State from the hands of her *Kotha Mucha* ... and walked on foot to the Kōt.'

She would have been tearing at her hair in order to dishevel it; and weeping 'aloud' would mean a loud wordless threnody.

Once at the Kōt she sent for General Abhiman Singh ('whose house was nigh at hand') and ordered him to summon by bugle-call an emergency assembly of all high functionaries, civil and military. This done she climbed to the 'second storey' of the Kōt, which I take to mean the one immediately above the ground floor. She sat there waiting, saying over and over again—

'that until the man who had assassinated so faithful a Minister should be discovered and put to death, she would neither take food nor taste water.'

Determination to revenge his death was already sharpening her grief to fury.

Quite soon the silence of the city's dark and empty streets was shattered by the blare of bugles.

First to respond to them was General Jung Bahadur with his six full-brothers. The nature of this urgent call to assembly at the Kōt required that generals bring their regiments with them, under arms. I do not know what vernacular term 'regiment' here represents but the strength of such a unit in Kathmandu was then nearer four than five hundred men. No one tells us how many troops were actually inside the courtyard of the Kōt by now. General Abhiman Singh, so conveniently 'nigh at hand', had been summoned not by bugle but by a message from the queen; he may well have left his two regiments behind and come with no more than his personal bodyguard; and I think we may assume that

Jung drew up the twelve hundred-odd troops of his three regiments outside the Kōt compound and that he too was attended inside it only by his bodyguard (armed with double-barrelled muskets).

As soon as Jung arrived and learnt what had befallen Gagan Singh he climbed the stairway to the second storey where he will have bowed himself into the queen's presence.

No one else was upstairs with her that we know of, except the four female attendants—and now Jung (and possibly one member of his bodyguard). Who, then, would be the source for what I am about to quote? Not Jung, certainly; and surely not the queen. The girls must have been questioned later, but by whom, I wonder. It is Jung's reported speech to the queen before the killing started:

> 'Addressing her he said that as he and General Gagan were known to act together as her special servants, that one of them had been treacherously murdered by their enemies, and it was probable that he himself would not be spared, and that in the end her two sons would also probably suffer, that the Maharaja had invested her with full authority as to all State affairs, and it was therefore incumbent on her to enquire searchingly into this affair and punish severely those who should be found guilty, in order that her sons might not become victims in the sequel, and himself might continue to serve her zealously in future, without sacrificing his life.'

This may well have been the gist of what Jung told the queen —with the double underlining of the danger to her sons that he seems to claim was inherent in the situation. But he was lying. First of all if anybody's sons were now in danger it was the dead senior-rani's two. Without much question Jung had been lying to her in this same vein throughout months of patient manoeuvring for position—with General Gagan securely in the lead (seven regiments) until his providential death an hour before. Jung was already ahead of his only other serious competitor for power, General Abhiman—though only by a single regiment at present.

The truth was that Jung—if anybody's man—was the heir-apparent's man, as Matabar had been before him. Did the queen not know this, or suspect it?

Jung now left her, went downstairs and out into the courtyard. There he called for the officers commanding his three regiments and warned them to be on the alert.

In the hour or two the queen must wait for all those functionaries to reach the Kōt she must have sat there puzzling out her
situation, now so changed by Gagan's death. With Gagan dead,
were Jung's protestations of loyalty and obedience to her orders to
be trusted? But if not Jung, was there anybody else of the necessary strength and ruthlessness that she could count on in his
stead? Needs must when the Devil drives, perhaps.

While Jung was upstairs with the queen General Abhiman, the
King's Man, had slipped out of the Kōt, crossed Durbar Square
with all its temples, and so to the towering palace just beyond it.
He went before the king. The latter knew exactly what the bugles
meant and if he had not responded to them it was because he was
deeply nervous of the outcome: it was he himself who had
sponsored Gagan's death. But Abhiman must somehow have persuaded him that his presence at the enquiry into it was imperative. Whatever it may be Abhiman now brought the poor timorous muddle-head back with him to the Kōt and sat him in a *dalan*,
a recess in the walls of the ground-floor assembly-chamber.

Some, but by no means all, high officers of State had assembled
by this time, most of them unarmed—except perhaps a sword for
ceremony's sake.

Upstairs, alone and waiting, the queen had grown increasingly
impatient. She came down to the assembly-chamber to learn that
Fateh Jung Sah (the senior-most member of the royal family) was
still awaited, so she called up one of Jung Bahadur's brothers and
ordered him to go and bring back Fateh Jung Sah urgently. It
sounds as if her next move was altogether unexpected: suddenly
she pointed at a certain Pande chieftain and commanded Abhiman
to put the man in irons. In the small closed community of Kathmandu she knew her enemies, and Gagan's (those men who en-
vied and despised him), and this was one of them. She knew too
that the king himself, her *cocu* husband, was in the background
of the plotting that had killed her lover. But the proper forms
must be observed, however summarily. Name the culprit, record
his confession, execute him. Let the ministers get on with it!

Abhiman had the prisoner put in irons, though this was quite
unnecessary: but for a Gurkha 'iron'—the metal, and by extension 'the irons' themselves—possessed a magical malevolence.

The interrogation of the prisoner began—who had killed the
General? Did he deny that he had at least abetted it?—and so on.
The Pande stubbornly denied all knowledge of it, and this so

enraged the queen that she thrust the Sword of State into Abhiman Singh's hands and commanded him to kill the Pande on the spot. Abhiman held back. At this point the queen seems to have left the assembly-chamber in a fury, to go back upstairs again. So Abhiman appealed now to the king for orders—must he carry out the queen's command to kill the Pande?

This put the king in quite a fluster. He did not want the Pande killed, whether or not he had had an active hand in Gagan's murder; the Pande was one of the King's Men, and the king had need of all the support that he could get. It sounds as if he were working up his anger so as to find the strength to defy the queen to her face.

'The Raja somewhat angrily replied [to Abhiman] that without enquiry and proof of guilt and recording the confession of the accused, it would be unjust to put to death such an old, long-employed, able and highly-descended servant of the State.'

Abhiman went up to tell the queen the king's decision. He laid the naked Sword of State at her feet and said that:

'as one Sirkar [embodiment of State] had ordered execution on suspicion, and the other ordered that it should not take place without the proofs of guilt, he could do nothing.'

The queen could not contain her rage—did Abhiman not know that the king had vested full powers in her, that there could be no need to get his special sanction for every little thing? And Abhiman was brave enough and rash enough to answer her:

'—"to yield obedience to the Rani when the Raja was present was not in accordance with good government", and left her presence.'—

We may guess that it was exactly for this reason Abhiman had fetched the king, because in his absence the queen might well accuse and kill at random. And the victims would all be King's Men, certainly, like Abhiman himself.

The young woman in the room above must have sat glowering, nerves all taut, what should she do? She sent for Jung. Had his brother returned with Fateh Jung and party yet? No, not yet. Then she would wait no longer. The chiefs and officers in the hall below must sit at once and determine who had done the murder, and until they named the culprit let no one leave the Kōt! Let the compound gates be closed and bolted!

Meantime the king himself had taken action—of a sort. Evasive action. He said that without the presence of Fateh Jung—that 'experienced and able man' as he described him (that timid tool, that old and decent, lazy man)—no satisfactory investigation would be possible. So he called for his pony, ordered two more of Jung's brothers to accompany him and they set off with attendants for Fateh's house. Once there the king despatched Fateh Jung and party to the Kōt forthwith, escorted by Jung's brothers.

It was already around 2 a.m. Fateh Jung had wasted four hours or so and had only this moment, under compulsion, managed to start out for the Kōt in answer to the bugles. Who shall blame him? Just as the king was deeply implicated in this murder, so was Fateh Jung. What if the queen's enquiry should expose their part in it? The king's life and person might be sacrosanct, not so Fateh Jung's. Yet to the Kōt he had to go.

The king himself had not the least intention of going back there —at least not at this time. Instead he rode with his attendants to the Residency compound gates, but the Residency-guard made him wait outside while a messenger was sent in the king's name to ask for an interview with Captain Ottley—

'for the purpose of conversing with him respecting the event of the murder of Gagan Singh.'

If Lawrence, that outstandingly able and experienced officer had still been Resident, he might well have 'had the courtesy to come down and give a hearing to the royal visitor'. That he did not has been crossly held against him by such as Mr D. R. Regmi, a Nepalese politician and political-writer of our time. But as we know, it wasn't Lawrence; it was his young assistant, Ottley, officially on leave, not even officiating-Resident, there only by the accident of the *ayul*. Ottley may have been inexperienced still, but he will have known enough to keep the Residency's nose out of this flash-flood of Nepalese power-politics. It was the very basis of the Anglo-Nepalese accord that there should be no Residency meddling with Nepal's domestic affairs. And apart from that, could Ottley have managed Hindi well enough to handle this alone? Quite likely not: he would have had to have the Residency's *Mir Munshi*—'head-clerk', 'interpreter'—with him. Ottley decided to have the *Mir Munshi* roused and sent to see the king at the Residency gates. That the king did not regard this as discourtesy is clear from what then followed.

The king addressed the Residency *Mir Munshi*:

'Today someone has murdered General Gagan Singh, the faithful servant of my Rani, by treacherously shooting him in his Chamber of Prayer ...'

—the faithful servant of his Rani—this is how the king now referred to her dead lover, *mari complaisant* that he certainly was not but yet must seem to be. And he went on to explain that the queen was at that moment investigating the affair; that she was greatly distressed, so that he too was determined 'to use every possible exertion towards discovery and punishment'—moreover he was anxious that the Residency *munshi* should go back with him to the Kōt—

'—in order to see and hear what passed there and to be able to report the issue of the investigation to the officiating-Resident.'

The *munshi* very sensibly prevaricated; the king was mad and must be humoured somehow. He said that there would be much delay in saddling his horse, that 'His Highness's' business was extremely urgent and must not be deferred; and that it would be best if he himself, the *munshi*, should follow in the morning.

The king agreed: he seems always to have agreed with the last speaker. How strange to find such meek irresolution in an absolute autocrat. But he charged the Residency *munshi* not to fail to turn up in the morning.

With this the king and his attendants set off for the town again. Did he really plan to go back inside the Kōt? I doubt it. But if he did, then he was easily dissuaded, because when the party reached Durbar Square—

'—the gutter in the street outside the Kōt was flowing with the blood which came from it—'

—and 'the people about', outside the Kōt, prevented him from entering, which must have been a great relief. He went back quickly to his palace.

Well before the king had covered the two miles or so from Fateh Jung's house to the Residency, Fateh Jung and party would be arriving at the Kōt. Jung Bahadur was there to meet them in the courtyard. He quickly told them what was going on—how the queen 'violently suspected' the 'ironed' Pande of Gagan's murder;

how General Abhiman had made all manner of excuses for not obeying her command to kill the prisoner out of hand—'notwithstanding that her authority and rule were in full force'. She was so 'highly incensed' by now, in fact, that Jung felt there was only one thing to be done—

'—wherefore to appease her and bring matters round it will be necessary to make away with both these persons. . .'

—the 'ironed' Pande, and Abhiman.

And here I stop again to ask myself who the Residency's source for this reported speech could be? Did Jung himself at some point volunteer it? If so he may later have regretted it. But at that moment we must not suppose that either Jung or Fateh would have seen anything unethical in Jung's proposal. Abhiman had disobeyed the queen: he too must die—though we may find it difficult to forget how infinitely to Jung Bahadur's personal advantage would be the death of Abhiman, and how little to Fateh Jung Sah's. Yet it was worth a try, perhaps. Jung continued:

'—which course, with your approval, I will effect, and then you may administer the affairs of the revenue and territorial departments whilst I remain in my post as *Jungi* General [Commander-in-Chief which Jung was not as yet] and act under your orders.'

Fateh Jung would have none of this, however. Fateh was a King's Man; Abhiman and the 'ironed' Pande were King's Men too. Fateh insisted that 'nothing should be done without due deliberation'—a proper enquiry must be completed first.

This answer will not have pleased Jung. He climbed the stairs to where the queen was waiting. Fateh Jung then joined Abhiman and the other high officials in the *dalan* just off the dim-lit assembly-chamber. The place, its vestibules and corridors, was now full of people. Everyone was waiting, and no one could have known what for.

On the floor above, Jung Bahadur was reporting to the queen on Fateh Jung's obstructive attitude. He stood beside a window overlooking the big shadowy courtyard down below, and standing there became aware that Abhiman's men were loading their muskets. He must have swung round to tell the queen because it was now she snatched up her Sword of State and hurried down the stairway to the assembly-chamber. Once downstairs she sought out Fateh Jung, shouting, 'Who has killed my faithful general? Name him! Quickly!'

The Residency text says, 'No one answered.'

Fateh Jung was trying to placate her, urging her not to be precipitate, assuring her that he would personally 'sift the matter well to her satisfaction'. No doubt he aimed at gaining time, time to think out how best to extricate them from this woman's dangerous fury.

The queen would brook no more delay. She had been getting ever more excited and hysterical, no longer recognising any need for 'proof of guilt' or 'signed confession'—so with no more ado she made towards the Pande lying on the dais and had already raised her sword when Fateh Jung and Abhiman and a chief called Dalbanjan came darting forward and between them managed to restrain her before she could bring the blade down on the prostrate man. Baulked in this way and seething with rage and exasperation as she must have been, she hurried up the stairway to the room above.

Oldfield's version of that night's events is based closely on the Residency's secret text (without acknowledgement) but with certain observations of his own to add. He says the queen 'mounted the dark and narrow stairs alone', for instance. The narrowness would be in the normal Newar tradition, and it obviously obliged the three men at the bottom of the stairway to wait below till the queen should reach the stair-head. Presumably they meant to follow after her, to calm her, if they could. They never got the chance.

'—shots were fired. . . .'

The Residency text says no more than that: no wondering where from, who by. Oldfield says, too vaguely to be of much help to us, that they were fired 'within the building'. The ground floor was dark and crowded. Even if the various factions had grouped themselves together—which I fancy would be normal practice—who could have used a musket or a pistol without the tell-tale flashes being seen? If anyone had seen the flashes, you might think that someone would have noted where they came from. No survivor of the ensuing slaughter ever spoke of it so far as I can find.

Shots were fired within the building. Both Fateh Jung and Dalbanjan fell dead and Abhiman was seriously wounded. He staggered back and cried out, 'Jung has done this treacherous act!'—then did his best to stumble out into the open courtyard where his men were waiting—but one of Jung Bahadur's brothers, Krishna Bahadur, 'nearly cut him in twain with a single sword-stroke'—a lateral swipe, it had to be, the ceiling being so low—and now Khadga, eldest son of Fateh Jung Sah, leapt forward from the *dalan*. He would probably not have seen his father killed (Oldfield says it happened in the adjoining passage-way) but he must have heard them shout that it had happened, and he would have seen Abhiman cut down and heard his loud accusing cry denouncing Jung. He grabbed at the small *kukri* in his girdle and made for two of Jung Bahadur's brothers, Krishna and Bam Bahadur, each in turn. Bam was in difficulties, struggling to free his sword-hilt of the rich embroidered scarf it was customary to knot about the hilt on ceremonial occasions such as this had seemed to be till now—but he could not get it free, he could not draw his sword; and was Krishna off his guard, perhaps, having only just this moment dealt with Abhiman? At all events Khadga now succeeded in landing a *kukri*-cut to Bam's and then to Krishna's head—and Bam, half-stunned and blinded by the blood, would have been easily des-patched had not his assailant suddenly been brought down him-self—'he fell, killed by a shot...' And once again the Residency text has nothing to tell us about who fired it nor where from.

What actually did happen? People lied so, afterwards. People do; and it depended upon who told the story and to what end. But what is likely to have been the truth?

We would have expected Jung to follow the queen downstairs when she came brandishing her sword and seeking Fateh Jung—but no one says he did, and Oldfield categorically says that he did not. Accept it. But when the queen came back upstairs again, her ears filled with the pleas for patience of those three ill-fated men, it surely has to be that she ordered Jung to shoot them down—it would be entirely in character; and in character for Jung to do so at her command (just as in the case of his uncle Matabar). And had Jung not already proposed to Fateh Jung that Abhiman must die for refusing to carry out her orders? So now the three must die. It would be so easy too. A standing-target. The three victims at the bottom of the forty-five degree diagonal of wooden-ladder steps. Range perhaps eleven feet. A double-barrelled musket snatched from a member of his bodyguard upstairs with him? Two balled-cartridges discharged at such a range could scarcely fail to kill two men outright and could seriously wound the third. They would have been looking up the unlit wooden shaft, watching the queen step clear into the upper-room—they could certainly have seen Jung as he replaced the queen at the stair-head (if my theory is correct and this is what he did). Only one of the three victims lived long enough to shout out that it was Jung. Abhiman, the wounded man. Any of Jung's enemies or rivals on solid evidence or none would automatically lay the blame on him, but in Abhiman's case I think this was no guess—he would have seen Jung firing. And from where else could these shots have been fired but down that steep and narrow stairwell whose sides effectively hid the flashes and sealed off everyone below (both friends and enemies) outside the target-area?

Once something of this kind gets started, panic or rage or the heaven-sent chance to kill off enemies and rivals takes charge, or in any case took charge inside the Kōt, and the next we hear is that a body of men cagily described by the Residency as 'usually attendant upon General Jung Bahadur' had stormed into the ground-floor Assembly-chamber from the courtyard and was firing indiscriminately into the *dalan* recess. This must be the origin of a report the Residency doesn't mention that Jung himself had 'mown down fourteen nobles, one after the other'. But a double-barrelled muzzle-loader is no machine-gun; it can't mow down fourteen men, for who is to protect the marksman while he sets about his cumbersome re-loading after each two shots? Honour where honour is due—Jung's bodyguard did the mowing down. But just as Jung would not have shot his uncle Matabar in May the year before unless at his sovereign's direct command, so Jung's men would never have stormed the building had not Jung directly ordered it— and this he could so well have done by shouting down to their commander from the window of the upper-storey, and giving them a specific target, what's more—the *dalan*.

The end was in no doubt at all. As soon as Abhiman had fallen and his men had learnt of it they quietly slipped away. One of Jung's regiments outside had little difficulty in forcing the gates and taking possession of the courtyard, then securing all the exits once again. So now, to follow on the slaughter of the nobles inside the Kōt, there began the general slaughter of the lesser victims, inside and out, spurred on, applauded by the queen herself—'a very fiend of malice', Padma calls her. She stood before her upper window watching the heady holocaust below, ecstatic, glorious, shouting, 'Kill and destroy my enemies!'

They did, and it was quickly over. It seems that some who thought their end had come 'were saved by the brothers of General Jung who took them by the hand and put them out of the Kōt through a small doorway at its back'. It seems also (this is from Padma too) that some of them less favoured nevertheless managed to escape by 'leaping down walls and roofs, others by crawling out through drains and gutters'—and he offers us this toothsome bit as well, how a group of them stopped for a second to 'throw stones at the queen before scampering off—' —but I doubt if she was hit, or we should have heard about it.

And in the midst of all this business the queen had quite made up her mind: Jung was her man. So she took time off to make him 'the grant of the Wizarut'—that is, appointed him prime minister, and gave him the command of all sixteen regiments stationed at the Capital; Jung in his turn presented her with his *nazr*, or ceremonial gift of acknowledgement.

Jung and his six full-brothers had triumphed, and come out of it unscathed, if we dismiss two unimportant head-wounds, Bam's and Krishna's.

Nothing that we know of suggests premeditation. For the queen it was her lover's sudden death that sparked things off; in Jung's case premeditation is hard to reconcile with his brother Bam's complete unpreparedness, witness the difficulty with his ceremonial sword. What started it all off, then? Spontaneous combustion? Not quite. Who really drew first blood inside the Kōt that night? And does it matter all that much who did?

For some, apparently, it mattered very much indeed.

The Residency document perplexes me. Since reaching Kathmandu where all this seems to live again I've worried over it a dozen times. The purpose of the document was to give the Governor-General in India the definitive 'particulars relating to the Massacre'. How, then, explain why it does not even seem to ask itself the questions it declines to answer for us? Who did fire those opening shots?

It would be normal for the Resident himself to take a hand in this definitive account of six months after the event, at least I should have thought so. He signed it, certainly. But in fact no Englishman compiled it; the prose-style would alone proclaim this—it is the purest *munshi*-English, fluent and well-managed as it is. Did the Resident get his *Mir munshi* to do it for them? Yet at the bottom of the document we find the word 'Translated' and have to start a bit of wondering on other lines. If the compilation was the Residency *munshi*'s work then why on earth should he set it down in Hindi, say (the language of the original is not named), only to render it into English and call it a translation? If it is not the Residency *munshi*'s work, then whose could it be? And we have to ask ourselves who—apart from the various pairs of interlocutors concerned—could have known and reported what passed privately between the queen and Jung in the upper room before it all began (a girl attendant, possibly? A member of Jung's bodyguard?); and then between the queen and Abhiman; and between Jung and Fateh Jung Sah outside in the courtyard; and finally between the king and queen next morning, as we shall be hearing in a moment. All these were private conversations that only the two dead men among the speakers (Fateh and Abhiman) would have cared to publicise if they had lived to do so. Who questioned whom and told the Residency *munshi*?

The Residency *Mir munshi* would be a well-educated, well-born Indian gentleman of the sort that could come closer to the king than any Christian could really hope to get. Had not the king begged him to come back to the Kōt 'to see and hear what passed' in order to report at first hand to the Residency? In fact the *Mir munshi* performed services of infinitely greater scope and value to the Company than his modest-sounding post suggests. He played the all-important role of 'Intermediary'.[1]

The Hindu-palace world adored the intermediary, all that sweetly furtive business of 'intelligence' carried back and forth and sideways, the watching and the waiting and the art of leaving certain things unsaid—and of course intrigue through sex. 'Politico-sexual hurly-burly' really does describe things at the palace in the 1830's and '40's. The basic principles they worked on had been laid down in the second century A.D. by Vatsyayana in his *Kama Sutra*, the 'Hindu Art of Love' and sexual politics. It was not lightly that Aldous Huxley spoke about this monumental work as 'Mrs Beeton's Book of Sex' for it is the very compendium of everything worth knowing (and trying out) on this absorbing subject. The *Kama Sutra* is as full of intermediaries as life itself should be, mostly old women in those early days. These old creatures would have to be well-versed in the science and art of

Kama—of Love, let's say, 'both procreative and recreative'. They would in fact be mistresses of the Sixty-Four Arts that all ambitious girls (not only courtesans, to whom the work is particularly addressed) would be eager to acquire.[2]

It is true that the British Resident would be unlikely to try his hand at sexual intrigue, nor yet his *Mir munshi*—but then the objectives would be different, requiring different techniques. His intermediary, master of such techniques, would be his *Mir munshi*, so quiet and unobtrusive, so conciliatory, tactful, clever, and above all sly. It is even doubtful if there would have been advantage generally in a British officer's dealing direct; he would lack Hindu finesse. For the ordinary officer the formula found best suited to the circumstances was the combination of British officer—'the Englishman with his authoritative voice, his nonchalant manners and broken Hindustani' as Richard Burton said—and his Indian *munshi*.

The Resident had his *Mir munshi*, then, and the palace had their own equivalent, the *Durbar munshi*, who was perhaps the only literate at court (where literate refers to the reading and writing of his own vernacular, though he might have a smattering of English too). In Lawrence's day, the *Durbar munshi* had been his constant visitor at the Residency, dropping in of a morning 'to pick up my sentiments' as Lawrence phrased it, on some matter of the moment.

All the same, even a Brian Houghton Hodgson or a Henry Lawrence would hold himself aloof from certain areas of activity. It would be his *munshi* who would recruit and control the Residency's paid-informers—if 'control' could be the term to use. How was a paid-informer for the British to keep his operations secret in tiny Kathmandu where spying was a passion and the criss-cross of its movements like shuttles in a loom?

So strict was the surveillance imposed on all connected with the Residency, so starved of accurate information must have been the Resident's *Mir munshi*—and yet perhaps obliged, in this case, to put together these definitive 'Particulars' about the massacre— could he have gone cap in hand to ask the *Durbar munshi* for his help? A long document, a lot of help (a lot of money?). Did these two *chers collègues*, heads together, puzzle it all out between them? Did the Residency *Mir munshi* agree that in the splendid cause of Peace, he too should withhold the answer to the unspoken question, 'Who shot those first three victims, who started it?' There was a reason for withholding it.

The fact is that since the night of the massacre six months earlier Jung's attitude towards the part he played in it had subtly changed. What had seemed obvious and unexceptional conduct then, looked somehow different in retrospect. Already in early 1847 Jung appears to have been focusing his eyes if not on London and an Embassy to the Court of Queen Victoria, at least on the advantages to him and (as he saw it) to Nepal of closer ties with England. He may have come to realise that to have started off the massacre by killing his three chief obstacles to power could look a little bit too pat—to a disapproving Englishman who kept his distances and wrote despatches. I am arguing that as soon as people came to realise that Jung, for reasons of his own, preferred the world to think that someone else had claimed first blood that night, an innocent and sensible conspiracy of silence imposed itself, in deference to Jung's known feelings.

It is a post-mortem of a post-mortem that I am here attempting. Jung was to offer Dr Oldfield (and a certain Captain Cavanagh as well) his final authorised version of his part in the massacre as he had retrospectively made it fit (as nearly as was possible) with his conception of what Victorian morality would find permissible. But this was some years later. It involved a few white lies that seem intended solely to exculpate himself from the killing of Fateh Jung Sah, Dalbanjan and Abhiman Singh.

At the time no one on the winning side—Jung Bahadur least of all—had suffered doubts or pangs of conscience. A faction-feud had suddenly exploded in the old familiar way. Survivors of the losing side would see it like this too, and no thought of moral censure would have crossed their minds. All would admit, in fact, that it had been the very model of a coup.[3]

Back at the Kōt at dawn on Tuesday 15 September 1846 the sun rose smiling on a queen all radiant from her noisy sleepless night, her grief now doubtless overlaid by the knowledge that this time her golden dream would really be translated into glittering reality. Her grateful new Prime Minister and Commander-in-Chief would see to it. There he stood sunlit too, his brothers grouped around him, his bodyguard behind him, and the sixteen regiments he'd just acquired now under orders to parade on Thandi Khel to greet and acclaim him.

Before they sorted out the victims, however (one hundred and thirty of them only? Or was it four-hundred-plus?), before they swabbed the bloody Kōt and courtyard down, the thoughtful queen required her Minister to summon Prince Surendra, Heir-Apparent, so that he might look upon the enormous mound of still-warm corpses piled up there together, higgledy-piggledy 'with no reference to rank', imagining that the sight of what she had achieved would strike the fear of God into him. So Jung conducted Prince Surendra in, knowing for his part that far from being fear-struck the boy they both had plans for would be overwhelmed with pleasure at the sight of all those enemies so freshly-killed. Freshly-killed anybodies would probably have satisfied him. Anyway he came—and gloated, I am sure.

This done, the sorting could be undertaken—separate piles for sheep and goats, I think—and later in the day all fifty-five of those whose 'names have been preserved' had been laid out in the hollow square Jung's sixteen regiments had formed for him. This done, Jung pointed at the carcases and shouted:

'Whatever they could do for you, I can do!'

—and the troops all roared their heads off, acclaiming him. He then busied himself consoling such officers as had lost relatives in the night's slaughter. The consolation took the form of immediate promotion.

19

After Jung had conducted the queen back from the Kōt he left her, to seek the king; to offer him too his *nazr*, the ceremonial gift. Jung found him with the heir-apparent and in a filthy temper, demanding angrily by whose orders so many of the highest in the land had been slaughtered in the past few hours. Jung answered him:

'All which has been done has been ordered by the Maharani to whom His Highness has made over the sovereign power'

—which so infuriated His Highness that he bustled off forthwith to her apartments to have it out with her for once.

Since her return to the palace the queen had changed into a white dress suitable to mourning—mourning for Gagan Singh: she did not mourn those others, though she remembered to give orders that Fateh's funeral should be observed with all the proper rites. But by the time the king came in to beard her he found her overcome by grief again. Despite it she could lose her temper and she evidently did, but all the Residency text can tell us about what must have been a stormy interview is that 'after some words passed' she issued him her ultimatum: unless he would forthwith put her eldest son upon the throne 'more calamities would ensue'. The Residency text winds up this scene with these words:

'As this conversation did not come to any satisfactory conclusion the Maharaja now mounted his horse and . . . proceeded towards Patan intending, as he said, to go to Kashi'—Benares.

Everybody in defeat or sulks or sent off into exile seems to head straight for Benares.

Perhaps delivering her ultimatum and packing off the king discomfited had calmed the air a little for the queen, and brought her back to humdrum earth. She summoned Jung and a certain Bhir Dhuj Bashniat—someone new who won't last long—and was soon busy organising the confiscation of the property of all those noblemen who had perished in the Kōt: this, and the issue of expulsion orders to their families, promising them death if they should be found hiding in Nepal when a ten-day period of grace was over. She added that each individual exile might carry with him only a small bundle of his personal effects. A final order: the heir-apparent and Mohila sahib, his younger brother, were to be kept under the strictest surveillance, night and day: 'Permit no one to approach them!'

The little princes in the tower.

Meanwhile Jung was quick to take his own precautions. Having sent a younger brother off to Patan to persuade the king to come back home, he saw to it that two other brothers would be the officers in constant attendance on the two princes, and he himself would be visiting them each day to keep an eye on things. If the queen had plans for them, then so had Jung.

As the weeks went by the impatient queen was forever after Jung to put those two imprisoned princes to death and cause the king to abdicate, and to lose no more precious time in setting up her elder boy as king—get on with it, in fact. We are not told how Jung contrived to satisfy her for so long with a series of postponements but by the last week in October the queen had reached the limits of exasperation and was prepared to lend her ear to what Bhir Dhuj Bashniat was telling her. In fact he managed to convince her that Jung had no intention of killing off the princes for her—

'because he was very attached to the Heir-Apparent and now he had become Prime Minister would never deal treacherously by him'

—so the queen had better set about destroying Jung at once. Then only could the matter so close to her heart be brought into effect. Bhir Dhuj was right, of course: the queen certainly will have remembered how first Matabar Singh had let her down (and dearly he had paid for it!), and now his nephew—each in turn raised to power by her alone, each with his broken promises. Very well,

232

then—Jung must die. And as reward for Bhir Dhuj Bashniat's perspicacity she had a grant of the prime ministry secretly made out in his name, his appointment to be publicly announced only after Jung was safely dead.

How should they do Jung in?

One grandiose proposal was that Jung and all his brothers should be required to sleep in the apartments of the doomed princes, to guard over them. The plan was not only to murder Jung, his six brothers and the two princes, but along with them the king as well. Why not? Too late now to consider the sacro-sanctity of kings. Destroy the hostile group 'on as broad a base as possible'. It was axiomatic.

Thinking it all over, however, the plotters must have decided that this solution of their problems was less simple than it looked. Jung and his brothers were a formidable lot, as their performance at the Kōt had demonstrated. The plan was changed to something that looked easier of execution, if more limited in scope. Jung would be summoned by the queen to attend her at the Kōt. This would look quite normal on the face of it, but the difference would be that young, presumably ambitious, General Wazir Singh—yes, promoted general since his father Gagan's death—would have introduced 'a regiment' of men into the Kōt itself. The day set for this splendid coup was 31 October 1846. The princes' turn would follow later.

It is now necessary to skip back a few days to explain that among those present to applaud the little secret ceremony that was to raise Bhir Dhuj Bashniat to power on Jung's assassination were not only General Wazir Singh but also one Vijay Raj Pundit, a Brahmin at the court—at least the Residency said that he was present. D. R. Regmi's version has it that this man learnt of the secret ceremony not at first hand but from a palace maidservant, and of the alternatives open to me I really much prefer the Regmi version—I suppose his variant is based on Padma Jung. It is the more tortuous, which is how it ought to be. I quote it here:

'In those days secrets often leaked out through the harem-girls who confided them to the men they conducted clandestine rela-tions with. It was not uncommon in the filthy atmosphere of the palace where sex-starved women sought amour indiscrimi-nately...'

—and there is no doubt that this was true, though I hardly think that they were sex-starved. Mr Regmi goes on to tell us that Vijay Raj Pundit—

'had long been a friend of Jung's [and that he was] thrust into the palace on [Jung's] recommendation to serve as private tutor, in which capacity he was also to trace and report to him all overt and covert movements of the queen.'

This too is highly probable; indeed Vijay Raj Pundit was soon to reap a very handsome harvest for having so punctually revealed the plot to Jung, complete with the time and date set for its execution. He was to be appointed to the *Raj-guru*'ship itself, which we may think of as equivalent to the Archbishopric of Canterbury.

On the 31st October in accordance with the palace-plan, the queen sent Bhir Dhuj Bashniat in person to desire General Jung to attend her at the Kōt—and we are told that having sent him off, she was herself preparing to leave the palace for the Kōt—but it looks as if she never went. Bhir Dhuj, on his way to deliver the queen's summons, must have been much disturbed to see Jung coming down the street 'with all his relatives and friends' and a whole lot of armed attendants with double-barrelled guns. It frightened him. How could Jung be here before even any summons had reached him? Bhir Dhuj delivered the queen's message over folded hands and Jung made the following reply:

'Mr Minister, as you have been appointed Wazir, what can I be wanted for?'

—at which Bhir Dhuj began to tremble. Jung then made a sign to one of his party who quickly shot the Bashniat dead.

News of this sort travels fast. There would be someone in the know to hurry off and warn Wazir Singh; it is certain that when Jung sent after Wazir Singh he had already left the city and was wisely making for the plains of India. But Jung himself had something more immediate to do than bother with Wazir Singh: he went straight on to the palace to confront the king. He found him sitting with the Heir-Apparent. Jung laid his turban at his sovereign's feet and—after exposing to him the queen's murderous intentions as they regarded both his senior-rani's sons and possibly the king himself—'requested either to be dismissed immediately

234

or to be vested with full authority to put to death the enemies of the Heir-Apparent'.

The king here did yet another of his bewildering pirouettes and 'wrote an order granting the power proposed with his own hand'— so the Residency said—'and affixed to it his private seal'.

Then, giving it to Jung the king embraced him and commanded him to destroy all his beloved son's enemies, who were by that very fact his own enemies. Jung was to do whatever he considered necessary for the welfare and safety of the rightful heir to the throne. The king said, and not for the first time, that he himself was going to Benares.

The first thing Jung did was to order a general Bashniat round-up and by nightfall the count of dead Bashniats was fourteen—so the Residency believed. According to Mr Regmi they numbered:

'sixty of which twenty were butchered in a room in the cruellest manner.' Mr Regmi adds 'this moment is called *Bhandarkhal Parva*'

—which he renders 'Massacre of the Strong'. Alas, not strong enough.

The moment Bhir Dhuj Bashniat fell dead the queen's cause was irrevocably lost, though she may not have recognised quite how irrevocably till that evening when Jung Bahadur waited upon her at the palace and delivered the Heir-Apparent Prince Surendra's ultimatum, doubtless Jung Bahadur's own, which the Residency describes as follows: 'Since she had become [Surendra's] bitter enemy, even to death, if she wished well to herself, she and her two sons would instantly quit the palace and proceed to [a Nepali village, specifically named] or go to the Plains'—which effectively meant to Indian exile. She was suddenly a beaten, frightened creature. She quit the palace with the two young sons she had planned so fine a future for, moved to some private house in the city and there began her preparations for departure into exile—and the king pirouetted yet again, agreeing to go with her, professedly on pilgrimage to expiate the bloodshed of the 14th September.

On 23 November 1846, the queen, her two sons and the king set off for Benares.

Prince Surendra, Heir-Apparent, was now appointed Regent in the absence of his father.

Little more is heard of ex-Queen Lakshmi Devi. Years later there were to be as many lines of far-away news as might be scribbled on the back of a fading picture postcard. Landon publishes the picture of her that I have in mind: a photograph. She looks sixty, but could well be ten years less. She was living in Benares still, her husband long since deposed by Jung but all the same permitted to return to live in Kathmandu. She had a new lover—the most recent of a string of them, his name Dalbahadur, an exile like herself, Nepali. She lived in open scandal with him. This had always been her practice and I suppose she saw no reason to change it just because she was in 'British' India. On this man she squandered all the funds allotted for her keep, not only grossly neglecting her two sons for her lover's sake but also abetting him in their corruption. The British intervened—not in her sexual life, of course, but by taking over the administration of her income.

What does she look like, in this fading photograph? A debauched and ageing woman, she sits before some heavy cast-iron railings in what must be a private garden. She is dressed in a *sari* infinitely fuller than the seven yards of Indian *saris* nowadays. It must be of hand-spun hand-woven muslin, very fine and white, and it is covered with little hand-embroidered flower-sprigs in the delicately-charming Indian manner. Her head sticks out above the muslin froth; her hair is thin (and dyed, I think); it is dragged back severely over her egg-shaped skull. Huge ear-rings. Great cavernous dark eyes, a fleshy nose, thick sensual lips and probably no teeth: the mouth has the upsetting sunk-in look of some sea-anemone closed and dark. Deep diagonals run from nose to sagging jaw-line. There is absolutely no expression on her face—but at the age of twelve or so, when they first presented her to King Rajendra, she must have shone with light and loveliness as if she were some little heavenly-body. Why should they have chosen her for him if she were less lovely than the stars? They had all the Himalayan world to choose her from, and for second wife much less attention would be paid to the requirements of caste and clan (some say she was a slave-girl). She probably continued beautiful for years, until the years so dangerously, violently lived caught up with her.

The day the Bashniat Conspiracy was quashed—it was her last 'throw'—the light that hitherto had burned in her, scorching, oxy-acetylene, quite suddenly went out and she was left in total darkness. Jung's brilliant incandescence now lit Kathmandu instead.

That same day, in token of the royal gratitude to Jung, the Prince-Regent Surendra Bir Vikram Sah, the 'Sun-born', was pleased to grant the family a patent of nobility suggestive of direct descent from Kshatriya stock of Rajasthan, if not quite 'Sun-born', then at least collateral, the second bluest blood of all. Thenceforth this family of the Konwar clan would be addressed as Konwar-Rana-ji. Full ennoblement to Maharaja with specific territorial appellations—and the grant in perpetuity of the prime-ministry would follow some years later, but already in 1846 the Ranas had effectively taken over for their hundred years of absolute supremacy.

20

More than two weeks now and the rhythm of my days has had ample time to get itself established. It suits me very well. Sun-up to nearing sundown I spend as firmly in the past as I can manage, alone and perfectly content to be. I've gone back and back to holy Pashupatinath, despite the dust and traffic of the road that leads there. It is the place I like the best. I walk a lot through other open country too, by pathways better made for walking, out into the ancient scenery. Tree-size poinsettias burst like great roman candles up, out and down, rhododendrons everywhere but quiescent at the moment—how lavish life is here. Mast-high bamboo-grooves shiver their foliage as a peacock in his pride shivers his brilliant fan-sticks, and there's nobody in sight. I love the silence of the walks through pasture-land.

I have visited the city-satellites, of course, the midget seats of gods and royalty we may think of as museum exhibits but that are simply 'home' to their inhabitants. I have visited Buddhist *stupas*. They look serenely satisfying but . . . There is a 'but'. Why should it bother me? It does.

A tourist handout tells us that 'a remarkable feature of Nepal is the religious homogeneity existing between the Buddhist and the Hindu communities who for centuries have cherished mutual regard for one another'. It says that the Hindu shrines at Buddhist Swayambhu, for instance, 'are the usual and at the same time unique feature of the Nepalese culture. It shows how the Hindu and the Buddhist religions have mingled together to form a vast cultural unity.'

The truth is that they haven't mingled in the least. Professor Snellgrove offers an analogy, in the planting of two different trees

238

in close proximity, the *pipul* (*Ficus religiosa*) and the *banyan* (*Ficus indicus*)—which are widely supposed to be the male and female of the same great fig. The towering *pipul* grows a single trunk; it scatters seed abroad to grow into independent trees, each with its single trunk. In Professor Snellgrove's analogy the *pipul* stands for Buddhism, 'its seed self-abnegation of which the philosophical counterpart is universal non-substantiality. The *pipul's* single trunk has been a sound monastic order.'

'Has been,' please note.

The *banyan*, on the other hand, female to the *pipul's* male, is insuperably productive, and here stands for Hinduism. Each branch can drop down tendrils that reach the earth and root themselves. In time a single *banyan* will be a wood that spreads and spreads, stifling the nearby solitary *pipul*, and this is what has happened in Nepal.

In the early centuries of our era Buddhist monks, strict celibates, were moving eastwards out of India to escape from Hinduism that held them in disfavour. Many settled in the Valley. In later centuries Muslims were invading India from the north, Hindus themselves were fleeing to the Himalayas for refuge, and many settled in the Valley. True Buddhism here was from that moment doomed. The Valley was too small for both these trees in such proximity: with no escape the solitary antisocial *pipul* could not for very long hold out against the proliferating *banyan*. What could the Buddhist monks then do but somehow come to terms with what was happening all round them? By the mid-fourteenth century, despite themselves, they had been softly overwhelmed, absorbed into the caste-system of the Hindu Brahmins, and even if the Buddhist monks were so respected that the Brahmins had assigned to them the highest caste and called them *Banras* ('honourable'), the fact remained that their acceptance was the beginning of the end for them. The end for them was when they finally abandoned their celibacy. There was no Hindu-Buddhist synthesis, no mingling, it was complete assimilation, and the once-Buddhist Newars were thenceforth Buddhist in nothing but the name. Professor Snellgrove adds that 'in order to realise the present abject state of Buddhism in Nepal, we should have to contrast it with Tibet. Tibet is still at heart a Buddhist country, but Nepal is Hindu through and through'.

The Lord Buddha himself (d. *c.* 480 B.C.) was easily absorbed as the Lord Vishnu in his latest avatar. And somehow or another a gravely heterodox Hindu system, absolutely crack-brained though demonstrably enjoyable, superposed itself upon the Valley. Tantrism, or Shaktism, with its marvels, magic *mandalas* or diagrams, the harnessing of gods to an adept's private purposes, the secret rites, and all those spells and ritual sex. All living women are here seen as sharing in the divine essence; in human women, as in goddesses of course, resides the *shakti* of their male counterparts, the gods. An extreme Tantric cult (*Kapalikas*) confidently locates the human soul in the Yoni—the female Yantra of the mystic diagrams that symbolise it.

It is not for nothing that in Nepal all women—like all cows and Brahmins—are exempted from the death-penalty. Women outnumber men here by two to one, or so they tell me.

When Vasishta, son of Brahma the Creator, went to visit Vishnu the Preserver in his 'Buddha' avatar, it was to question him about the Tara-Tantra cult. It had been born on Chinese soil, and it was in China that Vasishta found Vishnu-Buddha, surrounded by a million women in a state of erotic ecstasy. To strictly orthodox Vasishta this was such a shock and set-back that it had him crying out aloud '—but these practices are absolutely contrary to the *Vedas*!' A great voice then came to him from space, correcting him: 'If you seek Tara's favours'—the voice boomed—'it is through the Chinese rite that you must adore me.' Vasishta then approached Vishnu-Buddha in great awe and from his lips received this bit of wisdom:

'Women are goddesses, women are life, women are the adornment!'—and the Vishnu-Buddha charged him to practise what are called the Five M's—the initial letter common to them all in Sanscrit. They are the drinking of alcohol (*Madya*); the eating of meat (*Mansa*); the eating of fish (*Matsya*); the making of complicated finger-*mudras*—*mudras* are magical gestures, I always thought, though I've seen this 'M' rendered 'corn', and what is sinful about corn that we should be urged to eat it, I do not know. We may let this 'M' pass, perhaps, and get on to the fifth and last, and by far the most effective—*Mithuna*, or fornication.

Those temple-pornographs of carved and painted wood I have been so busy photographing in Durbar Square and holy Pashupatinath and elsewhere round about—they are not pornographs at all; they are the expression of sex as sacrament, though I'm not sure how this can be stretched to cover the little mannikin on one temple roofstrut because he lies masturbating all alone in his big white bed. Possibly he is supposed to demonstrate what not to do. Other examples strike my western eye as frankly funny in their adolescent way. For example there is one that surely was designed to get a schoolboy laugh: a street-porter with a baby sitting in the headsling basket on his back is busy fornicating with a lady on all fours, head down, skirt up, a baby at her breast still clinging on as best it may below. The Nepalese, who laugh so readily, do they not laugh at this?

I imagine that this *Tantra-Shakti* business has been striking chords of muddled music in the hearts of yet another sort of lost-soul westerner because I am sorry to report the presence of a third alien sub-culture in the Valley to add to the true soft-centre blown-head Hippies and the short-term experimenting drop-outs (I no longer count the blue-rinse ladies locked in Pullman-coaches, because I now realise they are only on what the airlines call 'transfer' to or from the airport). The third sub-culture, then, is represented by pink crop-head foreigners 'embracing' Buddhism.

I haven't said a word about this to Mussoorie partly because I am secretly disapproving, and also because I think he finds it the most natural thing in the world for foreigners to strive towards the nothingness of Nirvana* now that the Revolution has opened up Nepal's frontiers to them. But I do hear that Nepalese official-dom does not feel entirely as Mussoorie feels about it; entry-visas and the renewal of short-term (very short) residence-permits for those who look like Hippies are getting difficult to obtain, even for those who show they can finance themselves without shameless battening on kind-hearted citizens or peasants. Who knows, perhaps in time . . . ? And indeed it was to happen later, though not alas before I had to leave myself. Nepal, so long-suffering and patient with other peoples' foibles, finally grew sick of all those Hippies and got rid of them.

Thinking of this has made me think of Zena's being a nun now, and living in an isolated Buddhist monastery. From what I hear she is entirely serious and knows the difference between true Buddhism and the other thing. I gather from Mussoorie that her preceptors are Tibetan, lamas, true celibates. Refugees, no doubt. After all I don't think that I am going to try to get in touch with her. She has chosen a different world: why should she be asked to

* Sanscrit. 'The literal meaning of this word is simply "blown out", like a candle.' Yule and Burnell *Hobson Jobson*.

put up with a social call from me for no better reason than an agreeable auld lang syne elsewhere? And thinking about Zena makes me think about Mussoorie's 'lady who knows you, Peter'— his tease-lady. I shall do nothing about her either, and shall do my best to prevent Mussoorie's carrying out his threatened confrontation. Neither she nor I have any personal reality here; whatever she's up to—or I'm up to, for that matter—it is not going to be advanced an inch by our being made to meet. It could only make us both more foreign to the landscape, not less.

I have beaten the bounds a dozen times and more and each time note with pleasure how the countryside takes over from the city by way of huge turn-of-the-century white stucco Rana palaces, fat columns, colonnades and *œil-de-bœufs*. I've been inside a few, the rest I look at through the railings of their park-like gardens. The British Residency park that was really fully grown only by the last decades of the nineteenth century must have rung a gong to announce the bizarre idea of trees to be prized and loved as beauties in themselves and, by extension, as symbols of rich living (whereas the poor still think of them as firewood). The idea caught on, evidently: the treeless local landscape of Dr Oldfield's water-colours of the 1860's is now rich with Rana trees. Little post-Rana villas behind suburban-garden gates have mushroomed up meantime, of course, but we may ignore them and the foreign embassies so many house. There are a number of large new buildings we have to shut our eyes to in the suburbs, too. The mind boggles to think what would have happened to lovely homogeneous Kathmandu if there had been more building-money lying idle in the Valley since the Revolution and 1951.

Nightfall hides these few but awful horrors, though it can have brought no balm to Henry Lawrence at the Residency in the early 1840's; it only emphasised his prisoner's plight. No vivifying Mussoorie Shum Shere for him to visit or have round to visit him, whereas my evenings are so often enlivened by him, at a nephew's house, or else a cousin's—('...for cousin Singha Shum Shere —we may call him "Excellency"—I think perhaps a neck-tie, Peter. I'm glad to see you've got a jacket on this evening, anyhow. Is there a neck-tie in the pocket, possibly? No? Then look! A hat-box full of them to choose from!'). Or else Mussoorie will have invited family-members round to him, and from what I see of it his social life is sharp and lively. There must be other cliques, but for me Kathmandu society is Mussoorie and his lot—different evenings, different friends and family-members. They vary widely in their looks, from almost wholly Mongol to almost wholly Rajput-Indian. They vary too in size and age and in their handling of English. Where this concerns the older Ranas I think it must reflect a subtle difference in social standing. Probably the old-time Rana succession to the hereditary prime ministry is at the back of it. The succession-list, for which the rules were disregarded, reinterpreted or falsified as each successor played his tricks with it, gives the key, I think. My guess is that in general the highest education (here detectable in the excellency of the speaker's English) was reserved for those who, being close in line for the succession, would have the most need of it. But these nice indistinctions barely show in the social intercourse of every day.

Our conversations to begin with would go like this:

'I am very happy to meet the Maharajkumar-sahib's English friend, sir.'

'And I am very proud to meet the family-members, sir.'

'Maharajkumar-sahib was telling, you are much interested in our illustrious ancestor, General Sir Jung Bahadur Rana, GCB, GCSI, etcetera.'

'Yes, deeply interested. Particularly in stories handed down within the family. Personal details.'

Another voice chips in: 'So? I wonder if you know that he would go about the streets at night in thick disguise?'

'Like Haroon el-Rashid?'

'Yes, And how once he entered stealthily to some armoury, to test the vigilance of the guard. And Jung was just stealing some weapon from the walls when the guard woke from his doze, jumped up, attacked the thief, then fell back terrified on seeing who it was!'

'—and Jung was so absolutely delighted with this bold if somewhat sleepy guard, Mr Mayne, that he forthwith promoted him to sergeant. How's that?'

'Wonderful! Typical, I think, too.'

'Sahib knows the story of the narrow spar across the chasm and Prince Surendra orders Jung to turn his pony half the way across. . . ?'

'A brilliant horseman, sir!'

And I chip in with 'Brilliant!'

'—and next day they take away the spar and bring Jung to this place and order him to jump his pony over, so he jumps, and he and pony fall into the raging flood so far below! Does this kill Jung? It kills his pony—but Jung! Never! He swims beneath the torrent and is back next day!'

'—and then jumping down the wells at Prince Surendra's orders! And back next day!'

'The prince's girls survived the well-jumps less easily than Jung,' I commented, 'or so I hear.'

For Jung was always back next day, whether from some such murderous test or from dangers gladly entered into on his own. Once he subdued an elephant run amuck that terrorised the city; often, single-handed, he captured wild ones, or fought with leopards (an Oldfield eye-witness account supports this); or as a young man, bored with soldiering, he deserted, lived by his skill as gambler, went down to the plains of India with some thought of selling his sword ('He was a brilliant swordsman, sir') to Ranjit Singh, Lion of the Punjab, then thinking better of it came back home to pardon, each time to pardon.

But the best-loved and relished of all the rich apocrypha are the tales of Jung Bahadur's sexual exploits and excesses—something everyone can take rightful pride in.

'You know, of course, sir, that Jung Bahadur was a famous womaniser?'

'I'd heard so. Do tell me, please.'

'You like?' The speaker was looking round at the others, nodding.

'Of course. With details, please.'

'Well, sir. I think you do not know that the day they came to Jung to tell him of the great mad elephant that terrorised the city —he was in the bed of some prostitute!'

'They knew exactly where to look for him, you mean?'

'Yes. Of course they knew.'

'But in the sexual freedom of those days were prostitutes required?'

'So many will prefer a prostitute,' he answered absently.

'Less fuss?'

'No fuss.' This was a new speaker. 'And in modern Kathmandu, nine thousand girls, at least. Think of it, sir!'

'All young beauties,' someone else was saying, and here Mussoorie himself joined in:

244

'And everyone a student laudably working her way through college.'

'So that's the new idea, then!' I exclaimed, tricked for a second by his dead-pan face (but mocking now 'Oh Peter! *Really!*').

But someone else embarked upon another story of Jung Bahadur's exploits, evidently a favourite: how his roving eye had lit upon a palace-girl, and he perhaps too bold and forward. The young girl turned on him, haughty, threatening to denounce him to the king—

'And what he did? He laughed only! And laughing said to her "Some day, you wait. I marry you".'

'Tell the sahib what happened then! Tell him!'

'Yes, tell me. Did he ever marry this haughty little beauty?'

'Yes, sir, he did. Moreover she was to be one of the three wives who insisted upon performing *sati* on his funeral pyre, he who had expressly forbidden his wives to do so! He gravely discountenanced *sati*. He could not at that early period forbid the honourable practice. But it was known he frowned on it. He would say "We, the nobles, should set this example of forbidding our widows *sati* —and thus the common people will follow suit".'

'Three *satis*! Think of this, sahib! To honour him in death and bring great honour on themselves. Three! On his fire!'

At this point, a cousin-brother leaning forward cast a quick glance at a lady in the background. The ladies, if present at such gatherings, tend to stand back, in an archway possibly, by a door, beside a curtain. They are somehow at the social gathering yet not exactly of it. This seems to be the etiquette still in Mussoorie's section of Kathmandu high-society. This cousin-brother glancing sideways wished to whisper something that the lady should not overhear. 'You know that Jung was always telling everyone "Never miss a chance with any woman you can get—*any* woman!" '

'Yes,' I told him, 'and the *Kama Shilpa*, that ancient great authority on love, it says so too.'

'Oh yes,' he whispered, 'Jung was a great breaker of hearts. He is known to have kissed more than fourteen hundred different girls.'

'Was "kissed" the word you used, sir?'

'Sometimes we say "kissed",' another man explained in whispers. 'We who live so many centuries after Lord Krishna first entered the Valley, we ... Yes, it was the great Lord Krishna's coming that made the difference for us. Before he came it was mostly the Lord

Vishnu—just the one girl for him, though in her varied aspects. But when the Lord Krishna came from India, thenceforth men would try to emulate him—"Kiss and forget! Kiss and forget!" A hundred milkmaids, a thousand—the Lord Krishna adored milkmaids. "Kiss and forget." '

'Maharaja Joodha Shum Shere—he too kissed girls far and wide. His number was above twelve hundred. He admitted it.'

'And General Kaiser Shum Shere—yes, our cousin. Dead now.'

'Sad,' I said. 'I have been to his beautiful library, though.'

'Yes, sad. General Kaiser was present on one occasion at a talk of kissing girls but had to flee the room from fear that they would make him name his number, which was but a paltry nine hundred and something.'

This bit of conversation had a sequel to it. Running into Mussoorie an evening or so later on Joodha Road (the newspaper stampede again) he spoke of it:

'All that about kissing girls, remember? Yes, exactly! My poor cousin was a bit upset. Not seriously, of course, but cousin's wife was—seriously so. She had overheard. She later said to him "That talk of kissing and counting up how many, what can cousin's Englishman have thought of you?"—and he asked her in return "But my dear wife, what could have been said—if not 'kissing'? Tell me please."—and after she had thought a little she replied "You could have said 'winked at'." '—and Mussoorie burst out laughing, then added: 'And you know what, Peter? Since you're interested. Jung had made a standing offer. Twenty-thousand rupees to any girl who could oblige him to ... well, to ejaculate a second sooner than he chose to!'

'Did any girl win the prize, I wonder?'

'None. Or so they say.'

'He may have given them booby-prizes. A diamond bracelet, for example. For honourable failure.'

'History does not relate,' Mussoorie said. 'And do you know Jung's trick? Opium! A fine controlling-agent! Jung was a confirmed addict, though not intemperate.'

'How interesting! Do you think that Jung controlled King Surendra, calmed him, with opium too? I think it possible.'

'I wonder.'

A long letter from Jagut has catapulted me back all the way to Soon Saan.

Dear Peter—

I have been meaning to write but events have overwhelmed us and there hasn't been a moment free till now—so I'll cram it all in just anyhow to keep you up to date and so that you may be prepared for shocks on getting back here. (When is it to be?)

They found for the complainant—the Panchayat, I mean; in that boring case of the 'bewitched' buffalo. I knew they would: and so would I have, if foolhardy enough to meddle in the matter. Compensation assessed at five hundred chips. Compensation? What for? The polyandrous defendant was up in arms, be sure. Yet she was all compassion, lamenting a dear neighbour's loss—but death was wise Nature's way with animals—with man too, when his time is on him. Some say she gave the complainant a very meaning look as she uttered these words. The wrangle still goes on and everybody with a part in it feels deeply ill-used in his or her own way. You will understand now, even if you did not at the time, how prudent one must always be in matters of 'bewitchment'.

Our poor Fair Maiden seems to have gone into a decline. I wonder if she's got T.B.? I must have her tubercular-tested, like the Jerseys. Or is it only for forlorn love of Sir Launcelot that she is wasting? Sir Launcelot, by the way, has been on the rampage again these last few days. Absent without leave down in the Bin Nullah with that public-miller and one or two cronies.

Talk about 'Tirra lirra by the river
Sang Sir Launcelot'
Some one else has got a rod in pickle waiting for him too, and I'm sure you can guess who. Right first time! Jezebel! Nothing seems to have been coming right for anybody, somehow.

Now, alas, for very bad news. Two deaths. I fear the first of them will pain you, for he had become your friend, as everyone recalls. Poor Kalé, Bird-Fancier. Found lying on his side not far from home. Dead. No forensic explanation. None. I fear his beautiful half-sister will be disconsolate when next she comes of age. Perhaps I should replace him—for her sake: and for the other ladies' too; in their seasons. We ought to have someone 'at stud' and a younger generation coming up for recruitment into the Pariah-pack. None of us lasts forever. Perhaps his half-sister will be giving him a posthumous son in consequence of that unfortunate mishap she suffered, not to speak of their shameless love-making when released. I do hope so.

247

The second death: our poor leper-boy. They have consigned him: they promised me they wouldn't and then waited till I was absent for the inside of a day. I dare say they were right to do it and I was wrong to try to interfere. They say it was a very dignified ceremony—just the immediate loving family, all drunk, of course; but not to the point of dropping the litter or anything unseemly. They had wrapped a long cummerbund about him and weighted it with great stones. The poor boy's final shout was excellently rendered, so his father told me: it went ringing bravely round the valley. In he went, the waters closing over him, and no sign of him since then, which is good. We don't want *revenants* at Soon Saan. The boys have instructions to fish up-stream of him at present. But one must not dwell on sadness. He has gone and it is really better thus.

I haven't finished yet, though. More bad news to give you. Our handsome Punjabi tenant having quite recovered from his accident has been bitten by a mad dog. What a hullabaloo! Most people are sorry for him now and inclined to forget the strange rumours, but not Sarwa. He claims that our Punjabi had been trying tricks with some peasant's little daughter, a girl not all that far from here, down near the barrage. The father had suspicions, grilled his little daughter sharply, obliged her to identify the man, and with his sons went after our Punjabi. That's the story Sarwa's telling—but with no corroboration, I'm bound to say. And meanwhile I have to send the Punjabi down to Dehra Dun to get his daily shots against the Rabies. And this brings me to something else—Bal Bahadur, major-domo. I fear this is a very woeful situation-report on how things have been going on, back here 'at the Château'.

'Ô tout va bien, madame la marquise—

Ô tout va, tout va bien. . . .'

—remember singing that old song so long ago?—though I can't remember any more of it. Bal Bahadur has gone mad again! It has been terrible. He locked himself up in his cottage and every now and then would open up a window, just a chink, and point a gun out through it (a gun of mine, I may say!) threatening to shoot all comers, even me! It took two days to calm him. How lucky that I have a bit of pharmaceutical experience. We left him food on the window-sill; like leaving food for gods in temples, but this one ate it all. It did, well—you know—calm him: quite a lot, in fact. I was even wondering if perhaps I'd overdone it. Rather a relief the day he came out 'calmed' and of his own accord. But meanwhile Soon Saan had been in sorry straits, not only emotionally; economically too. Bal Bahadur is our Bank, you see: he keeps all our money, all of it! And he'd been refusing to release an anna. We've had to live on 'tick'. Grovel for 'tick' from tradesmen! Think of it!

But there's one good thing (two if you count the bumper rice-crop)—something that shows that after all, the major deities are on our side. *My new car has been delivered!* A dove-grey 'Ambassador' four-door saloon—that's the Austin or whatever it is: the thing assembled here in India from imported parts. We've got a Gurkha chauffeur too. I'm so relieved: a car again at last, even if it means the tightening of belts. It has been doing shuttle-service—daily Dehra Dun for the Punjabi and his anti-rabies shots; and at intervals Bal Bahadur (separate trips: he and the Punjabi cannot bear each other) for his shock-treatment. Lucky that the Civil Surgeon is a good friend of mine, and kind. I think and hope the worst is over now.

Send me a cable when you know your arrival date at Dehra Dun—I suggest the same morning train again—and you shall be met at the station.

Give my love to Prince Rice-Mill, will you. With love to you too. Ever yours. Jagut.

P.S. Everyone sends respectful salaams. Sarwa wants me to mention to you the matter of the Punjabi's smashed-up face that day when you were with us still to see it. 'Please ask Peter-sahib if he remembers what I told him then.' What *did* he tell you? Don't bother to answer, though. You can tell me when you get here.

21

The next time I was to see Mussoorie I took Jagut's letter along with me for him to read:

'Prince Rice-Mill indeed!' he exclaimed. 'Jagut knows perfectly well I've given my children my share in it! He's much better off than I am.'

I laughed, then said: 'By the way—just a second.' I had left a big square envelope in Mussoorie's hall when coming in and now went to get it: 'Did you ever see this? The year of Jung's embassy to London.'

'Show!'

'Jung Bahadur. A wood-engraving—a reproduction of one. It was in the *Illustrated London News* in summer 1850.'

He glanced at it. 'You can see it's by an English artist. The English have never been able to draw eastern people. Look! It's all wrong! And he's made him quite black, too!'

'I just wondered if you'd think it interesting...'

'How kind you are, Peter. But you see I only collect hand-paintings. And this is—a what?'

'Only a reproduction of a wood-engraving, really.'

'It was kind of you to think of me'—

—and indeed I did see. So I put the thing back in its envelope and recovered poise, a little, by saying: 'I bet you don't know all I know about that embassy to Queen Victoria.'

'What about it?'

'Girls and such.'

'Jung couldn't keep off it, of course.'

Lieutenant-Colonel Thoresby arrived at the Kathmandu Residency as successor to Henry Lawrence in the winter of 1846, having prudently awaited the recession of the *ayul* in the Terai, and he had missed the Kōt Massacre into the bargain. He remained in this post till 1850, so it was during his tenure of office as Resident that the great formative experience of Jung Bahadur's life was organised and the scene was set for the real Anglo-Nepali love-affair to start.

On 15 January 1850 His Excellency Jung Bahadur Konwar Rana-ji, Minister and Commander-in-Chief, Ambassador Extraordinary to the Court of Queen Victoria, set off from Kathmandu for London, leaving the eldest of his six younger brothers—Bam '*Kukri*-headwound' Bahadur—to officiate for him. His suite consisted of some seven high Nepali officers, among them his two youngest and favourite brothers, Jagut and Dhir, both colonels now and Dhir, the youngest, aged about nineteen. On top of this 'a bard, a doctor (*ayurvedic*, probably: a Nepalese) one Newar artist (whose name I do not find on record: was it Mussoorie's Bhaju Ratna who I've been calling (with Mussoorie) 'Bhaju—the Kid'?)—plus orderlies and a whole host of domestic servants. Accompanying Jung 'in political charge of the Mission' was the Captain Cavenagh of the Bengal Army who in 1851 was to publish a short and excellent 'Account'—on Kirkpatrick/Hamilton lines. A certain Mr D. Macleod, at one time pleader in the Calcutta courts, was attached to Jung as interpreter and private secretary.

The Governor-General received Jung most flatteringly in Calcutta—a full Durbar. A nineteen-gun salute greeted Jung's arrival, and nineteen guns again to signal his departure aboard the Peninsular and Oriental ship *Haddington*. Most of the ship had been chartered exclusively for Jung and party, very grand; but his grandeur could not save Jung from the indignity of being seasick, hopelessly and miserably, when they reached the Bay of Bengal. His son Padma Jung says he kept a diary and we have this quote:

'—the waves rose high like mountains and people sleeping on bedsteads were in danger of being rolled down.'

The diary must have been dictated, and if it is still extant I have not seen it.

Up the Red Sea, by the overland route from Suez to Cairo: thence by the river-steamer *Feroza* down the Nile to Alexandria. There they boarded the P & O steamer *Ripon*, all her fore-cabins and saloons reserved for Jung. In her they sailed for Southampton, via Malta and Gibraltar.

The travel-costs to Southampton alone amounted to £10,000, so a press-report announced with awe. Yet does this seem so much? Jung carried with him not only 'complimentary letters from the King' to Queen Victoria 'but' it was said, 'a quarter-million pounds sterling worth of presents'. Arrived at Southampton, Jung somewhat disconcerted everyone on the reception-committee by declining point-blank to stay the night in any hotel not emptied for his exclusive use, 'lest any food prepared by Christians should be mixed in with his own'. Jung got his way; and in the back-yard of his hotel was erected a tent in which four cooks worked away, observing the utmost secrecy in the dressing of the food and their masters in the eating of it. But against this squeamishness Jung's party

'cared not at all who should see them at their extraordinary ablutions. They wash after they touch anything. Not only the Hindu servants but also some of the chiefs were in the back-yard almost perpetually. They stripped, with the exception of a slight cloth around their loins, and they would wash themselves all over with about half a pint of water.'

In Southampton that Saturday onlookers may have been watching everything with wonder in their eyes, but they freely commented upon the meanness of the servants' clothing, contrasted with the magnificence of their masters'.

To London—and the visit-proper had begun.

London fell on him; the press was full of him:

'He is the first Hindu of high caste that has visited this country . . .'—and the public was quite unprepared for him as he drove down Piccadilly—'. . . in his rich oriental costume, profusely wrought in gold and glittering with diamonds, pearls and precious stones stated to be worth £150,000':

nor prepared either for his manner, which was

'regal and graceful and he appeared more like a polished European than Oriental . . .'

He was described as 'rather slight in figure but neatly formed; strong, firm and agile as a hart'.

So that's what Jagut is still as agile as! A hart! And yet I think not 'hart'. It is a creature far too timid for Jung then or Jagut now.

'Ibex' for both of them! Surer-footed, bolder, braver, better-fitted to their craggy mountain-country, and sharper too.

'The general is a handsome and most intelligent man, about thirty-two years of age, very dark with long jet black hair'—and another account contrasts his neat, firm, agile figure 'with his two short, or rather fat, brothers, who accompany him. His features are of the Tartar cast.'

This is from *The Times*, a letter from a correspondent in Calcutta who had evidently interviewed or met Jung there on his arrival from Nepal. This correspondent tells us that Jung—

'—has picked up a little English and to my great gratification told me what he had learned and I corrected his sentences for him and he repeated the alterations till he was perfect; after which he asked me to teach him others, carefully enquiring and noting the difference in addressing equals, inferiors and superiors—'

In London Jung was diligently increasing his range of English sentences, though alas we get no chance of hearing them in actual use and only three of them are known to me with certainty—because they are the three that he repeated back in Kathmandu to amuse his visiting English friend, Laurence Oliphant. Jung's English and French (wrote Oliphant) 'are less than rudimentary. "How d'you do?" "Very well, thank you." And then with great volubility, "You are very pretty."'

Queen Victoria was safely delivered of Prince Arthur, Duke of Connaught, on 1 May 1850, but her convalescence necessarily postponed for Jung his first audience of her—the piece of knowledge I'd showed off with to that chance-met Nepali gentleman in discussing Jung Bahadur and his relations with our queen. Meanwhile there were to be other social occasions for Jung Bahadur, such as an exchange of visits between him and the Duke of Wellington who bowled Jung over and was from that instant 'my friend'. The friendship finds an echo—eighty-one of them in fact—in a grand salute of guns on Thandi Khel reverberating round the Valley of Nepal in 1852, one for each year of the old man's life the year he died.

The exchange of noble visits by no means filled Jung's London days, however. Sumptuously housed in Richmond Terrace as he was, and wonderfully looked-after (which delighted him), he was discreetly left alone as well, when circumstances might suggest discretion. Jung and his brothers were discovering delights enough, and more, for the filling of their leisure hours. They lived it up, and the least of it was 'shopping'.

Shopping-sprees. Jewels of 'Messrs Morel's Jewelry Dépt [sic] in New Burlington Street'. Guns and rifles from James Purdey & Sons of South Audley Street—and pistols too. Pianos from Broadwoods. Violins and flutes from somewhere. Billiard-tables. Wolfhounds. A chandelier 'like a glass tree, the trunk of glass being nine inches in diameter, the whole affair sixteen foot high. It cost £800.' This is from a letter Dr Oldfield wrote from Kathmandu to his mother back in England.

Anything and everything was pounced upon and bought. 'Half of his purchases are quite useless to him,' Oldfield told his mother, but the violins and flutes were far from useless: Jung had four of his six 'beautiful misuses' (so described to Oliphant) taught to play 'The Girl I left behind me' and they later performed it for Oldfield. 'They really played very fairly, while one or two others danced.' Jung himself had learnt to dance the polka while in London, and a London music-publisher cashed in with sheet-music entitled 'The Coomeranajee Polka' and 'Long Live Jung Bahadur!' And later, back home in Kathmandu, Jung had what sounds like a Boys' Battalion taught to dance it in jigging couples one-two-three-HOP! which much disconcerted English visitors who saw the boys in action. For their polka-number the boys wore 'pen-wiper' costumes. And while western music fills the air on Thandi Khel I add that two Gurkha military bands under a British bandmaster were soon to learn 'The British Grenadiers' and play it full blast in the very early mornings.

Jung had knocked London cold. Thackeray wrote a jingle about him for *Punch* calling it 'Mr Mahony's Account of the Ball given to the Nepalese Ambassador by the Peninsular & Oriental Company'.

'At ten before the ballroom door
His moighty Excelléncy was,
He smiled and bowed to all the crowd
So gorgeous and immense he was. . . .'

Gorgeous, he certainly was! And glittering!

'Bedad his troat, his belt, his coat
All bleez'd with precious minerals.'

Jung took a box at Her Majesty's Theatre. Together with his

two brothers he was introduced to Opera, and how they loathed the 'abominable screechings'. But the little ballet girls were quite another matter. After the performance Jung and his two brothers would be round back-stage, hot-foot, and massive bits of jewelry would soon be changing wrists and necks.

The brothers ordered London suits, so dark and decent, no doubt from Savile Row. They had discovered the notorious Cremorne Gardens and other places frequented 'by such fast men as they showed themselves to be' (Oliphant). Wearing their London suits, in 'thick disguise' and recognised at once, they went—O joy!— and ogled at the ladies, boggled at them, and how the ladies boggled back at these Eastern princes too good to be true, too rich to be believable!

'Rana men have always seemed to prefer girls of the lower orders to high-born ladies'—has not Jagut Shum Shere told me so himself?

Jung was having the time of his life—scattering 'bleezing' bracelets left and right—'kiss and forget—kiss and forget'.

The pretty lady who did best of all out of these showers of jewelry and gold was a girl called Laura Bell. She was daughter of a bailiff on Lord Hertford's Irish estates, but had left home for wider horizons, 'first to Belfast—where she was a shopgirl for a few months—then to London where she got a job at Jay's Mourning Establishment in Regent Circus (as Oxford Circus was then called)'—I owe all this to James Laver. 'Here she attracted the attention of the Nepalese Envoy, HRH Prince Jung Bahadur'— Mr Laver's source makes Jung not only prince, but royal prince, and Jung would not have minded: rather the reverse. 'And before she had finished with him had mulcted him of the prodigious sum of £250,000.' There is a sequel: but something else comes first.

Discreetly insulated from all this fast-and-looseness there was Queen Victoria. As soon as she recovered from her accouchement and was strong enough she received Jung—received him with such grace and charm and majesty that she enslaved him, he who while bowing deeply to the concept of the sanctity of kings had hitherto had first-hand experience only of delinquents on the throne. She honoured him, she knighted him—Knight Grand Cross of the Order of the Bath. And a signal honour—she caused him to sit beside her at a drawing-room surrounded by her children. She was barely thirty—Jung just thirty-three. A comely pair: you might think them ill-assorted, yet a little thought may well have crossed Jung's mind—though hardly hers. A son of Maharaja Chandra Shum Shere confirms for me what the citizens of Kathmandu then thought (still think to this day): it is taken quite for granted that this majestic handsome couple had allowed themselves a moment's intimacy. Why else the Order of the Bath—if it wasn't in the bath-room? All this apart, however, there was probably no need for her Majesty to be informed of Jung's unfortunate involvement with Miss Laura Bell—enough that her Ministers of State should know, and Mr Laver rounds the story off as follows:

'—strange to relate the Foreign Office, anxious to preserve British-Nepalese relations on an amicable basis, refunded this sum to the Prince'—

—a quarter-million pounds sterling! Hurrah for British diplomacy! Up the Anglo-Nepalese love-affair! Nepalese history was to be transformed by the emotions that stirred Jung's heart and admiration and the union was destined to secure for Britain generation after generation of the world's best fighting-men, the Gurkhas, matchless recruits for our British and Indian Armies. For Nepal this *mariage de convenance* secured what still remains today the country's largest single element in her foreign-exchange earnings (except for rice exports to India)—the home-remittances from Gurkha soldiers serving overseas or down in India and, later, their pensions or those of their widows.

Throughout Jung's long victorious London visit there was one member of his suite who, while marvelling (with Jung) at the splendours all around him, hated it. His name was Kazi Kharbar Khattri, an ultra-orthodox Hindu to whom the presence everywhere of Christians seemed the deepest possible defilement. Careful as the poor man was to keep himself apart from the filthy beef-eaters, he felt himself polluted; yet, feeling this, he had to watch Jung's goings-on, how Jung was revelling in the muck-heap, adoring these Christian untouchables. How could the good old Kazi bear it?

When the party finally reached Kathmandu again, Jung's lurking natural enemies were to discover in the reluctant Kazi's testimony exactly what they needed to bring about Jung's downfall. Caste-defilement.

22

'All that pertains to external and internal defilement, bodily or spiritual, is the very beginning of a Hindu's education, both religious and civil.'

This is the Abbé Dubois again. What was true of India's deep south where the Abbé lived and worked so long, was equally true of Hindu Nepal—and still was true in 1850 when Jung went to London. To leave India at all meant braving the *Kala Pani*, the Black Waters, the river that could be seen to encircle India and the world. Crossing the *Kala Pani* meant defilement immediate and automatic, and loss of caste. Luckily caste lost in this way could be redeemed by pilgrimage to certain holy temples on one's return, there to go through the complicated rituals of re-purification, which naturally cost a lot of money. To cross the *Kala Pani*, then, was bad enough, but in Jung Bahadur's case he and his whole party had been exposed to pollution of an order infinitely more vile; they had actually entered and stayed in the Land of the Beefeaters. On their return to India the rituals of re-purification were to be correspondingly more rigorous and more expensive still. The job was, however, very satisfactorily accomplished.

Renewed and sinless, the party crossed to Ceylon to take ship from Colombo to Calcutta. It was in Colombo that Jung met young Laurence Oliphant, the son of the British Chief Justice of Ceylon. Jung promptly invited Oliphant to accompany him back to Kathmandu as his guest. It will have pleased the Company, this young man's employers. Oliphant, alert, inquisitive, bright enough, now Jung's bidden guest, first Englishman ever to be invited to Nepal as friend and not official. The book the young man wrote gives an inside-view: a light-weight's view no doubt, but the heavy-weights were locked behind the Residency walls and Oliphant's delineation of the local scene does help to fill things out.

When Kathmandu was almost reached Jung halted. He had to give the astrologers time to consult the stars and so determine day and hour for an auspicious entry. They got it wrong, as we shall see, but on 6 February 1851 Jung approached the city.

On that triumphant day one of Jung's brothers was assigned to Oliphant as 'conductor' ('—he took me by the hand in the most affectionate manner') and, writing a year after the event Oliphant can add a detail then unknown to him—that this same 'conductor' 'distinguished himself a week later by a base attempt to assassinate the minister', his brother. Well might Jung exclaim, indeed he was to do so later, 'Save me from my brothers!'—but for the moment he seems to have had no inkling of what they had in store for him, as smiling, affectionate Badri Nur Singh conducts young Oliphant into the Durbar tent set up for this occasion.

Oliphant now sees the king for the first time: King Surendra Bir Vikram Sah, sixth in line, aged twenty-two that year. He was sitting on a divan and was slung with jewels and 'gorgeously attired'.

'His countenance is not unlike those depicted on the walls of Indian towns, with the same large staring eyes . . .'—myopic, on the later evidence of Dr Oldfield. Oliphant continues his description:

'. . . thin twisted moustache, the full lips and thick bull neck . . .'

Oliphant probably already knew the young man's reputation so that he would read into his face the sort of character it went with:

'I thought the young man . . . seemed to have only just enough sense to gratify the brutal and sensual passions to which he is prey . . .'

and here follow stories of Surendra's murderous pursuits, including those in which Jung himself had been the intended victim.

'Whether the stories are true or not, I cannot say, but he looks capable of any wickedness.'

Capable no longer, though. His passions had been calmed. One wonders how.

258

But who was 'the old gentleman sitting with perfect sang-froid next the king?' Ex-King Rajendra, whom we last saw accompanying his wife to exile in Benares a few years earlier. Jung had pardoned him for having meanwhile led a damp-squib of an insurrection against him (though once and for all deposed for having tried it on).

'Jung himself was unquestionably the only distinguished-looking man in Durbar, wearing a magnificent robe of white silk embroidered with gold, and pantaloons of rich brocade which set off his slim figure to advantage. His turban was a mass of sparkling diamonds, and his whole person seemed to be loaded with jewels. His sturdy bodyguard, all armed with double-barrelled rifles [Purdey weapons, bought in London], stood close in behind his chair and were the only soldiers in the tent. The nonchalant way in which he addressed the Raja, with folded arms and unbended knee, betokened the unbounded power he possessed over the State.'

The fact is that Jung's experience of London had brought him to look down upon the little world of Kathmandu. It had already 'become highly repugnant to him to embrace' the king, or even bother to take his shoes off when in attendance on him. He spoke of his feelings in more general terms, too, which must have fed Oliphant's sense of national pride, and this it was that caused him to abandon his simple young-man's narrative prose-style for a bit of carefully-turned Victorian purple, putting these words into Jung's mouth:

'Why should I attempt to tell these poor ignorant people what I have seen [in London]. It is as ridiculous to suppose that they would believe it as it is hopeless to attempt to make them understand it.'

Yet Oliphant had noted that on entering Pandit Vijay Raj's presence—Jung's old friend who had saved his life with timely warning of the Bashniat Conspiracy and who was in consequence Raj-Guru—Jung would make profound obeisances, touching first his own forehead and then the foot of the man he wished to honour.

Oliphant went everywhere with Jung and Dhir, best-loved and only trusted brother: to their respective houses, to court, to see the

Resident, on big-game shoots. It was at meal-times only that he seems to have been required to keep his distance. At a shooting-picnic, for example—'retiring a few yards from me, for a Hindu may not eat in the presence of a Christian, Jung and his brothers were soon deep in the mysteries of curious viands . . .'—of which they brought him some to share, with grapes and pomegranates—'. . . Jung always helping me with his own hand.' Young Oliphant did not bother to ask himself how else Jung could feed an 'untouchable' without the instant pollution of their own food too. Back at Soon Saan I have watched Jagut's Brahmin cook do exactly this as well—drop the workers' helpings on to each man's proffered plate from a height judged ritually safe.

Dhir bustles in and out of Oliphant's narrative '. . . jovial, light-hearted, thoroughly unselfish, brave as a lion, always anxious to please and full of amusing conversation'. He comes in whistling the 'Sturm March', challenging him to a game of billiards in Jung's new billiard-room at Thapathali. In Dhir's own palace he proudly shows his dogs off—

'bull-dogs, terriers of all descriptions, a collection worthy of the most ardent votary of the Fancy . . . His manner was more thoroughly English than any native I ever knew, and both in appearance and disposition looked as if he was an Anglo-Saxon who had been dyed by mistake . . .'

—so I take it that Dhir's features were less Mongol than Mussoorie's, for example. In other respects, character, 'disposition' and the rest, Mussoorie is for me Dhir's reincarnation, Dhir's spirit having passed first to his own son Deb, and then from Deb to his son Mussoorie, tying family-history together with a strong *fil rouge*. And Jagut? He is for me great-uncle Jung Bahadur, tamed, calmed and civilised.

Ten days soon passed and on 16 February 1851 Bam Bahadur, Jung's next younger brother, who had deputised for him throughout the year-long absence on the London visit—Bam who had tasted power in fact, and found how much he liked it—Bam went to the new Thapathali palace in a strangely nervous mood. It was nearing midnight and 'after sitting over the fire for some time' told Jung that he had a secret on his mind that had kept him sleepless for the two nights since he'd learnt it. All this I take from Oldfield, no doubt direct from Jung. Bam knew this secret from Badri Nur

Singh, Oliphant's 'amiable conductor'—and also from a first cousin of theirs: these two had visited Bam to tell him on the unimpeachable authority of Kazi Kharbar Khattri, the godly Kazi, that Jung had lost his caste in London '—by eating meat and drinking wine with and from the hands of Europeans, as well as by other acts incompatible with his caste as a Hindu'. Bam said he knew himself to be entirely innocent of plotting against Jung— but dared he hope that Jung would believe him? He told Jung that he had pretended to agree with everything the others said, so that in the day or two that he still had in hand he could 'with great tact and skill draw out all the details of the plan and show himself most anxious to further it'.

Bam's mind was in a torment now, or so he told Jung: he had the lives of two beloved brothers in his hands: Jung's could be saved only by betraying Badri Nur Singh. Well after midnight he ended up by revealing that the plot was due for execution early that very morning. A hired assassin was to shoot Jung on his way from Thapathali to the palace. Jung's severed head was then to be handed over to their brother Badri Nur, and the latter would himself show it to the troops.

Padma was later to maintain—as doubtless had Jung himself in speaking of it—that his uncle Bam was 'guiltless but wily'. In any case Jung bestirred himself that early morning. Armed posses, each a hundred strong, were immediately despatched to round up the conspirators: answer no questions, cut down all who might resist, bring the king's younger brother, Mohila sahib, to the Kōt at once, along with Badri Nur and their cousin—and for the two last-named the orders were 'alive or dead'. They were to bring old Kazi Kharbar Khattri too.

Within two hours all four prisoners 'heavily chained' were in the Kōt before the assembled chiefs, and by that very evening 'a paper clearly implicating them was found [for 'found' perhaps read 'drafted'] and all the guilty had confessed'. The king and ex-king Rajendra were both present at the Kōt but took no active part. The king, however, said that his brother Mohila sahib should suffer the same penalty as all the others—and in fact the grand council's verdict was unanimous: death for all—but with one dissenting voice. Jung's own. Blinding, then, as an alternative? But Jung objected to the blinding too. He had scarcely taken power in 1846 when he embarked upon an overhaul of the country's penal code. For instance he had abolished capital punishment except in

261

the case of murder and high treason; he had also abolished the old-time mutilations, and was very loath indeed to revise such practices as blinding, no matter what the crime. He was supported in his decisions by his mother (dead Matabar's sister). She has been described as a woman of irreproachable character who since the Massacre had consistently influenced her son 'on the side of clemency and mercy'.

Jung had other considerations too: he could not bring himself to lay violent hands on a royal prince—for him royalty was sacrosanct. Moreover Padma Jung explains that Mohila sahib was so weak by nature that he had been easily 'birdlimed by these cunning men'. Jung was content, in fact, to debar Mohila sahib from ever coming to the throne, and to get the British to receive the prisoners and confine them down at Allahabad in India.

Oldfield, whose account I have mostly followed, has a shrewd comment to make—that a plot like this could never have matured so fully had not the conspirators been assured of considerable support from the chiefs and others. People had been deeply shocked to hear the stories of Jung's fraternising with Europeans: news of what the old Kazi had revealed had spread like bomb-blast. Oldfield corroborates this in writing home to his mother about Jung's eating meat and drinking wine with Christians while in London 'and flirting extensively with English ladies'. Moreover everyone in Kathmandu could see with his own eyes a sort of confirmation of Jung's alleged partiality for the English in his too easy, too close association with, for example, Laurence Oliphant. He made no attempt to hide his affection for the English, and at Thapathali he had now displayed life-portraits of the Queen and the Prince Regent, cheek-by-jowl with photographs of his little ballet-dancers. A great many of his subjects were quite honest in their belief that Jung had sold himself to the British, and with him their country and its independence.

The Kazi's revelations drove Jung into frenzied rage—'gross and malicious perjury!' is how someone translated Jung's furious outburst into English. So although the Kazi had played no active role, yet he must suffer the supreme humiliation, so awful that no one cares to tell us exactly what it was, but it involved being 'subjected to a disgusting degradation' at the hands of two drummer-boys—untouchables, pariahs—all this in the presence of a large assembly who would witness the outrage to the old man's honour and his loss of caste. But no further punishments were to be inflicted on him. Jung had learnt clemency.

When in December 1852 another plot against him had been discovered, firmly scotched and the lives of the conspirators spared again, Oldfield wrote to tell his mother that:

'Since Jung had been to England, he has, in my opinion, become [one word illegible] humane, and mistaken leniency will, I am afraid, one of these days cost him his life.'

What would Jung have said to this? When well-wishers remonstrated with him, begged him to be more prudent, to punish treasonable acts with death, his answer was a question:

'What would *The Times* say?'

23

Success when once achieved is seldom very interesting to look at from outside, and for the person who achieved it the cost of staying on top can well prove too burdensome to be worth the trouble, except where money-money-money is the measure of success.

When Jung seized power he took his opportunity at the first *Panjanni* that came round to kick out every 'undesirable' office-holder. At this annual *Panjanni* ceremony each man's record for the previous year, from the highest in the land to the most humble, would be reviewed and his incumbency confirmed or else revoked. Jung had thus filled all key appointments with his brothers and relations, in the normal way. But now that he was in, he found to his dismay that no one (Dhir Shum Shere apart, perhaps) had any understanding of his simple plans for bettering Nepal, nor interest in them either. What did they care for good intentions? Jung, starry-eyed from England in 1851, was disillusioned all too soon, and then frustrated; and then, quite frankly, bored.

How 'great' was he? Great men achieve things, what did Jung achieve? Perhaps through the rosy spectacles of Victorian imperialist self-advantage Jung could be seen as 'great' because he was all-powerful in the Himalayan world that he inhabited, and Britain could depend upon his loyalty as a friend (and on his Gurkha man-power). We can hardly claim that his post-massacre achievements were more than modest. And the man himself? I had hoped somehow to clothe his bones with a bit of flesh and blood, to realise him as a living creature under all that jewelry and swagger: and for a moment, following up his actions and his movements on the night of the Kōt Massacre he seemed to me to live again. Perhaps it is that violence can hold our horrified attention much better than can the absence of it—Peace. The city, the whole country, knew stability at last, because of Jung. Peace at home and other peoples' wars abroad were to provide the nation with an income and an occasional outlet for Jung's superhuman energy that even after death would power the eight unremarkable Rana prime ministers who were to follow him.

Peace and quiet. God! how quiet and boring it had all become, not only in the city and round about, but in Jung's own palace and in the gingerbread-Gothic villas of the Residency compound. Poor Dr Oldfield had cruel abstinence to face as well. In the early days of 1851 his wife had yet to join him, and my guess is that he was not the type to find solace with the maid-servants. One of Oldfield's letters to his mother touches on this. It is written from Segauli, the one-horse town in British India where the 1816 Treaty with Nepal had been signed. For Oldfield on a fortnight's spree from Kathmandu, Segauli seemed *La ville lumière* itself:

'I have been enjoying myself very much down here and feel almost spoilt for the monotony of Nepal. However I have no doubt I shall soon fall into the old Nepalese habits of quiet and hermit-life.'

Some years later Oldfield's successor as Residency-Surgeon, Dr Wright, sat bored to death in his turn and speculating about the Ranas—how did they amuse themselves? It was an unfathomable mystery to him. 'They had no business except playing at being soldiers', no outdoor games; they never went out shooting—except (occasionally) big-game, down in the Terai. No literature to occupy their endless leisure (the Residency prisoners at least could read). Cricket? Degrading. Walking was beneath their dignity and was long to remain so as we know (Jung's sons would daily cover the two or three hundred yards to their English tutor's house and home again, on horseback, with attendants). Dr Wright, like Dr Oldfield, fails to list sex among the recreations, but it certainly helped the Ranas through their empty days and nights.

Something would happen every now and then to stir the air a little. A minor war, for instance: in 1855 Nepal invaded Tibet. Jung jumped to it: Dhir Shum Shere too (he particularly distinguished himself in fact). But this diversion did not last for long and the only thing about it that sticks in the mind is that Jung. with the solid backing of his Brahmin friend the *Raj Guru*, decided that for the purposes of feeding hungry fighting-men at great Himalayan altitudes, the useful Yak was far from being bovine; it was actually a 'kind of deer' whose flesh was both admissible to Kshatriya Hindus and fortifying.

Peace again. I'm not sure what year it was that Jung had organised a little more excitement to divert himself with, but the second London visit he then planned was necessarily cancelled: Jung fell sick down in Bombay where he and his suite were to have taken ship for England.

On 1 August 1856 Jung suddenly resigned the ministry and handed over to his next younger brother, Bam. He had grown 'wearied of the toils and responsibilities of office' (Oldfield). Yet there was a little matter that was exercising his mind a lot these days, a little weakness that he might be said to share with his self-made contemporaries in England whose desire was now for pedigrees to lead them proudly back not to some far-off Smith or Clerk or Tailor, but to origins more worthy of their new-won fortunes.

So, here in Kathmandu, Jung was pestering the king for his ennoblement. He quickly got it. It only cost the impression of the king's red seal for Jung to be not only Sir Jung Bahadur, GCB (with other English honours coming later in the queen's successive lists), but at the same time His Highness the Maharaja of Kashki and Lamjang, two minute territorial divisions in far-western Nepal from which (this was to be the presumption anyway) the family had sprung. And it was very soon revealed that the family itself was of the finest Rajput lineage. Mr Regmi, who does not care for Jung at all, says everybody knew that Jung was born a Khasa— which he suggests was nothing to write home about in terms of the Nepalese tribal social-register. A government official in Kathmandu explained to me that the Sahs and Ranas were really only 'country-bumpkins' when each snatched power in turn. He added: 'I expect they wanted to seem a little grander.' I see nothing wrong in that: we've all been at it, always.

What some have questioned since about the *sanad* to which Jung caused the king to set his seal (by now Surendra was fully tranquillised and did what he was told), was that Jung had had embodied in it not simply his elevation to hereditary maharaja of a new princely state with the title 'Highness', but also a clause that granted to Jung personally, and after him his heirs, the hereditary prime-ministry in perpetuity. In return for all this honour Jung graciously allowed that the king was in direct descent from the god Vishnu, which made him semi-divine, a condition which also made it quite improper for him to play a part in any mundane matters—or to be gazed upon by his subjects, except when taken in procession for this purpose, like any idol. No ordinary mortal, of course, was allowed into the presence.

Oldfield, who surely knew Jung's plans for the succession, says that on Jung's death the ministry and the title would pass to each of his surviving brothers in order of seniority, and then to his own sons. The idea behind this was presumably to reward the brothers for the part they had played in his own rise to power, but basically to ensure that a mature, experienced Rana family-member should succeed him. Meanwhile his eldest son, Jagut Jung, would be of an age to manage the affairs of state in his turn. No more co-regent mothers to take charge during a minority.

To consolidate the Rana position further still, in 1854, when the younger-generation Sahs and Ranas were growing big enough to marry, Jung had started welding the two families together in indissoluble wedlock. That year, for instance, his heir, Jagut Jung was married off to King Surendra's eldest girl. In the same year Jung himself was marrying the daughter of an important member of the royal family, and next year, her niece. In 1855 Jung's second son was evidently old enough to be brought into play, so he was given King Surendra's second daughter. And two years later Jung's oldest still-unmarried daughter was given to Surendra's son and heir.

Some years before all this, but with the same sharp eye to the future, Jung had engaged tutors for his sons, determined that the boys should start their lives better equipped than their own father had been, for Jung had found his lack of letters a serious handicap. Oliphant notes how Jung, by 1851, had been diligently applying himself to his 'Alphabet': and in time, they say, he was sufficiently master of his alphabet to carry on the simple sort of paper-work that was called for in his day—in the vernacular, of course. He had given up learning his useful English sentences. Who was there in Kathmandu that he could say to 'You are very pretty'?

In May 1857 Bam Shum Shere died—the brother Jung had put into the ministry when he resigned from it. Jung now promptly resumed the ministry himself. He had been very piqued meanwhile by the British Resident's correct but obstinate refusal to deal with state affairs through anyone but Bam, whereas Jung had aimed at meddling, and playing *eminence grise* as much or little as he fancied. So Jung was back again and would have been as bored as ever, but the Indian Mutiny had suddenly broken out and this perked him up. He was immediately offering his Gurkha army to his friends the British, and he himself would lead it into battle. And in fact the British, as things went worse and worse for them, most gratefully accepted Jung's offer. Jung and his Gurkhas surged down into India, and their contribution to the outcome of this dangerous situation was signal, though it scarcely endeared Jung to the Indians. I imagine, in fact, that there were to be residual memories of this when India helped the Sah king to overthrow the Ranas in Nepal's Revolution of 1950.

The Mutiny was suppressed; and there is a story that I cannot vouch for, though widely credited at the time, that the British rewarded Jung for all he did by allowing him to loot Lucknow's immensely rich quarter of the courtesans and prostitutes—the *Chakla*. Jung certainly arrived back home with a mass of jewels as booty, to which he was soon adding more when Nana Sahib, a prime-mover in the revolt against the British, appeared in Nepal as a refugee. Nana Sahib had hurriedly collected together all the jewels he could carry with him in his dash to safety. With him he also took his latest, youngest wife, a girl thirteen that year.

Jung loved jewels, and it must be said that in acquiring Nana's hoard he did not hesitate to take advantage of a defenceless man's position. Among the jewels that Jung bought off Nana sahib at remnant-sale prices was a famous treasure—'—a long necklace of pearls, diamonds and emeralds ... perhaps without a rival in the world' is how Landon describes it. Jung obliged Nana sahib to accept a mere nine lakhs for it, nine hundred thousand rupees, the price that gives the jewel its present name, *Nau Lakha*. There are photographs of Jagut and Mussoorie's mother wearing this astonishing piece. It comes down to her waist.

1857 had been a peak year for Jung Bahadur: he was to say of his part in the suppression of the mutiny (Indians today refer to it as their First War of Independence) as the high-spot of his career. He was now a grand old man of forty, and nothing would disturb the pattern of his life thereafter. The Brahmin Nana sahib had disappeared into the blue. Jung had acquired not only Nana's jewels but on top of them his little wife as well: Kashi Bai, thirteen that year. What would Jung care if a hundred years later Mr Regmi should loudly label him 'unscrupulous'—a Khasa daring to defile a Brahmin girl! Little would Kashi Bai have cared, either: she was shrewd beyond her years and extracted a very handsome settlement out of Jung.

There was one more little stutter of excitement left for Jung: in 1876 the Prince of Wales—later to be King Edward VII—visited Nepal at his invitation. A great success. The prince's suite included Dr Freyer, surgeon. Dr Freyer examined Jung (did Jung feel his health was failing?) and his verdict was that 'fat was gathering round the heart, and that as soon as the quantity reached a certain point, death would be instantaneous'.

I don't know if death was instantaneous when the end came in the year following, 1877. The grand old man was sixty. He died while he and Dhir were out of Kathmandu, on tour somewhere. Dhir and Rana Udip were now the only two surviving of the seven full-brothers. Somehow Dhir kept the news from breaking at the capital until he himself should get there with Jung's body. Rana Udip, the senior of the two survivors, was then installed as His Highness the Maharaja, Prime Minister, and Jung's body was carried in state procession to holy Pashupatinath. Despite Jung's strict injunctions, three of his wives committed *sati* in the flames that roared upwards from his funeral pyre. A heat-haze will have hovered shimmering above.

24

It is believed that Rana Udip was born in 1825 and that Dhir was some five years his junior. So by 1884 Rana Udip—Maharaja since 1877—was fifty-nine. He was ineffective, rather soft and silly, and tending in advancing age towards withdrawal into a nothingness which sounds less spiritual than lazy. Dhir was quite different; he was tough, energetic and determined: and on top of commanding the army it was really he who ruled the country. He could easily have rid himself of Rana Udip if he had chosen to, but he was quixotically set upon carrying out his beloved brother Jung's expressed wishes for the succession (each of Jung's brothers in his turn, and then his sons)—at least while Rana Udip was still alive.

From the outset Dhir had imposed 'a kindly but iron discipline' upon his seventeen sons, so determined was he that the boys should take all profit from the education he had given them through private tutors. He will surely have let them understand, if only tacitly, that the future could be theirs: for had not Jung, some time before he died, already turned against his own eldest son and struck his name off the Rana-succession? And was he not concurrently showing special interest in and special favours to Dhir's own eldest boy, Bir Shum Shere? Years later this was to be confidently interpreted (by Chandra Shum Shere, through Landon's pen) as showing Jung's intention to divert the succession from his own unsatisfactory sons to Dhir's much more worthy Shum Shere boys. And when Jung died and Dhir was quick to pack off into exile Jung's eldest boy, the dispossessed Jagut Jung, it will certainly have looked to everyone as if he were clearing the field of future competition.

As things turned out Dhir himself never came to power. He died in Autumn 1884, predeceasing his elder brother by a year.

Who was now to succeed when Rana Udip, last of the Jung brothers, himself should die? Jagut Jung, whom Rana Udip was seen to have recalled from exile as soon as Dhir was dead? Or would it be a Shum Shere...?

God save us from our brothers? God save us from our nephews and cousin-brothers too! But one dark November night God did not choose to save old Uncle Rana Udip from his nephews—nor Jagut Jung from his first cousins, those seventeen Shum Shere brothers.

At 9 p.m. on 22 November 1885 the hard-core Shum Shere brothers' striking-force was heading for their uncle's palace. The eldest brother, Bir, whose privilege it would be to usurp their uncle's and their cousin's place, was to take no part in the night's preliminary business, if only for the look of things. Instead he would be visiting the queen-mother and her boy the child-king.* This would give Bir an alibi and also would enable him to take these two into protective custody as soon as the initial deed was done.

In their uncle Rana Udip's private apartments, the old man was lying face down on a divan with a pillow to support his breast and raise his head. He was 'facing east', it seems: perhaps this made a subtle difference. He was dictating a letter, heading it with the holy invocation that is standard at the top of letters—*Ram Ram*. Rana Udip was *Ram-Ram*'ing at his lazy ease; two maid-servants were busy shampooing his feet and legs as he lay there on his stomach, and oh! the restful ritual, the kneading and the pressing and the light-handed working as if of so much dough—'the pleasing wantonnesse' as Mr Terry wrote in 1616 (I know of Mr Terry from *Hobson Jobson*).

Three of Jung's daughters were present too—including the one who was by now dowager-queen: also with them was the child-king's uncle. A peaceful, soporific scene, but it was interrupted by a knocking at the door. A senior courtier had come to say that Khadga (toughest of the hard-core Shum Sheres) desired an interview with His Highness their uncle in the matter of 'an urgent

* King Surendra's grandson: Surendra himself had died in 1881.

despatch from the Viceroy' just received via the Residency (who possessed the only cable-line in Kathmandu).

The door was opened to him—and Khadga, Chandra and three other younger brothers all trouped in. Jagut and Mussoorie's father, Deb, had evidently been excluded as 'unworthy' of a part in so significant a mission. Bir, the eldest brother, was absent at his alibi, of course. The Shum Shere striking-force was armed with rifles. The youngest of them present, Dambar, was muttering a little nervously about the rifle that he carried: an interesting fire-arm of a somewhat novel type, or so he said as dropping to one knee he aimed this interesting firearm at their uncle, pulled the trigger, point-blank range—BANG!—and missed. His bullet had merely grazed the old man's forehead. So Khadga had a shot him-self and killed him: or it may not even have been Khadga's bullet that did the trick, because the other brothers were taking pot-shots at their uncle now—which all can see does conveniently distribute blame. Under this volley their uncle fell 'to the floor', which must mean fell out of bed, unless he had jumped to his old shaking feet meantime. Uproar! The witnesses all ran for it, naturally enough. They feared the customary massacre, and even if women and royalty were exempt from being killed, you never knew. The dowager-queen made straight for the British Residency. In India, some years later, she met and so fascinated a certain William Digby with her story of the monstrous Shum Shere brothers and the killing of Maharaj Rana Udip (who was her uncle too, we may remember), that he quickly wrote a slim volume all about her sufferings and the flouting of Jung's plans for the succession, from which her personal favourites among her nephews had been ex-cluded.

Jung's biographer-son, Padma, had stories to tell of how he was pursued by relentless enemies as he too fled to asylum at the Resi-dency. Yet Padma did at least survive: their eldest brother, Jagut Jung, did not. The Shum Shere brothers tracked him down and murdered him, along with a young son.

It happened that the British Resident was away from Kathmandu (he was living it up for a welcome spell in Segauli, *ville lumière* that Dr Oldfield had so much enjoyed some forty years before). The Residency-surgeon, in temporary charge, received the refugees and started off the flow of cables—his cable to the Resident in Segauli; the next from Resident to Viceroy, Delhi; from Viceroy, Delhi to Secretary-of-State, Whitehall; from Secretary-of-State back to

Viceroy to close the series with the words: 'Nepaul. I approve.' In fact, while ordering Colonel Berkeley the Resident (now back in Kathmandu) not to surrender the refugees, the Viceroy had had no steps to recommend, beyond just 'wait and see'—and this is what Whitehall had approved of.

Colonel Berkeley simply waited, and was already seeing a new prime minister acclaimed—Maharaja Bir Shum Shere Jung Bahadur Rana, soon to be Sir Bir, KCSI, by Queen Victoria's grace.

25

I had gone round to Mussoorie's to pick him up: we planned a walk in the early-evening air. There is a whiff of winter on it now. Not cold: I manage very well without an overcoat (I haven't brought one, anyway) but I'm happy to have a second blanket on my bed. I'm happy in a more general sense as well, though I cannot think what life here would be like for me without Mussoorie and the intermittent feel of 'home' that visiting his house has given me. His presence here turns Kathmandu into a warm reality for me—for so long as I am in his company. But living as I must in some anonymous hotel, eating anonymous food in modest public restaurants, it's not the same as being part of life. Mussoorie was telling me the other evening that he's due to leave quite soon. He will be off for a winter visit to his eldest son and family, down in the Terai, near their rice-mills and the Indian border.[1] He was showing me a photograph: his son with wife and children. The wife is beautiful (perhaps all Rana wives are beautiful?). She was grandly born a Thakur, Mussoorie told me, and he was pleased with me because I knew that his own mother had had a Thakur mother. Yet although he loves this daughter-in-law of his he is not completely satisfied with her because despite his son's, her husband's, very Mongol looks, all the grandchildren she has produced for him 'are just like little Indians, Peter! Charming, yes. I grant you that. But I'd so wanted them to come out little Jung Bahadurs. Never mind; I love them just the same. By the way, do you know the test of the true-blue Mongol?'

'The fold to the upper-eyelid? The epicanthic fold?'

'Yes, but not only. The real Mongol always has a sort of

274

medallion the size of a big coin on each of his buttocks. On Mongol women's buttocks too, of course. Pale-ish to mid-blue.'

'You'd have to get their drawers off them to test them.'

'Peter! What a thing to say!' He was laughing his characteristic ho-ho-ho, one small hand laid on his stomach. 'True, however. Youth, youth... !'

'"Youth, youth!" indeed! From all the talk I hear you Nepalese never give in, but I suppose there comes a day...'

'I can't speak for others,' he said, smiling, 'but for myself... Perhaps the world would come to an end.'

We had left his house already and were walking without any very fixed objective but in the general direction of the Rana-palace belt outside the city proper. Ranas are of course allowed to walk these days, and Mussoorie obviously enjoys it. We chatted as we walked. The subject was now more rarified than sex, and with the old Bombay days in mind I was asking if he still practised the old spiritual austerities:

'Of course I know that you can still cross your legs behind your neck: you told me so. But that business of reversing the peristalsis of the lower bowel and sucking water in...'

He stopped me: 'That's got nothing to do with spiritual matters! It's simply a process of Hatha Yoga. Muscle-control in this case. A scoundrel who had studied it could do it, where a saint who hadn't studied it could not. But yes, I could suck in water. When in form. Child's play, really. Well, not quite, perhaps.... But I was capable of a much more testing feat than that when at the height of my powers. Now years ago, alas. I could expel air through my phallus—*just* enough, and only once, I'm bound in honesty to tell you—to blow a note on a conch-shell... *booo-o-o-o...!*' He broke off to say, 'That's Cousin Kaiser Shum Shere's library across the road, but of course you know that.'

I like to have Mussoorie pointing out for me Cousin-This and old Uncle-That's great white stucco palaces in what is now the suburbs of the city. But Cousin This and Uncle That are dead, and their palaces look dead to me—when I'm alone. Mussoorie gives them each a little shot of life again.

On our way home Mussoorie asked me, 'Did I ever show you the palace where they kidnapped father? There! That's it! That palace! It was one of Maharaja Bir's.'

We walked towards it, then stopped and stared.

On 26 June 1901 Maharaja Deb Shum Shere, prime minister since early March that year, following the natural death of his brother Bir Shum Shere, went to the Nepal High School he had himself founded just those three months earlier. There was to be a prize-giving ceremony. Deb's bosom friend and cousin-brother, King Prithvi Bir Vikram Sah, accompanied him to this unprecedented function. Bunting, banners, mottoes everywhere, the school was dressed for the event at which the prizes were to be presented simultaneously in pairs by the prime minister and king, the students being ushered up onto the dais in pairs, one left, one right.

Escorted by his normal bodyguard, a hundred and fifty strong, and warm with prize-giving, Maharaja Deb now left the High School for the palace that Mussoorie pointed out to me. The king went with him, though with no special business there himself. He was to be a grave embarrassment to everyone as things turned out.

Deb had specific business: he had agreed to join his brothers at this palace to arbitrate in a dispute among the family-members over the division of so valuable a property as this. Deb and the king went in, Deb himself unarmed, but as was customary indoors he was closely attended by two riflemen. The main bodyguard would wait outside. Fateh Shum Shere, a younger half-brother, was in command of it.

All this I take from a statement Deb was to make five months later to an official of the Government of India: and on Mussoorie's showing I can add that a prime minister would normally place a son of his in this key security post of commandant of his personal bodyguard, but Deb's oldest boy was not quite old enough. It is only fair to add that the younger brother Fateh, who in consequence had been appointed, had been warning Deb already (or so family-tradition has it): 'Don't trust our brothers; in particular don't trust Chandra!' But would Deb listen to him? No. He was cross, and merely countered with a question: 'Are you trying to undermine our family unity?'

Deb's statement continues. He and the king had reached the third courtyard inside the palace. A younger brother had been deputed to await him there. (They had been seventeen in all, remember; there were fifteen of them still.) Mussoorie says this brother stopped in front of Deb, right arm outstretched across Deb's chest, deflecting him in through a doorway. Deb was to say to people later that it was this extraordinary action—'a gesture of *command!*'—that told him in a sudden rush of comprehension that he had been trapped. Who, otherwise, would dare 'command' the Minister?

Stairs to an upper-storey; successive doors to huge successive rooms now opened and all promptly closed behind the maharaja—behind the king as well. Deb's two-man bodyguard was in attendance still. Deb was now ushered into a room much smaller than the others. This door closed too, but the riflemen were left outside. Inside it the senior among his brothers were awaiting him. Deb said that he was already opening the subject that had brought them all together here, though he knew now it had only been a ruse, when suddenly 'the Maharaja's own brother Chandra ordered [one of the others] to seize the Maharaja, which he did, seizing him with his arms round the body.'

Deb was thunderstruck. 'What is this you are doing?' he shouted to his captor: and then to Chandra, 'What are you doing to me?'—and it was now the brothers caught hold of the king and without ceremony 'pulled him out of the room'. This done the brothers in question came back in, armed now with rifles which Deb was sure they must have taken from his riflemen outside the door. Chandra himself, prime mover in all this, seems to have left them at this point, and it was Dumbar Shum Shere (the one who fired the first shot at Maharaja Udip and missed) who was spokesman. He addressed Deb Shum Shere in these words: 'Maharaja Chandra'—Chandra in that instant had appointed himself prime minister and maharaja—'has ordered me to inform Your Highness that it is owing to your too much contact with the king . . . that you have suffered this misfortune.'

Deb remonstrated with him: had Deb not isolated the king even more carefully than had his predecessors? 'So have I made the king more powerful or less powerful? And when you came to me in the time of Bir Shum Shere to assist you . . . did I not help you? So how can you say I am against the Shum Shere family?' .

The Viceroy made it clearer still, in a despatch to the Secretary-of-State for India: 'During his brief term of office, Deb Shum Shere is said to have been active in introducing reforms. He had instituted a Nepalese newspaper. His views on education were liberal, and he had taken steps towards the abolition of slavery. It seems not improbable that these progressive measures contributed to his downfall.' All the Viceroy knew of Chandra was that he would be presumably 'another brother of Deb Shum Shere'. Just the same the Viceroy thought it an improvement in Nepal politics

277

if deposition of a prime minister entailed exile instead of death. His cable finished: 'We cannot do anything at present,'—nor did he, apart from recognising Deb's successor Chandra as readily as he had recognised Deb himself when Bir had died those few months earlier.

All this happened around 4.30 p.m. and Deb was taken to 'a larger room' and kept there till the curfew gun at 9 o'clock; he was then hurried out of Kathmandu in a shuttered palanquin. On the road to their first-night stop up in the mountains a messenger came after them with a letter for Deb Shum Shere from Chandra telling him that he had been obliged to depose him 'by order of the king so as to save the Shum Shere family'. Next morning, when the exile and his guards resumed their journey, the commander of the escort—who was now to leave for Kathmandu again—came to Deb, his uncle, and said, 'Your Highness always used us well . . . why then were you going to expel us?'—for this is what he and others of them who were fond of their uncle Deb had been told he planned to do. The nephew added that they had had to go to Chandra for protection against him. Deb was outraged; he had had no thought of such a thing. His bodyguard commander, Fateh, had obviously been suborned in some such way as well.

Back in Deb's palace his senior wife, Jagut and Mussoorie's mother (her older co-wife was dead by now) would have heard the guns on Thandi Khel—but whom were they saluting? She knew all too soon. She and her ladies must have been shaken and alarmed. We are not told if the palace was surrounded or if the ladies were under constraint of any kind. But Mussoorie says that even at this tragic moment, his mother (who was with child) had a sad unselfish thought for her poor husband. For the first time in his adult life there would be no woman in his bed that night. Was it she, perhaps, who contrived to right this sorry situation? We know from secret official exchanges that two of Deb's 'concubines' (so described) did manage to get to him at once (and many others later), so he was not left unconsoled for long.

It took the party twenty-six days to reach the township of Dhankota in far-eastern Nepal that had been chosen for Deb's place of exile. By some date in October his senior-wife had joined him there. Deb's mind was in a ferment. Exile! Exile was no easier for him because he was at liberty to move around (though always with a guard of fifty soldiers with a colonel in command, and a second colonel in personal security-attendance on him).

278

Towards the end of October 'mother' was safely delivered at Dhankota of another elder sister to Jagut and Mussoorie whose turns come later. Deb could now finalise the plans for his escape. He would slip across the Indo-Nepalese frontier, to Darjeeling; his ladies and (he hoped) his personal fortune would later follow him down to India. He wrote to Chandra indicating that a place called Ilam (where there was a fort and a small garrison) might serve him as a more salubrious place of exile than Dhankota. Chandra wrote back granting him permission to go and look. He went. And from Ilam he moved down to the small village of Maipokhri, the home of a certain sergeant-major of Military Police named Agham Singh. Did Deb already know this man, perhaps? Agham helped to organise the escape to India. From subsequent despatches I learn that Agham Singh gave Deb his sword—no doubt the very sword that figures in the story as it was handed down within the family.

Riding out of Maipokhri eastwards by the track that Agham Singh had told him of, Deb must have timed things carefully. He was well-mounted; his guards were not. Suddenly Deb spurred his horse into a gallop and left his escort standing, the only one who managed to keep up with him—though only momentarily—was a horse-boy, clinging to the horse's tail:

'Maharaj, Maharaj!' the horse-boy shouted: 'Stop, Stop! I cannot... If I let go and leave you, they will kill me! Maharaj, I beg you!'

Deb did not stop. The Indian frontier was a matter of a few miles distant only. He swung round in his saddle and with a quick back-handed sword-cut docked his horse's tail: the horse-boy fell away and down a slope, still clinging to the severed tail as if it were a fly-whisk. The fly-whisk would explain how Deb had done it and the horse-boy could not be held responsible. Deb was free.

PART THREE

26

Rail-head, Dehra Dun. The long clanking night from Delhi to the foothills was behind me now, and the current morning too, or most of it. I was pleased to see Sarwa, surly First Switzer, waiting beyond the ticket-barrier. He was waving, even smiling. He had a middle-aged Nepali with him whom he introduced as Rana sahib's new driver.

Out in the station-yard the tumbledown Chakrata bus was at it once again, busy being stuffed with peasants, and I could look on undismayed because a brand-new dove-grey Ambassador saloon awaited me. This time arrival was not tinged with apprehension. Let Sarwa and the driver direct the stowing of my baggage; I would get in behind and we'd be off and I could sit back in happy silence and watch the skyline. But as soon as we were off Sarwa turned round in his seat beside the driver and started talking in a very smug and self-important voice:

'That Punjabi *goonda*! Sahib remembers?'

I said, 'yes, yes,' a little irritably. I didn't want to talk. Moreover though Sarwa might dislike the man and envy him his looks and radiant vitality, I rather liked him just because of them.

'Sahib has heard what now has happened?'

'Rana sahib has told me. In a letter.'

'But *now*, only? Sahib knows it?'

'Oh yes, I know it. Your own story, wasn't it? The girl down by the barrage and then her brothers caught and beat him.' It was Sarwa's air of personal victory that I didn't like. 'And then a mad dog bit him . . .' I had a sudden anxious thought. 'Is he all right? All those injections?'

'Who knows?' asked Sarwa of the air. 'He did not wait to finish those injections.'

It was obvious that he proposed to tell his story in spite of me, so I made a show of not attending as he embarked upon some drama more recent than any I had heard of, and a moment later he had me listening intently—the Police? They came to get him? But what for?

'Stop it, Sarwa,' I told him sternly. 'You've been listening to . . .' and then I couldn't for the life of me remember the Bridegroom's real name and had to break off rather lamely.

'If sahib does not believe, may he be pleased to listen to what Rana sahib will tell him.'

Sarwa, surly now and trying not to show it, had turned back to face the hairpin bends and the roadway swinging like a pendulum. I would sit back in my corner and seek peace again.

From here, as from Soon Saan, it is not the Himalayan giants bordering Tibet that form the skyline but lesser peaks, seven thousand feet perhaps, yet for all that big and near enough to mask their betters. As often as the wooded foothills let through glimpses of the high-lands up above I tried to spot the little town, the 'hill-station' that Maharaja Deb's youngest son by 'mother' had been named for—Mussoorie. I knew that it was visible at night from Dehra: you could see its winking lights. But by day I could make out nothing.

When Deb escaped to British India and reached Darjeeling (no more than a few miles from the point where he had crossed the frontier into India), he had his plans already formulated. First, he would ask the British Commissioner, Darjeeling, to arrange an early interview for him with the Viceroy and Governor-General. Deb would say that apart from guarantees from Maharaja Chandra that his family and fortune and all movables would follow him to exile, he had only one representation to make: 'that he may be allowed to live in British India, residing at Calcutta and Darjeeling, till he can build himself a house at Dharbanga'—a princely State of which the maharaja was his friend. At the same time as Deb was working on the Commissioner, Darjeeling, he was also writing to the British Resident at Kathmandu a good deal more explicitly: 'My object is that I should be allowed by the Viceroy to fight against Chandra Shum Shere,' and Deb even added that he hoped to enlist the Viceroy's active help in doing so. He did not know, but surely might have guessed, that already, months before, the Viceroy had addressed a message to the King of Nepal, Deb's dearest friend, expressing lively satisfaction at His Majesty's appointment of Chandra Shum Shere in Deb's stead.

His representations to the Viceroy cleared the first hurdle easily enough: he was most welcome to make his new home in India; but at the second hurdle they came to grief. How could Government have failed to note that his two successive choices for an Indian home were so handy for the frontiers of Nepal? Deb's guileless letter to the Resident at Kathmandu quite overtly confirmed the obvious suspicion. He had in mind the staging of a come-back *coup d'état*. Government, accordingly, would see to it that the distinguished exile settle somewhere so remote from Kathmandu and its lines of communication as to make intrigue as difficult as possible.

The hill-station Mussoorie must have been proposed to him: it would offer him the sort of hill- and mountain-country, and the climate, he had been accustomed to at home. At all events he came to have a look: and there, four miles outside the little town, he first saw Fairlawn Palace. Well-sited on a ridge, big gardens, splendid views, abundant water. He fell in love with it and bought it.

In due course Deb's senior wife—'mother'—was allowed to join her exiled husband. She brought their children with her and a regiment of ladies, *talimés* and lesser palace girls and what the British called his concubines, and a host of male attendants. The baggage-train that followed after her brought all the 'movables', fit furniture for palaces, no doubt, household equipment, stores, stocks of the rice she was accustomed to, the chutneys and the pickles and traditional preserves of every sort. No question then of import-permits: but when 'mother' and her ladies crossed the British-Indian border, the frontier officials may have wondered why these pretty ladies, with their neat small heads, small hands, small feet, all looked so monstrously fat. If they had only dared to search the ladies' persons they would have learnt that they were all wound round and round with cummerbunds stuffed full of jewels, just as the Soon Saan leper-boy had had his cummerbund stuffed full of heavy stones to sink him. They say within the family that the priceless jewel, *Nau Lakha*, was smuggled out in a great crock of chutney. *Nau Lakha* certainly reached India safely, and Deb was certainly to sell it to his friend the Maharaja of Dharbanga, though only for a song. The weakness of an exile could be traded on, as

Nana sahib's own weakness had been traded on when Jung Bahadur coveted and bought this self-same jewel in 1857.

Maharaja Chandra Shum Shere is for me 'the wicked uncle'. For the King of England, Secretaries of State for India, Viceroys, he was gallant ally, great gentleman and statesman, and indeed he played the part supremely well in public places. Having done his bit in killing off the uncle and later on in grabbing everything so easily from Deb, he could afford to make a show of magnanimity. He treated Deb correctly, if with less than generosity, once he had had him exiled. Deb for his part did as everyone in Kathmandu expected of him; he organised a plot to kill off Chandra when en route through India for a visit to the Viceroy. But unlike Chandra, Deb had no talent as assassin or conspirator. The British foiled his plot quite easily.

The two brothers were to meet again, but only once, Calcutta 1908, when Chandra could not forbear to express his lofty disapproval:

'So, Your Highness. You escaped and tricked me of your person.'

Deb, too, was a stickler for protocol, even between brothers. He replied:

'*Your* Highness tricked *me* of my rightful kingdom'—and 'kingdom' was the word he used.

This confrontation had witnesses in some of Chandra's sons, and one of them has told me how for the first time in their young lives he and his brothers saw and heard their formidable father worsted. Chandra flushed dark red. The sons were secretly well pleased. They had been fond of Uncle Deb.

'Mother' died in 1909. Deb never ceased to mourn her. Not, naturally, that he abandoned women. Nothing of the sort. And he took another wife. She was an Indian princess. The children hated her and I expect she hated them, though as an Indian perhaps she did not know a Gurkha proverb that John Morris quotes. It exactly fitted her position and it goes like this: 'Seven co-wives are not more worrying than the dust on one man's feet, but even a single step-child is like a nail in the heart.' She had inherited a bag of them. They mocked at her behind her back: they called her 'Long-nose', long noses being very ugly, small slightly flattened noses beautiful. Long-nose had big liquid eyes, however: that much was noted and reluctantly admitted.

One night Long-nose's sleep was troubled by a nightmare in

which she lay awake beside her husband in their enormous bed. The two of them were evidently alone in it that night: often other beds with other ladies in them would be pulled up close on either side, with one across the foot of the great mother-bed. Father liked company. But for Long-nose's story to be true, that night Deb and she were quite alone. In the semi-darkness of her nightmare a door was opening and an old crone coming in, a witch-like creature. Long-nose lay watching, horrified, incapable of crying out or moving as the crone approached, took hold of Deb and dragged him from the bed and to his feet beside it. For some seconds he stood swaying. Then he toppled slowly forward to the floor and there lay prone and motionless. Long-nose was suddenly awake. But to her infinite relief she found Deb sleeping peacefully beside her. Thus reassured, she went to sleep again. But she was roused again, this time by Deb's movements in the bed. He was easing his legs out of it, then sitting on the edge of it, then slowly he stood up. He swayed a little. A moment later he had toppled forward to the floor, to lie there prone exactly as Long-nose was to claim that she had seen him in her nightmare. He was mumbling what sounded like: 'I can't get up. My leg...'

A stroke had partially paralysed him.

Doctors, nurses, silent servants, the huge place was like a hospital and Deb's condition filled the children's days with drama.

Deb got a good deal better but was less than ever reconciled to exile and he constantly sat dreaming of Nepal. He wrote to Chandra: 'Your Highness, I am growing old and am now a broken man. Pray grant that I may see my country once again before I die.'

Chandra felt the stirrings of compassion, or else perhaps he didn't, though the answer that he gave suggested it. However, in his apparent readiness to acquiesce he was altogether vague where details were concerned. So Deb must humiliate himself and write again, begging that His Highness fix the date, the length of visit, point of entry, name his conditions and restrictions, anything, just so that he might look upon his country once again. A long silence followed this, but finally Chandra did reply, and this is what he wrote:

'Just as no jungle can contain two tigers, nor one scabbard two swords, so there is no room in Nepal for me *and* you.'

Mussoorie has demonstrated for me how it was when father got this letter; how father's eyes and lips closed tight, how his face crinkled and his mouth fell open, though for a while no sound came out of it. And then at last a terrible despairing *ohhh-h-h . . . !*, lips rounded and protruded to allow it to escape. And father burst into a flood of tears.

He died in 1914 at the age of fifty-two and Fairlawn was divided up amongst the children. Long-nose must have had a share of it as well. The older daughters would be marrying already; the younger sons, now being of an age for a princes' college, junior-school, were packed off there as boarders.

In providing for his family Deb had not of course forgotten all his concubines, now widows. Amongst them was the concubine the children loved and called 'aunty' who had been loving 'mother' to them all ever since their real mother died. They were not as nails in the heart to her, who had never been Deb's wife. This aunty had a mind to invest her small inheritance from Deb in real estate and, looking round for something that appealed to her, she lit upon the valley that the maps call Kata Pathar. She lacked the funds to buy the place outright, so she put down half the modest sum agreed and was to pay the balance later. She then installed a manager to work the land for her. But year followed year and the manager just sat there doing nothing, and then didn't bother to be there at all, and aunty, growing old, lost heart and yearned for home, as Deb had done before her. The Valley of Nepal. She petitioned Maharaja Chandra. No matter was too small for him to wish to exercise his power upon it: would His Highness graciously allow this humble exile to return? He graciously said yes.

And Kata Pathar, the half-paid-for, half-forgotten little valley in the upper reaches of the river Jumna? With Chandra's kind permission and aunty's blessing it came to Jagut, provided that he settle up outstanding dues. He did so.

He was now possessed of three giant mango-trees perched on a rocky shoulder otherwise quite bare; a hovel that a squatter-hermit occupied at present; high empty hills, an empty valley. He inherited the water-channel also: the *kul* that hitherto had been required to do no more than quench the hermit's thirst. And he inherited the waters of the river down below that the hermit had been using for nothing but his ritual ablutions. With Jagut in control, the waters were soon put to work the slow marvel of fertility that is now complete and that so astonishes and delights the eye. Soon Saan.

27

Soon Saan in time for tea—not quite by tea-time, all the same. The light begins to fail a good deal earlier than when I left here all those weeks ago, and the evening's programme has to start that much earlier too, being harnessed to the sun. Since my arrival had been harnessed to a railway time-table instead, they had held up tea till I should get here, and sitting in tea-corner it seemed as if I'd never left at all, with nothing changed and everything precisely as it should be—if you except the sun's position in the sky at such an hour. And yes: this too—poor dead Kalé's sister's silhouette has changed a lot. I could see her down below us on the cobbles, spread out and bulging.

'Yes, she has conceived,' said Jagut comfortably, looking at her too. 'We now await the outcome with great confidence. A son, and worthy of his uncle-father, may he rest in peace. Sad, wasn't it? But come, Peter! Shoes! There's no time for the real Grand Tour this evening, but we'll manage an inspection of our headworks before dark, if we hurry. Snake-sticks! No. Not that curvy one: yours is the straight one in the corner.'

He had unhooked his odd old bird-beaked cap and stuck it on his head and was now choosing a pair of shoes from the pile beside the mango-stairway.

'But I haven't told you, have I? A freak storm struck a few nights back. Bin Nullah in full spate. It washed away the head-works of our *kul*. By dawn the lily-pools were nearly dry. The water-snakes were writhing ... what? You thought we only had the one? Oh dear me, no! Many, many, many! And the goldfish all agasp! We made the headworks good as fast as we were able, but meantime the lily-pools were suffering a terrible attack.

Kingfishers! We saw at once that it was either them or our poor goldfish. I hated killing off such lovely birds but I just had to. Shot the lot! Eight!'

He had finished putting on his shoes and now bounded down the stairway to the cobbles. A kind word for the expectant-mother, the evening's orders for the tall thin Rajput Tuman Singh, with Jadish straddling his shoulder. There was a woman passing near whom I don't intend to name, nor shall I speak to Jagut of what I saw her do. On seeing me she stopped and gave a gasp and made a covert gesture at me, then set off at speed again. She was warding off the evil eye, and it startled and upset me, particularly as Jagut, as he led the way across the threshing-floor, was saying, 'This business of our headworks: it's the first time in Soon-Saan history such a thing has happened'—and then with lowered voice, 'In the matter of the headworks, here too the locals see the hand of . . .' he mouthed a silent 'Mahasu' at me. 'Everyone is asking "Why this danger in the air? Who has enraged him?" And it's true, our whole autumn has been sinister and fraught.'

'Yes, it is true.'

'They say he hasn't finished yet. He stops at nothing. Have I told you what he did to the unhappy Raja of Bhirat? Only planted a tree in the royal stomach so that it should grow up through his throat and choke him! That's all. Though in fairness I must admit that for once his cause was righteous. The Raja had been killing off all babies within a radius of miles, oh yes, a veritable Herod! So that he himself could gorge on mothers' milk. But don't alarm yourself. It was centuries ago now, though as alive today in the public consciousness as if it had been yesterday. Yet we poor mortals must go plodding on, despite you-know-who. This is our new shop to-be, for instance.'

Men working on a new construction just beyond our private mill were getting to their feet to make *namastes*. Jagut *namaste*'d back and I dutifully did so too.

'It's to be a general store. A Supermarket, as you might say nowadays. To engender competition and keep our prices down. Moreover I'm trying once again with a *neem*-tree sapling. See it? Very tiny still in its barbed-wire entanglement. To keep despoilers off till it is big enough to fend for itself.'

'Tooth-brushes?'

'We certainly hope so. And its leaves will offer us a sovereign specific. Poultices for boils, carbuncles. If only the sapling can survive to tree-hood. Its predecessors never have.'

I had never before been so far along the *kul* as Jagut was now leading me, way past the zig-zag down to ford and public mill, but he was coming to a halt.

'Look! We've arrived. Our reconditioned headworks.'

A pool of barely-moving water, fed by a waterfall above it, here forms a small natural reservoir that spills across its curving lip in an unbroken sheet of water. A gutter of cemented stones leads from this reservoir and gently draws off water for our *kul*. Could anything be simpler? Jagut was on his hunkers, poking at the structure. 'Holding up well,' he commented.

The evening sun still lit the hillside across the gorge from ours, but down below, beyond the ford, the nullah-bed was shadowy already, and soon the shadows would be broadening and rising, floating out the sunlight to the sky. Rameshwar-houseman would be busying himself with mugs of *lassi* and rehearsing his news-bulletin. Jagut interrupted these pleasant thoughts by saying:

'It would be nice to make our way home by the nullah-bed, wouldn't it? This is the best way down into it: keep well left so as to avoid Niagara: a little tricky certainly, but with resolution. . . . Better use the same rocks as I do. Watch me. First to this rock, *thus.*'

A drop beside Niagara, quite sheer, but to a landing wide and flat enough. I followed him, a grumble on my lips.

'Now this one—and the third will take us to mid-stream.'

Jagut, on Rock Two, prepared himself with resolution for the next.

'Rocks Three and Four. I call them Scylla and Charybdis.'

A leap, and he was safe on Scylla. I had made Rock Two myself meanwhile, and with a boldness that I scarcely knew was in me. I could see at once what he was up to: not only showing off, but testing me as well. I must steel myself to pass this cruel test, but snatched a moment's respite:

'Sarwa was telling me a most unlikely story on the way from Dehra Dun. About your Punjabi tenant. He swore that it was true.'

Jagut had stopped and turned, as indeed I had intended. 'What did he tell you?'

I repeated Sarwa's story.

'White-slavery and all that? You know what village gossip's like. They *want* a drama—so they make a drama. All we have to go on is that the little girl from the up-river village has never re-appeared; and our brash Punjabi's gone for ever! At least I hope it's to be forever. Soon Saan hated him.'

'I'd like to hear the details, all the same.'

'Some other time. We'd better get along or we'll find ourselves benighted. It's difficult enough by daylight.'

'That's what I've been thinking too.'

'Rock Four! Charybdis!'

A leap.

'Rock Five! And this one ... even I ... even *I* cannot! Here we must admit defeat and take our shoes off. I see you're wearing socks. And then ... you'd better watch me carefully ... a slither down ... and slip into the water here ... quite shallow. Next ... because the channel deepens sharply just beyond ... this bit's rather difficult ... *a final leap!*'

He leapt. Lord Vishnu's Leap, the leap encircling the world in one, unseen angels to support him, bear up his splaying arms and legs.

'—to dry land!' cried Jagut from the further bank and turning back exultant.

'You're on the wrong bank now,' I told him, flat-voice.

'But not for long. Rocks Six, Seven and Eight are nicely cal-culated to get us back to *our* bank just above the ford. Rock Eight's the very devil, though.'

'Wouldn't it be simpler, and much quicker, now it's getting dark, to walk down the *wrong* bank—that's a sort of track behind you, isn't it? Then we could cross to *our* bank at the ford itself.'

'You haven't got the point at all. It's much more fun, my way.'

'Oh yes, it's fun all right.'

'Save your breath to cool your porridge. You'll need every bit of concentration for the work in hand. Rock Two! To Scylla now! *JUMP!* That's the way. Good! *Ohh–h ... ! Don't look down!* Are you all right? Sure? Now for Charybdis ... *shabash*, Peter! Well jumped! Next the slither—and it's really not worth rolling up your trousers, you can't roll them high enough anyway, and we can dry them off at home. I would have told you to wear shorts if I had thought of coming back this way before we left the house. The slither ... good ... prepare yourself to leap!'

'I can't leap that far. Not out of the water. And the water's icy ...'

'Nonsense. Have a try.'

I tried, and half succeeded, reached land with dripping trouser-legs, then went on strike.

'You can do as you please, Jagut. I'm taking the wrong-bank pathway to the ford and going home the proper way.'

I unlooped my shoes from round my neck, took out my socks, eased my wet feet into them, put on my shoes and started off without another word. I could hear Jagut laughing merrily behind me, but when a few yards further on I turned to look, I saw that he was coming with me.

Home again and dark by now. The windows of Bal Bahadur's cottage were shuttered tight, no lamp-light gleaming through the chinks. ('He sleeps nearly all the time these days,' said Jagut. 'We keep him well sedated. He's not right yet.') Across the threshing-floor and underneath the mango and the pleasuredome it cradles (I'd be up there in the morning), then out onto the cobbles. I chose my favoured mushroom with its lingam back-rest, stuck out my feet, let willing hands take off my shoes and socks, stood up to have a bath-towel wrapped around me so that I could slip my sopping trousers off for someone else to take away. Rameshwar was arriving with our mugs of *lassi* and his evening bulletin. Lean back against the Lord and listen!

But nothing world-shattering had happened to us in the hour or so Jagut had been absent: 'Drink up your *lassi*, Peter. We're running late this evening. Now for a hot tub!'

I sniffed the wood-smoke on the air and said, 'A hot tub will be very welcome.'

'You look tired. It's all that travel. Shumbhu's supernumerary on Shampoo-hour this evening. I've detailed him for you. He has good fatigue-relieving hands.'

'That will be very welcome too. Thank you.'

Lobster-red from soaking in the tub but the dirt of travel gone now; my *loongi* neatly tied (with practice I have learnt to tie it neatly now); a light-weight sweater against the noticeably cooler airs of evening and the *khasto* round my shoulders. People have begun to wrap their heads up in a woolly scarf, I see, though they go bare-foot still. I also saw that a folded blanket had been laid across the bed and blessed Mrs Midget for it; or would it be the Fair Maid I should bless? I blessed them both; and Sarwa and the Bridegroom, who had meanwhile unpacked my things between them. And Jagut. I was brimming with good-will and blessed him too. A pile of books and papers on the dressing-table had a big stout envelope on top of it. It was labelled 'Jagut' and contained a batch of blow-ups from the set of Soon Saan photographs I'd taken on my autumn visit. I would give them to him when I joined him in tea-corner for a *chota-peg* and shampoo-hour. But when I joined him both his arms were being oiled and pulled and kneaded, so he had one of the attendants put the envelope aside. 'I'll look at them tomorrow morning, in the light. How nice of you, though, Peter.'

Supper. Night-cap tea in formal drawing-room, dim-lit by the camel's stomach. I was drowsy.

Early bed. I turned my bedside lamp off and a moment later Kalé's sister arrived to settle on her doormat, moonlit and bulging.

The Seven Sleepers on the back verandah were settling down as well: I could hear their murmurings. I lay there in the darkness thinking—in the morning I shall talk to Jagut about a sacrifice: perhaps I'll say it's an excuse for feasting Soon Saan, and it is partly that, of course. But it is also that I'd like Soon Saan to feel that you-know-who is being handsomely propitiated, and if people really think that I'm to blame for anything, then they can see that I am making what amends I can. We'll use the Durga-devi temple—at least I shall propose this—because so far as I'm aware you-know-who boasts of no temple of his own, and such things are so much better done in temples than just anywhere. The resident-*jogi* can be allowed to think I'm doing it for Durga-devi, and he will be wrong. But I see now that since I have to make Soon Saan party to this small deception, Jagut must be told as well, because if I don't tell him, someone else will do it for me. So I have to risk his laughing at me anyway. Together he and I can work out all the details in the morning. Though the first day of my return, I don't want to talk, or even think, of leaving here yet I can't stay long this time. We have to have some rough date for the sacrifice in view from now: we have to find and buy a big un-blemished billy-goat (there may be rules about the choice of beast that make things difficult); and though I hardly think we'll need to book the altar in advance, yet the *jogi* has to be consulted. I wonder who will act as executioner. I should like, myself, to honour Sarwa with the task, but I expect that as a Rajput he will have to cede the honour to some Nepalese. This head-off-with-a-single-stroke technique is very Nepalese, and the sacrificial *kukri* it is done with specifically so. Jagut will decide about it, I am sure. I think the sacrifice should take place on the day before I have to leave: the village can then feast upon the victim that night. I don't fancy a huge billy-goat myself; and least of all when freshly killed, and though perhaps it would be proper to be served a bit of liver, or his kidneys, as a sort of starter for my final dinner here, yet I'm hoping Jagut will remember that he promised me a goose. And that would be the night for her appearance as *pièce-de-résistance* on our dinner-table. I wonder how they'll be preparing her. The Second Lady of Soon Saan is bound to have some good ideas, but something puzzles me. Of course I know that Brahmins can't take life of any sort; how then can the Second Lady escape defilement in cooking what a Kshatriya has killed? Perhaps in fact she just directs proceedings from a decent distance.

Sleep had meanwhile stilled the back verandah murmurings, Kalé's sister on her doormat was already deep in it. Now that I cocked my ears I could hear the river raging far below us as I settled down to sleep myself.

28

Next morning when Jagut came to the pleasuredome to fetch me down to breakfast he had the envelope of Soon Saan blow-ups with him, and although he thanked me generously he said that actually he had very little use for photographs himself these days; I would have noticed, possibly, that the albums in the drawing-room all stop short before the war. I said yes, I'd noticed this; but since I had taken all this lot in any case, so as to have a record for myself, I'd simply wondered if he'd like one too. He said no again, politely, but did make a show of keeping two or three (to please me, I expect), of the house and lily-pools.

'But I'll tell you what, Peter. Those portraits of everybody; why not hand them round? Most of them have never had their photos taken in their lives. And anyone who has will certainly not have seen a portrait of himself much bigger than a postage-stamp, whereas these big ones. . . . They'll love them.'

I said, 'What a good idea!' with as much show of enthusiasm as I could muster, though disappointed that my attempt to make a gesture should have failed. Perhaps father had instilled it into his sons, as boys, that princes do not accept presents, in case there should be strings attached. 'I'll hand them round after breakfast,' I told him.

'Better let Sarwa do it for you. He'll know where to find them all.'

I should have liked to do the distribution myself, but never mind. Jagut may have meant that it would not look correct for me to go to cottage doors when the husband might be absent at his work. I briefed Sarwa carefully instead:

'Give photographs of children to their parents. Wives—in the absence of their husbands—may be given the husbands' photographs as well as their own. But otherwise see to it that no one gets a photograph of anybody else.'

I had the risk of magic vaguely in my mind, I think (it is vaguely at the back of everybody's mind here, I dare say): wax-mannikins with needles in their eyes and hearts; and would not photographs be better still, if someone ill-disposed could lay hands on those of enemies?

I went up to the pleasuredome to watch Sarwa at the distribution. The news of what was going on had spread instantly and everyone came running to the farmyard and surrounded him. In fact they mobbed him. But he is young and strong and was able to control them with a few well-planted slaps. Indeed where I had been prepared for Soon Saan to react with simple pleasure to all this, the response has been electrifying. Delight unbounded!

All day, since then, my sitters have been going about their work in a golden dream, their portraits in their hands to show again to others, or to contemplate again themselves. And as for me, I emerge transfigured. In October, to begin with, Soon Saan came to stare at me in speculative wonder, a White, and all the rest of it. Then, later, when accustomed to my continuing though always outlandish presence, people seldom looked my way, unless I spoke to them. I was simply Rana sahib's guest, to whom perfunctory *namastes* should be accorded twice a day. But now I suddenly exist for them; I have acquired a personal identity and a status of my own. I am by special appointment Soon Saan's Official Photographer.

Two of my sitters did not turn up at the distribution as I knew when Sarwa brought their portraits back to me. As the first of these was the Punjabi tenant whom I knew had left us, it was no surprise, though silly of me not to have extracted this from the batch before handing all the rest to Sarwa. He did not look at me: I did not look at him.

The second of the photographs was Jezebel. I turned aside, aloof, not wishing to be lured into discussion of this lady, nor to let on that I knew exactly who she was, her real name, her husband's name and face and character, their children's names, and her official lover's. She undoubtedly is pretty.

It was Jagut that I spoke to about Jezebel.

'You know, she hasn't even bothered to come to claim her photograph.'

'How do you know?'

'*From* her photograph. Sarwa has brought it back to me.'

'I meant how do you know that the lady in the photograph that Sarwa brought you back is she?'

'Have a look at it yourself, if you doubt me.' We were in tea-corner. 'I've got it in my room.'

'*No, no, no!*' he said quickly. '*Don't* get it. I don't want even to know who you *think* she is!' A pause. 'Or did Sarwa tell you? Peter! You've been gossiping back-stairs!'

'No I haven't. Sarwa didn't volunteer it, either. I know it for myself; just by using my eyes and ears, plus a process of elimination. Don't worry, though. I've already promised you not to write a thing that could serve to identify her. I know, just the same. I think I can say that I am almost omniscient by now.'

'Oh you are, are you? Then let me tell you that you're nothing of the sort. I had meant to keep this from you—keep right off Jezebel with you. But since you reiterate your promises of deep discretion, I shall relent. Will it shock you to be told that Jezebel is no longer with us?'

'You don't mean she's . . . ? Not *dead*?'

'She is far from being dead. It's that her husband . . .'

I interrupted him—to tease: 'Shall I name him for you? And their children?'

Jagut raised a hand to stop me:

'Her *nameless* husband has been at last aroused. To everyone's astonishment he turned, the worm! Not only turned, but gave her a walloping black eye!'

'Jagut!'

'She's made off in a rage. Forever. Destination Kathmandu.'

'And Sir Launcelot? How will he have taken this?'

'With great relief, I fancy. She has been a hard, exacting task-mistress all this time for him, and he is not strong.'

Dawn, noonday, dusk; dawn, noonday, dusk. The darkness counts for little more than sleep, though each evening we concede an after-dinner lamp-lit hour for tea, with sopari nut for digestive and to clear the palate. Then bed. The river Jumna grumbles out its lullaby for us each night, and is in the background still when the first sharp horizontal shafts of sun transfix the house and set

Soon Saan ablaze with day. I get up slowly and shuffle to the pleasuredome. The farmyard noises will be starting soon, and next we'll have the violent winged commotion as the poultry-pens fling open. But till then I sit placid in the pleasuredome awaiting Rameshwar with the tea-tray, and I listen to the river grumbling below. I do more than listen. By leaning out across the foot-high parapet as far as I dare venture, I can just get a sideways glimpse of tumbling waters, way down the precipice beyond the kitchen fly-screens. I do this every morning now, as if offering it a bit of homage. It informs life here, the river. We depend upon it (and its tributary Bin Nullah) not just for irrigation. We can fish in it, and bathe in it, receive its absolution; we can look at it and listen and at all times be aware that we rely on it. And what a potent lure it seems to be! That strapping handsome girl who married Tuman Singh—the tall thin rather handsome Rajput—she harnessed Jumna to her private ends by threatening that she'd consign herself to the river if Tuman would not marry her. And marry her he did and, now that he's been trapped, he certainly adores the children she has given him. 'Yet many a time and oft,' says Jagut, 'I've heard Tuman moan "she's gobbling me up, consuming me!"'

Though Jumna was in this way cheated of the strapping girl those few years back, it can expect an offering from time to time, the most recent being our leper-boy.

Occasionally the offering may be a Shivaite *jogi*, though these are mostly buried, sitting up, as I know from their sarcophagi at the nearby Durga temple: but then such *jogis* as the river has received across the centuries were always dead already, which makes them less acceptable as offerings, I'm sure. While doubtless much preferring humans, Jumna is certainly not above accepting animals as better than no offering at all. A neighbour's cow, for instance. She can easily find herself consigned if she makes a habit of marauding someone else's vegetable-patch. Poor thoughtless holy creature, her sanctity won't save her if her owner's back is turned that day. Into the river with her, gagged, bound and helpless, and never a soul to hear her muffled moos.

Heady with my new-found status in the village, I have been advancing my success in other ways. Phase 1 of my present plan is now complete: I have had the two Switzers sing into my Sony tape-recorder. They cannot really sing at all but since they don't know this, it has no importance. It has been their reaction to the play-back that has mattered: it was exactly what I was hoping for. Stupefaction. So Phase 2 was an automatic process—the Switzers' spreading of the word about my Sony and its magic powers. Soon Saan is now agog to have a chance to sing into it. So I have asked Jagut if he would mount an All Soon Saan Festival of Song (Phase 3) and he has readily agreed.

'Why not? It may be quite amusing for us, too, if it doesn't go on too long. We'll get them all onto the upper verandah—as many as there's room for at a time. We can do it in relays. And they can sing in turn. No, no, they won't be shy. You can then play back the tape for them as grand finale. Moreover just to build you up a bit (your portraiture has done a lot for you already, did you know?) I shall be telling them that each separate song costs five rupees in operating-charges—and that that of course explains why each song has to be so short. They'd sing into it all night if we allowed them to. You think the batteries will hold out? It would be very up-setting if they didn't, and the singers further down the list had no chance to get their songs in. We dare not risk that sort of disaster.'

'No risk of that. I've got spare batteries with me.'

'While I think of it,' said Jagut in an off-hand voice. 'Have you any film left for your camera?'

'Masses. But I thought you weren't much interested in snaps these days.'

'Not for me. For those whose snaps you never took.'

'Oh, I see! I hadn't thought of that. I was concerned with a selective record only. Have there been complaints? Sarwa never told me.'

'He was instructed not to tell you, but the underprivileged have been complaining piteously. We did not want you to know of this, however, till I could check about supplies of film. It would have embarrassed you so if you had had no more.'

'Now that I know, I'll soon put things right. Shall we have Sarwa bring complainants to me, say half a dozen at a time?'

'I'll tell him.'

'Then there's something else I want to ask about, Jagut. I'd like to be allowed to make a sacrifice. A billy-goat, I thought.' And I came clean about the whole business, even the evil-eyeing bit, and the small deception over you-know-who and Durga-devi that I meant to practise.

Jagut laughed, but nicely; he said it was an excellent idea:

'And of course we'll use the Durga temple; we'll fix it with the *jogi*: a pure formality. The temple will expect a small donation. And we can let the *jogi* have the severed head to feast on.'

'Exactly!' I said. 'I wonder if we ought to start looking out from now for a fine unblemished billy. I don't know exactly what "unblemished" means in this context. It may not be so easy to find what we want. He must be big enough to make a bold impression— so that the feast that follows can be a real feast, though I don't care much for goat myself, except perhaps a kid . . .'

'Never fear. The night the village feasts on billy, it's to be Mother Goose for you and me. I promised you. Remember?'

Of course I remembered and felt a bit ashamed at having dropped what surely sounded like a hint.

I do not want to think of leaving, and Jagut hasn't said a word about when he plans to leave himself for his winter in the plains, yet I must bring the subject up quite soon. In a day or two, perhaps, but meantime our programme of events before I go is spoken of in terms of D-Day minus. For example it is now agreed that the night of D-Day minus 2 we shall hold the Festival of Song. And the afternoon of D-Day minus 1 can be consecrated to the great sacrifice to you-know-who. There is, however, a little detail of my proposing that Jagut does not like.

'No, Peter. Sarwa would not be at all a proper choice for executioner. He lacks all expertise, and should I be weak enough to let you have your way and should Sarwa need two blows, or more, to get poor billy's head off, it would be gravely inauspicious and go far towards nullifying the good expected of the sacrifice. It might well be taken to mean that you-know-who rejected all appeasement. By the way, no sign yet of a suitable unblemished victim, but the search goes on. Excitement mounts about all this. I am being asked if you are very rich. I tell them "yes, of course. And Peter sahib is not the man to be fobbed off with an inferior animal. Nothing but the best."'

I said: 'Of course, I do see. It's only that I thought. . . .'

'Peter!'

Jagut was at the door of my room, looking in on his way down to breakfast. 'Good news! A goat has been located who will fill the bill. Something special, by all accounts. He will be with us by tomorrow morning, latest.'

'Oh good!'

But even as I said it I was thinking in dismay—well, that settles that!: because two days before I'd made a firm decision, that I should do again as I so often do: allow events to make decisions for me. In this case the arrival of the goat would irrevocably mark the dawn of my D-Day minus 3. I had gained an unexpected bonus while the search for billy still went on, and I must be content with that. Tomorrow the final count-down would begin.

I joined Jagut in the dining-room.

'Today is D-Day minus 4,' I told him. 'I've got three whole days ahead of me before I have to leave.'

'Why must you go so soon?'

'I must.'

'I can't see why.'

'You'll be going yourself quite soon, won't you?'

'Fairly soon. But with this spell of milder weather I may stay on a bit. Can't you stay on till I go?'

'No. My mind has been made up.'

'Have second thoughts, then.'

By after breakfast I was having second thoughts: I even went to Jagut's quarters with it vaguely in my mind that if he should again urge me to stay on I would allow myself to weaken. But Jagut wasn't there. I found the Bridegroom dusting down a staircase. Ominous.

'When does Rana sahib leave for the plains?'

'In a week from now, sahib.'

D-Day minus 3. No goat.

'Don't get fussed, Peter. He'll be here tomorrow without fail. It's a long way he has to come, you know.'

'I had hoped we'd have him here nicely ahead of time. To fatten him up a bit.'

'They say he's nice and plump already.'

'Have any of our people seen him? Tuman, for example?'

'No. But the owner has assured us.'

'The owner! *Huh!*'

'But listen. We've got our programme of events to think of now. If today is D-Day minus 3, that makes tomorrow minus 2, and the night of minus 2 is what we've fixed for the Festival of Song. I was going to suggest that you and I sit in our usual places in tea-corner. The singers can then all enter by the mango-stairway and range themselves down the length of the verandah. And then as each man—or woman—comes to the head of the queue to sing his song, he can exit down the other stairway; and the next in line can take his place in front of us. A sort of endless chain of singers.'

'Yes, but the goat? Everything really depends on his arrival.'

'Forget about him. He'll be here on time. Don't fuss.'

D-Day minus 2. Throughout it I was waiting for the goat till in the evening the Festival of Song was round our necks. Who but a madman would have thought up such a thing? It lasted hours. They sang, they sang, both high and low, and gruff and shrill, the noise of it, some thirty of them in succession, boys and girls (the older people mostly didn't come). Some I'm sure sang more than once, by nipping up the mango-stairway for a second go, like the endless chain that Jagut had been speaking of. They filled the peaceful Soon Saan night with din, and in the making of it quite forgot their daily selves. A *prima donna*, every one of them for two or three delirious minutes, and for the grand finale play-back as many minutes more again, each in turn could hold a stage that none of them had ever dreamed existed.

Oh the footage that we must record and then play back to them! The demands for extra time, encores, replays, how sick we grew of it, yet felt compelled to go through to the bitter end. I was touched by it, however, and doubly touched when later Jagut told me that one of them had said that if Peter sahib should yearn for Soon Saan from across the seas, he could always play their songs again; and his spirit would be transported here again. Others, on the other hand, were asking when they could expect to get their songs sent back to them:

'I suppose they think that it can all be printed somehow, like their blown-up portraits.'

D-Day minus 1. The day scheduled for the sacrifice.

By eleven o'clock, no goat. My mid-day, still no goat. I was alone in tea-corner, drinking beer. Rameshwar came and placed a big red-leather book beside me on the table. It had *VISITORS* embossed in gold on it. Something visitors must sign before they leave. So soon now. I opened it and turned the pages. People had written little pieces, even verse, in Hindi or in English; some had drawn pictures. Must I try to do the same? What could I write that wouldn't look self-conscious? Then my eye caught this:

'Oh! A nice place this is! I like this place very much. When I was coming, and in the way to this place, I was thinking really a soon saan place, a solitude. But when I reached to near the house, I felt very happy and named it in my mind as a Heaven.'

—and then this:

'I will like to spend the rest of my life in this heaven. Oh God! How cruel are you to me, to deprive me of all this pleasure!'

What could I say but ditto . . . ditto . . . ?

And still no billy-goat.

After lunch I said to Jagut: 'If he doesn't turn up within an hour, or two at most, what are we going to do? We can't not have our sacrifice, after all my song and dance. They'd be perfectly within their rights if they should try to sacrifice me instead—or should we send a posse out to kidnap the goat's owner and sacrifice him in *my* stead?'—which reminded me that I had meant to ask when the last recorded human sacrifice had taken place, so I asked him now.

'I think the last I read of was when you were with us earlier this autumn. *The Hindustan Times* reported it: from Bikaner. Didn't I show it to you? No, no. I'm wrong. There's been another news item since then, from somewhere in the Saharanpur District, quite near us, in fact. A father sacrificed his five-year-old son, or so the distracted mother complained to the police.'

'Like Abraham and Isaac. Except that God sent them a goat . . .'

'We'll get our goat. Stop fussing! Yes, Rameshwar? Excuse me, Peter. It *is*? *At last*? Peter! God's sent our goat! They've just been sighted. They're on their way!'

'*They?*'

'Yes, billy and his goat-herd! They say he's huge. Let's go out to greet him, shall we?'

29

A fine great animal! Almost as tall as the small boy who had brought him in. Black with white shoulders, great arched neck, and head set boldly on it. We stood regarding him. Tuman, armed with the Fair Maiden's scissors, was neatly snipping out a four-inch section of the creature's thick black mane at the point where the sacrificial knife would fall that afternoon. The goat looked magnificent to me, but I wanted to be sure of things:

'Has anybody competent to do so checked carefully for blemishes? I don't want any murmurs afterwards. Black *and* white? Does that pass, Jagut, do you know?'

'Such things don't blemish him.' Jagut turned to Tuman for confirmation. Tuman too was satisfied. 'Yes, he's absolutely all right, Peter. And perhaps this is the moment for you to pay for him, with so many here to watch. Have you got the money on you? Give it to Tuman, then. Let the people see!'

So handsome was our billy that even Jagut was impressed. He said: 'His beauty quite apart, though, his price alone is going to do your *izzat* a lot of good, Peter.' *Izzat* is the honourable esteem in which we wish the world to hold us. 'Not that any extra fillip could now be necessary.'

I gave Tuman Singh the money, watched by the goat-herd and an important cross-section of Soon Saan.

'You will now be looked at with double awe,' said Jagut.

'Do they really have so much respect for money, then? In places where it's mostly barter, I'd have thought that...'

'It's not the money. It's the princely extravagance they have just witnessed that will count for them. I've long since got you classed for them as "noble". I think I told you.'

'Yes, you did. And thank you again.'

'We should dress up just a bit, and then we'll set off, shall we?'

'What will you wear?'

'A jacket would be thought appropriate. Otherwise just shirt and trousers, shoes. And socks, today, I think.'

Off we went.

'As we can hardly keep formation down through Bin Nullah,' Jagut decided, 'we won't draw up our procession properly before we reach the temple precincts, but just for the look of things, let us two nobles lead the way.'

This side of the ford, Rameshwar and his brother and the various other fathers caught and picked up their small children so as not to have them wet their sacrificial finery in the crossing of the ford. For Jagut and me it was the ceremonial pick-a-back.

Not all Soon Saan could take time off to be with us, but we must have numbered upwards of a score, to include all children big enough to enjoy it and to run and scamper. Jagdish was in his usual seat astride his father's shoulder, and it was Tuman, too, who bore the sacrificial *kukri*. The pigman-executioner at present carried a big tray of carefully selected fruits, fit offerings for gods (or demons). This he did in his capacity as extra gardener. Rameshwar and his brother carried trays of altar decorations, flower-heads (amongst them blood-red hibiscus trumpets), cones of blood-red powders, a few wax candles, bits of tinsel and the rest. Bal Bahadur was with us in the end, having earlier expressed reluctance. He walked slowly, in a trance.

Just before we reached the mango-*tope* that surrounds the temple clearing, Jagut halted us so that we might draw up in procession and make a proper entry on the scene. We had to wait for Bal Bahadur to catch us up. At the head of our procession the small goat-herd and the goat himself; then Jagut, with me beside him; Bal Bahadur; behind him Tuman with the *kukri*; Rameshwar and his brother; the pigman. The others followed as they pleased, and the children skipped and scurried, eyes flashing with excitement.

Someone must have warned the *jogi* of our imminent arrival. He now came out of the little lime-washed temple and stood motionless on the wide raised pavement that stretches out in front of it. There is no doubt about the *jogi*'s personal authority, so tall and slender, wiry, his ram-rod posture. He was in *camiz* and *loongi*, *kavi*-coloured, pinkish saffron, his neck slung with the canonical *rudrakshas* seeds. As we drew nearer still the *jogi* was advancing slowly, head up, lips composed, his eyes not looking at us, as if taking no account of us till we should reach the steps up to the pavement. I had to stop below while Jagut went on up, then he too stopped. I think this was to oblige the *jogi* to advance towards him, in any case the *jogi* did so and they exchanged the proper greetings. This done, the *jogi* had the grace to come forward a pace or two to bring him within greeting distance of the donor of the goat. We made our dignified *namastes*.

There then followed *pujas* in the temple from which I was of course excluded. Does my untouchability bother me at all? It does a bit; not much. I was left out with the children and the goat-herd and the goat. Rameshwar's little girls were playing with it, stroking it, and pulling at its ears. It bore with them (a docile, even-tempered beast), then shook them off and took to cropping foliage instead.

The *pujas* seemed to take a lot of time. I expect the *jogi* wished to exercise authority—over Jagut in particular—for as long as he could make it stick.

Jagut and the *jogi* were at last emerging from the temple.

'*Puja* satisfactorily performed,' Jagut told me. 'Now for the business of the afternoon. Mahatma-baba, are you ready for the goat?'

'The *bakra*, yes. Ah yes, I see him there.' Mahatma-baba came on forward, erect and willowy, shoulders squared, black beard impressive, his skirts swinging to the movement of his naked legs. 'Would Rana Sahib be pleased to have his men bring the animal to me?' He then shouted to the goat, to summon him: '*Aiyye, bakra*-maharaj! Kindly come here to us! Yes, a fitting victim, a fine animal.' He motioned to a man behind him: 'The powders. I am ready for the powders.' Then with some powder cupped in one palm and the free hand grasping goat-maharaj by one uncomplaining horn, he briskly rubbed the powder into the ridge of stiff black hair that bristled down the spine. Mahatma-baba then released his hold and goat-maharaj was suddenly less docile, leaping from the pavement and off among the appetising foliage of some bush.

'Bring him back!' Jagut commanded.

'Let him have his last munch, Jagut. Go on. Let him.'

Jagut let him; but then they brought him back and hoisted him up onto the pavement, goat-maharaj protesting somewhat.

'And now,' began Mahatma-baba, cupping his palm again to receive more powder and at the same time taking one of goat-maharaj's ears: 'Now for the assent.'

'Powder, Mahatma-baba?' Jagut queried. 'In Nepal it's always done with water.'

'I prefer the powders,' Mahatma-baba said in fluting, priestly tones, and was promptly blowing little spurts of powder into goat-maharaj's placid ear. 'I'll have the left ear now. Please turn him slightly, someone. *That* way.'

Someone turned him slightly and he stood there quietly enough. His short rebellion was evidently over.

Jagut said, 'Mark my words, Peter. They'll never get him to give assent like that. Never!'

'Assent? Assent to what?'

'To being sacrificed, of course. I thought you surely knew.'

'So that we can kill him with a clear conscience? Like in the old days in Nepal, confessing to some crime you haven't committed so as to justify the king in killing you? And anyhow, how *can* goat-maharaj give his assent?'

Jagut was grinning now. He said: 'A signed confession is not required of animals. Simple assent suffices. You'll see in a moment. We have to go through with this rigmarole, I fear. It would not be at all proper otherwise. Goat-maharaj must wag his head to indicate assent. Mahatma-baba! It's no good, Mahatma-baba!' His voice had edges of exasperation. 'Here! Let me do it. Tuman! Water!'

Tuman hurried to us with a small saucer of it.

'Thank you. Turn his head up!'

Tuman without difficulty turned goat-maharaj's head up sideways. Jagut caught one ear and in a second had dribbled a few drops of water in. 'One ear amply suffices,' he assured the *jogi*. 'Watch!'

We watched. Goat-maharaj was instantly assenting, once, twice, thrice; his great head wagging sideways, sharp hoofs tattooing on the pavement; formally assenting, yes, but off he went again, hop, skip and jump, to be followed by the Soon Saan group whose task meanwhile had been to decorate the altar. They chased him, surrounded him, and brought him back. They kept hold of him this time, a man to each curved horn.

The hibiscus flowers and powders certainly made a very festive altar-display. Lit candles here and there embellished it, stuck to the stonework with a dribble of their own hot wax. I congratulated those responsible and they smiled warmly back at me. How nice to be the giver of the goat and to receive their smiles. The pigman now had the sacrificial *kukri*. He went off to a puddle to wet the blade, then tried its cutting-edge, a finger to it, a blade of grass. He seemed satisfied. I watched him execute a practice swish with it, cutting a swathe of whistling steely air. He caught Jagut's eye and smiled and did another swish.

Goat-maharaj was meanwhile resting in the grass. His keepers left him to it. The pigman judged it time to take his shirt off and I was asking him on which side of goat-maharaj he would be standing: 'You'll warn me, won't you?'—and he nodded. He came up to Jagut now: 'If Rana sahib is ready, then all is ready.'

'Peter? Ready? We are ready,' he announced and to the *jogi*: 'All is ready, Mahatma-baba.'

The *jogi* gave his orders.

'Have goat-maharaj stand up to face the altar.'

The two keepers lugged him to his feet and faced him properly, but as soon as they retreated to let the executioner approach, goat-maharaj was on his fore-knees as if he might be praying, though he was really cropping grass. Or was he sniffing at the discoloured patch immediately before the altar, the patch that had been bloodied by earlier sacrifices? His keepers got him to his feet again. But he was down again.

'He's offering *satyagraha*,' I said to Jagut. *Satyagraha* is something powerful like 'soul-force' and offering it is the standard means of getting what you want by doing absolutely nothing, in this case by not standing up for long enough to let the pigman chop your head off. O sly goat-maharaj!

The pigman cursed aloud.

An acolyte now grabbed goat-maharaj's back legs and lifted his hind-quarters up as high as he could manage and goat-maharaj was threshing with his sharp back hoofs, and unless someone else would help the acolyte he could not hope to hold on any longer, but no one came to help, and goat-maharaj had threshed his back legs free and he himself was all docility again. Moreover, by a stroke of fortune, he was nicely centred on the altar now. It was the pigman's chance, he seized it and stepped forward the necessary pace, his shining *kukri* raised in a two-handed grip—

'Wait, wait!' I shouted, fumbling with my camera. 'One second, please!'

But who would wait at this stage? The waiting-stage was over; it was blood, blood, blood that everyone was after now, including the little girls beside me with their lichee-eyes wide open. . .

WAHANG-G-G-g-g-g. . .! Hrrpp-p!—a throttled throat noise. Whose throat? The pigman executioner's? Goat-maharaj's, as his head flew forward to the altar, neat as a trophy gouting blood? But nothing to the blood his headless body was now gouting as they picked it up, up-ended it, first gave the altar a quick squirting with it, a crimson water-spout, and then directed it into the big waiting wooden bowl on the altar's lowest step. Slowly goat-maharaj was emptying himself to the glory of you-know-who.

Someone had picked the head up and set it neatly on the altar, facing outwards among the flowers and tinsel and the powder-cones. Someone else had now unstuck a candle and was somehow fixing it between goat-maharaj's horns, a little flame in sunlight.

Peace had descended on us all. Now garlands for the principal celebrants and a blood-red *tika*-mark between the eyebrows, placed there by the *jogi* (one for me as well). Head-off-at-a-single-stroke, a beautiful performance. All will be well with us!

'May I congratulate the pigman, Jagut?'

Yes, I might: and Jagut did so too.

'Don't I have to make a donation to the temple's poor-box?'

'Yes. The *jogi* is the temple's poor-box. Give him three rupees. And after all I wonder if there's any need to leave the severed head for him to feast on? We have not yet quite forgotten Saraswati-the-Good and her pilgrims' rest-room and the improper use he put it to. I'll tell Tuman to make sure the head comes back with us.'

We made farewell *namastes*. A highly satisfactory occasion. Flushed with sanctity we all walked home, this time with goat-maharaj in two separate pieces, bringing up the rear.

At my request, because it was my last evening, although the light was failing rapidly, we made an abbreviated tour and I designed it. It excluded the Snake-Alley short-cut home and all hazardous wall-scaling and the like. We came back along the path that overhangs the river, then through persimmons, guavas, past the pig-sties. Under a tree a snow-white drift of feathers gleamed at us in the gathering dusk. Jagut pointed to it, saying: 'The scene of this morning's tragedy. Mother Goose. I meant to ask you how you wanted her prepared and I forgot,' and I said, 'Never mind. We can safely leave that to the Second Lady of Soon Saan. She must have her special ways of cooking goose.'

At this Jagut stopped and turned on me, quite sharply:

'It is *I* who have the special ways, I'll have you know! And don't you go complimenting that woman on her cooking, either! Because it isn't *hers*. It's *mine*. She knows nothing, nothing! Two of my guests once over-complimented her and it's gone straight to her head. You've only made it worse; you didn't start the rot. She has become intolerable. Does she think she's God? She no longer deigns to listen even, be it prayers or threats. So if you've found the food disgusting it's entirely because of her; and you'd be doing me a favour if you'd kindly tell her so, instead of handing out your misplaced praise. I am seriously considering her demotion, and getting the First Lady up here from the men's kitchens.'

By this time we had reached them. There is a terrace at the back of the ochre cottage whose ground floor houses them, and on this terrace, hooked and swinging from a six-foot tripod, was goat-maharaj, being neatly skinned by experts.

'Ah! That reminds me,' Jagut said. 'There's *our* feast to attend to, too. Look, Peter. You go on and start your *lassi* and I'll join you in a moment. I want to nip into our kitchens to make sure the Second Lady has not already ruined Mother Goose for us.'

I protested a bit: 'Despite the Second Lady your food is consistently and absolutely marvellous, Jagut. I only wish I'd realised before that it is you who make it so. I'd have begged you to teach me how you do it.'

He said: 'Sometimes I think that you're more flatterer than friend.'

Jagut held me back a moment on the way downstairs to dinner.

'Just before we go in. Actually I promised not to tell you, because the staff all wanted it to be a complete surprise for you— and I fancy that it will be. And that's why I feel I have to break my promise. Otherwise who knows how you might react? And you *have* to react with joy and absolute amazement. Understand?'

'But what must I react to?'

'It's that for years they've all been getting at me to make a proper show, a really princely show, for guests. And I've never given in. But for once, this time, because they want to honour you in your—how did you describe it: your new-found status?—I've given in at last. I've let them have the run of what we call the "Silver-Room", *carte blanche* to plunder it and dazzle you. Even I don't quite know what we must expect, except that it will be their notion of how to set a banquet-table fit for princes. So be warned.'

We went into the dining-room.

Heavens!

It was awash with candlelight. The table (which can easily seat eight) was practically invisible for silver candelabra sprouting their great branches, for three-foot silver palm-trees heavy with their silver coconuts; and fitted in below the major pieces, were smaller centre-pieces designed for modester occasions, along with a mass of other silver, cake-stands, cruet-stands, flower-baskets, flowers, fruit and trails of maidenhair. Two clearings at the edges of this flowering silver forest had been left to accommodate our *thalis*, but this time not the simple silver trays of everyday: these were massive inch-thick solid-silver ovals, all edges smoothed and rounded, the near side a concavity to serve as big shallow platter, the far side being built-in bowls for all the different garnishes.

I looked as Jagut; then at Rameshwar, whose triumph this must be. He dropped his eyes demurely. Framed in the open service-hatch were Sarwa, the Bridegroom and the bacon-cook, all watching. They must have had their fingers in this splendid pie as well. I mimed amazement, joy!

How right to go too far once in a while! How right for just the two of us to sit down to a gala goose so meltingly delicious!

After dinner, sated now but dazzled still, we went into the big dark drawing-room and sat on there far longer than had been our custom hitherto—till I caught Jagut squinting at his watch.

'Oh Jagut . . . Don't say D-Day's dawned at last!'

'Not dawned . . . But it's begun.'

In the morning when we came out on the cobbles after breakfast, the car was standing ready.

'Is it time for me to go?'

'It's just gone eight. You can safely give it half an hour.'

How could I fill that horrible half-hour? Jagut would have his bits of business to attend to. My business here was over now—unless, perhaps, I went upstairs again to make a last compulsive check before they brought my baggage down.

Sarwa was there and helped again, the opening of empty drawers and cupboards—'But sahib, we've looked already. Everywhere. There is nothing left behind.'

'There might be something. . .'

'Nothing, sahib!'

The Bridegroom had come in, to help take my baggage down and load it.

Ten minutes passed somehow.

I went downstairs, to find Jagut on the cobbles with the tailor-master. I waited till he'd finished with him and then said: 'I really think I'd better go.'

'But why the rush?'

'I . . .'

'Have they loaded on your luggage?'

'Yes.'

'All right, then. I'll come along with you—as far as the Rice Bowl. Just a sec': I'll nip up for my stick.'

I was aware of people gathering around, of feeling emptied, then of Jagut coming down the mango-stairway, stick in hand.

'They've come to see you off,' he said. 'The proper way would be for you to make them a *namaste*, just one for all of them. You can turn about while making it. Yes, that's the way. Perhaps for Bal Bahadur a hand-shake.'

Jagut was in the car by now and I got in beside him. The car moved off. This meant disturbing Kalé's sister, who had chosen to take her rest immediately in front of it.

'You'll write to tell me, won't you—when her happy event takes place?'

'Of course I shall.'

The leafy tunnels underneath the mango-trees were dark and luminously green. Out into the sun again in silence. We were nearing river-level when Jagut broke our silence.

'How does that Matthew Prior thing go, do you remember?'

'What thing?'

'The bit that goes . . .' His lips seemed to be rehearsing it: 'Yes, that's it. But I have to switch it slightly. Listen, Peter. Carefully. It's something for your note-books:

"Be to my virtues very kind;
 Be to my faults a little blind." '

'Oh Jagut! Do you still mistrust me?'

'No-o . . .' Then, to the driver: 'Stop!'

The Rice Bowl and the Soon Saan boundary-wall with gateless opening. Jagut got out. I got out too. This business of good-bye. I started trying to thank him but he cut me short:

'No, no! But you'll come again next year. . . ?' and I said brightly, 'Yes, of course,' believing it, or with half my mind believing it, but could I ever come again? 'Of course I'll come,' I told him.

'Next autumn. Don't put things off.' He stopped: then said: 'Time's running out a bit. For us.'

He was fiddling with his snake-stick and I saw with some surprise that it was not the one with so pronounced a curve to it that he had always used. It was the straight one I had come to think was mine. He saw me looking at it. He said:

'My only consolation at your going is that I can have my nice stick back once more. No, no, Peter! Don't apologise.'

He smiled. I think I tried to: I know that I was keenly conscious of the winter sunshine on my skin and that my Indian Summer was behind me now.

Jagut said: 'With our dear Narpat gone . . . And Bahadur. And those others . . . And Mussoorie lost to us in Kathmandu. So far as our little lot is concerned it looks to me as if you and I are certain for the Finals.'

Bibliography

PADMA JUNG BAHADUR *Life of Maharaja Sir Jung Bahadur, G.C.B., G.C.S.I. etc. etc. Prime Minister of Nepal and Maharaja of Kashki and Lamjang* (Pioneer Press, Allahabad 1909)

JEREMY BERNSTEIN *The Wildest Dreams of Kew* (George Allen & Unwin, London 1970)

CAPT. ORFEUR CAVENAGH of the Bengal Army *Rough Notes on the State of Nepal, its Government, Army and Resources* (W. Palmer at the Military Orphan Press, Calcutta 1851)

WILLIAM DIGBY *1857, A Friend in Need. 1887, A Friendship Forgotten: An Episode in Indian Foreign Office Administration* (Indian Political Agency Press, London 1890)

ABBÉ J. A. DUBOIS *Hindu Manners, Customs and Ceremonies* tr. and ed. Henry K. Beauchamp, C.I.E. (Oxford 1906)

BYRON FARWELL *Richard Francis Burton: a biography* (Longmans, London 1963)

FRANCIS HAMILTON (formerly Buchanan) M.D. *An Account of the Kingdom of Nepal and of the Territories Annexed to the Dominion of the House of Gurkha* (Edinburgh 1819)

SIR WILLIAM WILSON HUNTER *Life of Brian Houghton Hodgson, British Resident at the Court of Nepal* (John Murray, London 1896)

BHUWAN LAL JOSHI and LEO E. ROSE *Democratic Innovations in Nepal: a case-study of political acculturation* (University of California Press, Berkeley and Los Angeles 1966)

COLONEL KIRKPATRICK *An Account of the Kingdom of Nepaul (in the year 1793)* (London 1811)

PERCEVAL LANDON *Nepal* 2 vols (Constable, London 1928)

JAMES LAVER *The Age of Optimism* (Weidenfeld & Nicolson, London 1966)

SYLVAIN LÉVI 'Le Népal: étude historique d'un royaume Hindou' *Annales du Musée Guimet, Bibliothèque d'Études* vol. xvii (Ernest Laroux, Paris 1905)

DOM MORAES *Gone Away: an Indian Journal* (Heinemann, London 1960)

JOHN MORRIS *A Winter in Nepal* (Hart-Davis, London 1963)

DR H. A. OLDFIELD *Sketches from Nepal: graphic life at the court of Jung Bahadur* (London 1880)

L. A. OLIPHANT *A Journey to Kathmandu* (London 1852)

JOHN PEMBLE *The Invasion of Nepal* (Oxford Univ. Press, London 1971)

D. R. REGMI *A Century of Family Autocracy in Nepal* 2nd edn. (Nepali National Congress, Nepal 1958)

LEO ROSE—an article for *The Times*, London, special report on Nepal—14 April 1973—entitled 'Final Political power is still kept firmly in the hands of the monarchy'

DR (CAPT.) N. K. SAGAR *Kama Sutra: the Hindu art of love* (Capital Book Co., New Delhi, undated)

CAPTAIN THOMAS SMITH *Five Years Residence at Nepaul* (London 1852)

D. A. SNELLGROVE *Buddhist Himalaya* (Bruno Cassirer, Oxford 1957)

C. THORSEBY (Resident) 'Some particulars relating to the Massacre which occurred in Kathmandu in the building called the Kōt in the night of 14th and 15th September 1846' (Unpublished, available for inspection at India Office Library & Records, London)

DANIEL WRIGHT (ed.) *History of Nepal: translated from the Parbatiya* trans. Munshi Shew Shanker Singh and Pandit Shri Gunanand, with an introductory sketch by the editor (Cambridge University Press 1877; Susil Gupta, Calcutta 1958)

YULE AND BURNELL *Hobson Jobson: A Glossary of Anglo-Indian Colloquial Words and Phrases* (John Murray, London 1903)

Notes

Chapter 7

[1] There should be no distinction between *jogi*, in the Hindi, and the Sanscrit *yogīn* it derives from, but I make one in my own mind. A *yogi*, in the form we know it in the west, is an adept of the *yoga* system of meditation and austerities that are to induce miraculous powers over elementary matter. But for every true *yogi*, it would be possible to count ten thousand *jogis* who make a living with little or no mortification of the flesh.

Chapter 11

[1] Permits numbered 153 between 1888 and 1923: an average of, say, 4 a year. They would have been issued to Government of India officials paying courtesy visits to shoot tiger, rhinoceros, etc.; engineers and technicians; some friends of the British Resident or his staff, with an occasional British royal plus suite. *Landon*.

Chapter 12

[1] I am referring here to the most brilliant man the Company ever sent to Kathmandu, Brian Houghton Hodgson. He spent from 1820 to 1843 at the Residency in various capacities, latterly as Resident, and filled his infinitely empty working days with his researches in a dozen different fields of scholarship. Sylvain Lévi admiringly records him as 'grammarian, geographer, ethnographer, geologist, botanist, zoologist, archeologist, jurist, philosopher and theologian—and in every branch he excels'.

Footnotes cannot do this great man justice. Those concerned to know about his place in oriental scholarship may read Sir William Wilson Hunter's biography of him. His most notable contributions to Anglo-Nepalese relations were his skill in keeping the Gurkhas from attacking when the British were so sorely tried with other enemies in 1838 and the following few years, and in recognising the Gurkha fighting-man's potential value to the Company. His reiterated insistence upon this bore its fruit only when he had long since retired from service, a sick man.

Chapter 15

[1] In Gurkha sexual morality, marriage-lines don't count for much and although the Brahmin girl's son was illegitimate this was not because his parents were not married. It was because they could not in any circumstances have been allowed to marry. It is by proper regard to a couple's respective caste that the legitimacy of their children is determined, and by every application of the caste-laws this child was disqualified, even if in this case the Brahmins ruled that his adoption put things right.

[2] The charge was that Bhim had tried to rid himself of the senior queen's powerful anti-Thapa influence at court, but that the poisoned dish he had intended for her had been lapped up by the wrong victim, her infant son (her third). The infant died. In fact Rajendra is thought to have poisoned the little thing himself so that the blame could be laid on Bhim Sen.

[3] Indian newspapers openly charged King Rajendra with having done it. His reaction to this 'libel' was to threaten the British Government with war if they did not seek out the journalist responsible and subject him 'to the most barbarous punishments', adding that if he could lay his hands on the actual poisoner he would 'have him skinned alive and rubbed all over with salt and limes until he dies'.

Chapter 17

[1] A monthly allowance of Rs 100 was specifically granted to the Resident's British staff in recognition of this 'awful isolation'. In Smith's case the allowance represented 20% of his monthly salary, which was Rs 500. Lawrence's consolidated monthly earnings were Rs 3500.

Chapter 18

[1] Colonel Kirkpatrick's account of 1793 was based most certainly, and probably to a large extent, on information patiently put together by his 'intermediary', for whom the Company had managed to get permission to visit Nepal the year before. He was Maulvi Abdul Kadir Khan, 'an intelligent and zealous servant of the Company who resided some time in Kathmandu'. The circumstances were special: in 1791 the Gurkhas found themselves

at war with infinitely more powerful neighbours (the Chinese) and in risk of being overrun, so they had appealed to the British to send troops. The British were reluctant to take arms against the Chinese and offered instead to mediate—on terms that involved a trade-agreement with the Gurkhas. The Gurkhas, hard-pressed, reluctantly agreed. The Maulvi was sent ahead to draft agreements; by the time Kirkpatrick was setting out for Kathmandu the Gurkhas had had second thoughts and had hastily concluded peace with China (involving some loose sort of acquiescence to Chinese suzerainty). When Kirkpatrick reached Nepal he was 'met with cold disdain'. In fact the Gurkhas kicked him out within eight weeks of his arrival.

[2] N. K. Sagar's most useful translation and commentary stresses the work's value to modern man, and especially modern woman. It includes details of these Sixty-four Arts, among which were the usual social accomplishments (such as the Art of Magic for the Entertainment of Guests). But the truly industrious and ambitious girl would set her sights much higher—on Masonry and Engineering, on Chemistry and Metallurgy, Agriculture and Gardening, Mineralogy and the Colouring of Crystals; and on the Art of Wearing Clothes in such a manner 'as to disguise the private and other delicate parts of the body while dancing or making any violent movement'. But more important still for many would be Art No. 64: The Art and Science of Capturing the Property of Others by Means of Mystic Charms or *Mantras*.

[3] Jung Bahadur's final 'authorised' version of it went like this: Of course Fateh Jung and Co got killed, but not until the massacre was in full swing; and it was 'a sepoy' that shot them. What had started all this off was Fateh Jung Sah's son's attack on Jung's brother Bam with a *kukri*; Bam's life was saved by a *deus ex machinâ*, Jung in person, making 'his first appearance on the scene of bloodshed', as Oldfield loyally records in support of his dear friend Jung. It was Jung, upstairs till now, who dashed down, saw his brother's grave predicament, seized a rifle 'from a sepoy' and shot Bam's assailant; and it was Dhir Shum Shere, Jung's beloved youngest brother (Jagut and Mussoorie's grandfather) who despatched the young man, cut him almost in two halves with his sword. If anyone should ask why Fateh Jung Sah's son should have been trying to avenge the death of a father still very much alive, he must ask elsewhere.

In fact Jung claims to have given this version or something like it to the Resident two days after the massacre. We cannot know if he told the truth because the Residency Records for the period from 24 August to 17 October 1846 are blank. I imagine that Jung was lying; if not, the Residency's definitive 'Particulars' of six months later would surely have made some reference to what he told the Resident. It doesn't. Landon's casual comment sums it up, perhaps: 'Upon reflection Jung Bahadur seems to have re-called in better sequence the incidents of this massacre . . .' Landon was inclined to think that Jung's son Padma's 'temperately-written account represents more accurately the course of events'. Jung's own comment sums it all up too (Oldfield quotes it): 'The Mas-sacre originated in the violent conduct of the Rani. (Jung) always maintains (that) she was holding supreme power at the time, and she should be held responsible for it.'

Chapter 25

[1] Of all the foreign aid poured into Nepal since the 1950 revolu-tion, the one completely successful operation seems to have been the World Health Organisation's eradication of the Anopheles mosquito from the Terai strip. The dreaded *ayul* that had claimed so many lives each year between March and November proves to have been no more nor less than a specially virulent form of what, since 1740, we had been calling 'malaria'—the consequence of breathing the 'bad air' of marsh-lands.